Working Your Way to the Nations

A Guide to Effective Tentmaking

Jonathan Lewis, Ph.D., Editor

To Bob & Andrea,
May God bless you in this
life as well as the next, as you
pursue his glory in the ways
God allows and leads.
With love in our lord,
Steve & Laura
Spinella

William Carey Library
P.O. Box 40129
Pasadena, CA 91114

Editor: Jonathan Lewis
Technical Editor: Susan Peterson
Technical Assistant: Patrick Roseman
Illustrations: Dona Kacalek
Cover Design: Jeff Northway

© 1993
by World Evangelical Fellowship

Published by:
William Carey Library
P.O. Box 40129
Pasadena, CA 91114
Telephone: (818) 798-0819

ISBN 0-87808-244-1

Printed in the United States of America
First Printing October 1993

Table of Contents

Foreword

Working Your Way to the Nations: A Guide to Effective Tentmaking, edited by Dr. Jonathan Lewis, is the first-of-its-kind book of essays on effective tentmaking by experienced and knowledgeable missions specialists from around the world. Dr. William Taylor of the World Evangelical Fellowship Missions Commission should be congratulated for his support of this project.

Tentmaking is a subject of strategic importance to world evangelization. The concept is biblical, historical precedents abound, and today's mission context demands it.

On the one hand, we thank God for the fact that the forces of Christianity, and specifically the results of mission outreach in this century, have combined to reduce the number of non-Christians per serious Christian believer from a ratio of 50 to 1 in 1900 to less than 7 to 1 in 1994, and that ratio continues to drop.

On the other hand, despite the opportunities created by the collapse of the Soviet Union and the openness of Eastern Europe, there will still be a massive and growing body of non-Christians in the world—utterly outside the reaches of traditional missionary approaches.

While the current mission workers will always be needed, new kinds of specialists such as tentmakers must be deployed, and in large numbers. In particular, the mission work force needs men and women who are trained to penetrate people groups which are highly resistant to the gospel. These groups are usually not reachable by traditional missionaries. An *unreached people group* is a people group in whose midst there is no viable indigenous Christian movement strong enough to bring the rest of the population to "faith and obedience in Christ" (Rom. 16:26) without outside help.

The strategic shift required in today's mission context is to focus on mobilizing, training, fielding, and monitoring an army of men and women *called* to serve as tentmakers, to plant a pioneer church movement in the midst of every unreached people group.

The number of unreached people groups is said to be 5,310 located in 145 countries. In 1995, there will be an estimated 3.88 billion non-Christians within these countries—96 percent of the world's non-Christians. If we think of the unreached peoples as the target of Christian witness, we might conceptualize the center portion or bull's-eye of the target as an aiming tool in missions efforts. This bull's-eye is the so-called *10/40 window*, now made popular in the mission circle by the AD 2000 and Beyond Movement. The bull's-eye group of countries contains only about 79 percent of the world's non-Christians; nevertheless, the 10/40 window serves as a valuable aiming tool. This window is home to practically all of the world's largest gospel-resistant belts: Islam, Hinduism, and Buddhism. It includes 23 of the 30 countries (77 percent) which are classified as unevangelized. Further, about 82 percent of the world's poorest of the poor reside within this window.

Tentmakers are what the Apostle Paul describes as "Christ's ambassadors" (2 Cor. 5:20). These ambassadors must be (1) physically, emotionally, and spiritually self-reliant; (2) adaptable; (3) biblically literate; (4) alert to the emerging mission context; (5) trained in meeting needs vital to the people group they seek to penetrate; (6) trained in long-term and low-profile evangelistic skills; (7) equipped with broad new strategic thinking; and (8) prepared with a special strategy for responding to opportunities presented by need. This book will help tentmakers prepare to meet these qualifications.

In the pages that follow, veteran tentmaker and missiologist Wilson elucidates the inevitable connection between tentmaking and the Great Commission, and relates tentmaking to a biblical basis. Ogawa digs deeper into the tentmaker's biblical and doctrinal foundations. Cortes lays out the strategic deployment of tentmakers. A large portion of the book is rightly devoted to the discussion of what it takes to be a tentmaker (namely, the tentmaker's internal encounters): spiritual readiness for cross-cultural ministry (Lee), personal preparation (Vance), necessary skills training as an evangelist and a discipler (Chew), and coping with stress (Calderon). Tebbe, Goldsmith, and Acosta focus their studies on the tentmaker's external encounters: field dynamics, understanding the host culture, and intercultural adjustments. I am especially happy that the book emphasizes the importance of accountability structures (Hamilton) and of the local church as the tentmaker's base (Christensen). Numerous tentmakers of yesteryears have fallen due to the lack of accountability and nurturing.

This manual, without question, will serve as a flagship of resources for tentmakers. An appendix provides companion books and materials so the reader can explore the subject in more depth. Probing questions and Action Plan Assignments given for each chapter are designed not only to help the reader more easily comprehend what is presented, but also, in the process, to engage the reader to test his or her *calling* to become a tentmaker.

May the study of this book place a holy burden on each and every reader to prayerfully consider the most challenging profession of all—being God's ambassador as a tentmaker—to reach the unreached at this historic moment in God's timing. What has happened in the former Soviet Union and Eastern Europe in the past several years is nothing short of a miracle. God is sovereign and is in control of history. God will continue to crack open the seemingly impenetrable walls, and we must utilize God-given creativity to seep through small openings to gain accessibility, to the end that every remaining unreached people will see a viable Christian movement in their midst.

Tetsunao Yamamori *
President
Food for the Hungry

---

* Former director and professor of Intercultural Studies at Biola University, Dr. Yamamori has authored, co-authored, and edited numerous books, the latest being *Penetrating Missions' Final Frontier: A New Strategy for Unreached Peoples* (1993, Downers Grove, IL: InterVarsity Press). He is a staunch proponent of tentmakers as strategic missions manpower.

Preface

Bill squirmed in his seat as the missionary continued his impassioned plea for laborers for God's mission harvest. This happened to him every time he heard a missionary preach. When he was 18, he'd attended a national missions youth conference and, with hundreds of others, had offered himself for missions service if God should call him. He'd dreamed about being a pioneer, sharing the gospel in an area which had no gospel witness. Now, four years later, that dream seemed remote.

When Bill found out most missionaries had to spend several years in Bible school or seminary, followed by a couple more years raising financial support, he lost heart. How could he give up his career in computer science? Hadn't his pastor even affirmed that his abilities were truly a gift from God? This commendation had been borne out by Bill's excellent performance at the university and the job opportunities awaiting him upon graduation, almost anywhere he wanted to work.

"You can even serve God with your vocational skills...." The words snapped Bill's attention back to the missionary on the platform. "You don't have to be a professional minister to be a missionary. In fact, there are many areas of the world where professional missionaries, as such, can't enter. God is using *tentmaking missionaries* to reach these people." The thought took Bill's breath away.... "Could God really use me and my computer skills in taking the gospel to those who haven't heard?"

Who Should Study This Material?

Thousands of young Christians around the world have been challenged by the Great Commission and have expressed a willingness to serve as missionaries, should God call them. Yet most of these young people don't enter the missions task force. There are a number of reasons. For some, the main barrier is the long, often expensive professional ministerial training which is required of most career missionaries. For others, it's the fear of raising financial support under situations which may be less than favorable. For still others, life's circumstances haven't allowed them to pursue a missions career. For young people in these categories, this course offers a way to explore tentmaking as an accessible route for lay ministry in Christ's Great Commission army.

Other Christians have committed themselves to mission and have pursued regular channels for service. Somewhere along that road, they have been challenged to minister in countries where they are not allowed to serve as professional missionaries. They must enter these countries as tentmakers. For them, this course offers some practical guidance as they explore the possibilities.

Millions of other Christians from different parts of the world have already traveled to foreign countries as contract workers, skilled technicians, professionals, and representatives of foreign companies and governments. Most of these Christians don't know that they could be effective ambassadors for Christ as well. Even those who are conscious of this opportunity may not be successful in ministry because they lack essential skills. The sad truth is that the promise inherent in this vast army of Christians is largely wasted because believers are not aware of their potential or are not equipped to be effective tentmaker missionaries. For them, this course offers a way to get on track and develop their capability as cross-cultural ministers.

Last, but not least, this course is for the leadership of local churches who want to be on the cutting edge of what God is doing in the world of missions today. Tentmaking isn't just a way to channel a few young people to the mission field. It is the strategically critical path to placing hundreds of thousands of witnesses among the hundreds of millions of unreached people within countries which prohibit regular missions. Mission agencies will not be able to accomplish this deployment of workers on their own. It will take tens of thousands of local churches with the specific vision of nurturing tentmakers, to begin to tap the vast potential of lay workers for God's harvest among the unreached.

Course Objectives

This course is intended to help Christians in local churches throughout the world, as they plan and prepare to become effective, cross-cultural tentmakers. Participants will examine the issues surrounding tentmaking and will evaluate their own readiness. Based on this evaluation, they will outline a goal-oriented plan and timeline that they can pursue within an accountability structure. The process of composing the plan and determining to whom tentmakers are account-able is clearly delineated. Ultimately, this course is intended to see tens of thousands of new tentmakers from around the world recruited and prepared for Great Commission service.

How This Course Came Into Being

The need for a course aimed at orienting and training potential tentmakers within the local church was first articulated by architect Loh Hoe Peng of Singapore. As a consultant to the World Evangelical Fellowship (WEF) Missions Commission and head of its task force on tentmaking, Mr. Loh conducted research with over 40 organizations worldwide to determine the need for and possible content of such a course.

Based on this research, the course content was outlined by WEF Missions Commission staff, with the good help of Dr. Donald Hamilton of TMQ Research in California, and Mr. John Cox, Chairman of the Council of Pickenham Ministries in London. A 12-chapter format was chosen in order to fit easily into the traditional Sunday school "quarter." Twelve authors with ample experience in tentmaking were selected to write the primary content for each chapter. The complexity of compiling a work with 12 authors from 10 different nations posed an editorial and organizational challenge. The variety of cultural perspectives lent by these authors was important, however, for the work to be truly international and applicable to churches around the world. As the manual goes to press, relevant translations are being planned into Korean, Chinese, Spanish, Portuguese, and French.

Acknowledgments

As editor, it was my responsibility to lend cohesion to the material through extensive editing, creation of transitions, formulation of questions, writing of assignments, and development of tables, figures, and illustrations. This process would not have been possible without a very cooperative roster of authors and a competent technical staff. A great deal of credit belongs to Ms. Susan Peterson of Fort Collins, Colorado, who was the principal technical editor for the material. She was responsible for proofreading each chapter, formatting the material, and creating the figures and tables. Mr. Patrick Roseman was the primary "reader" and went over each chapter meticulously. Mr. Jeff Northway, a computer graphics expert, composed the cover art. Our talented illustrator was Ms. Dona Kacalek of San Jose, California.

A fine group of students led by Mr. Ed Mattson, Missions Elder of Community Bible Fellowship in Portland, Oregon, tested the materials in a seminar setting. Their response was particularly helpful in gauging the usefulness of the material and its effectiveness in a group setting.

Heartfelt credit goes to Dr. William Taylor, Executive Director of the WEF Missions Commission, for his constant and enthusiastic encouragement throughout the project. Mr. Galen Hiestand and Mr. Dwight Gibson of the WEF North American office are greatly appreciated for their faithful pursuit of funding for the manual's development, as are the donors who responded to their appeal.

Computer equipment and office space were generously provided by Mr. Mark Sprenger, President of OnGuard, Inc., a "kingdom company" in Fort Collins, Colorado. The marketing campaign to get this manual into the hands of those who most need it was undertaken by Mr. Ken Hoornbeek, President of Advanced Interactive, Inc., another "kingdom company" in Fort Collins with a heart for missions.

My sincerest thanks and appreciation go out to each of these people, without whose involvement the conception and production of this manual would not have been possible. This has truly been a team effort. We trust it will multiply greatly, contributing to the mobilization of tens of thousands of new tentmakers from around the world and the completion of the task our Lord left to us 2,000 years ago. Maranatha, Lord Jesus!

Jonathan Lewis
Editor
October 1993

How to Use This Manual

Working Your Way to the Nations is a course of study—a means by which Christians with a tentmaking interest can be guided in the fulfillment of their calling. Whether the course accomplishes this purpose, however, is largely up to each student. Becoming a tentmaker is not easy. It will require a great deal of effort, discipline, sacrifice, and dependence on the Lord.

Working Your Way to the Nations can be used for individual study, but the greatest value will be derived from its use with a group of like-minded individuals. In this context, questions and issues can be discussed for increased depth of understanding and insight. The group also provides an encouraging, supportive environment and a degree of accountability.

The heart of the course is in the Action Plan Assignments at the end of the chapters. These include self-evaluations and exercises which help define the individual's readiness for tentmaking. This assessment is then linked to a dynamic, goal-oriented plan with a timeline and an accountability structure. When created within a church, this plan clearly articulates mutual expectations between its leadership and the tentmaker, thus allowing for a healthy, successful relationship to be fostered.

The Action Plan Assignments for each chapter are charted in the Personal Action Plan in Appendix A. This chart provides a space for the individual to note the action which is to be taken as a result of fulfilling each assignment, the date the course of action is to be commenced, and the target date of completion. A column is also provided to note to whom the student is accountable for completing the action step indicated (see Appendix A for details).

Group Leadership

Each study group should have one or more *facilitators*. The facilitator's primary tasks are to hold members of the group accountable for studying the material and to aid the discussion process. Ideally, this individual should have missions responsibility within the church or training institution where the course is being led. The facilitator does not have to be a tentmaking expert, but cross-cultural experience is helpful. Since the end product of the course is the Personal Action Plan for the tentmaker to follow, the facilitator or other suitable "mentor" may provide an essential, ongoing, accountability relationship.

Following are guidelines for organizing and conducting a study group for this manual.

"Working Your Way to the Nations" study group checklist

1. Plan the logistics of the course

- **When.** The course is designed to be scheduled into a Sunday school "quarter," but it may not "fit" into the Sunday school hour. Each discussion session requires a *minimum of one hour*, with two hours being even better. If the first session is used to introduce the course and distribute materials, you will need 13 weeks to complete the course.

- **Where.** A location conducive to group dynamics is important. Seating should be arranged in a circle in a place with a minimum of distractions.

- **Who.** Target those with a specific interest in tentmaking *and* persons involved in maintaining the missions ministry of the church. The ideal group size is six to 10 individuals. Larger groups should be split for discussion purposes.

2. Promote the course

- **Word.** Word of mouth may be the best way to identify and recruit those who have an interest in the course. Don't overlook the less obvious persons.

- **Pulpit.** Ask for time to give announcements from the pulpit, or ask the pastor or the missions leader to promote the course.

- **Flier.** A flier giving the meeting dates, time, place, contact person, and a phone number may be appropriate for inclusion in the church bulletin or for general circulation.

3. Order a manual for each member of the group

The "workbook" format requires that each participant (including spouses) have a personal copy of the manual. To help you determine how many copies to order, set an early cut-off date for registration. For ongoing training, the church may wish to keep several manuals on hand.

4. Carry out the plan

The first session is very important, since you will be introducing the material and giving instructions for the course. Allow members of the group to introduce themselves and to explain their interest in taking the course. To introduce the material and provide a vision for the course, read the Foreword, Preface, Student Guidelines (page x), and Table of Contents within the group. Go over expectations (see the "Study Group Covenant" below). Emphasize the importance of reading the material, answering the questions, and carrying out the assignments. Explain that it may take two to three hours to do the reading and assignments each week. Answer any questions students may have. Pray for each other and for the course.

Group Accountability

Without question, one of the biggest problems tentmakers face is lack of accountability to others for their ministry. You can begin solving this problem by fostering a sense of accountability within the study group. Below is a suggested covenant to which each group member should agree.

Study Group Covenant

I agree to make myself accountable to the rest of the members of this study group in the following ways:

1. I will study the assigned chapter each week. To the best of my ability, I will answer the questions and do the Action Plan Assignments.

2. I will attend each group session when physically able to do so.

3. I will participate in the discussion and share insights the Lord gives me through my study.

4. I will give moral and spiritual support to the other members of the group through encouragement, exhortation, and prayer as God enables me.

Signature _____ Date _____

Steps to Follow During Each Group Session

The following suggestions are modeled after a group that meets once a week for 90 minutes.

1. **Open in prayer.** Ask for the Holy Spirit's control of the session, the discussion, and individuals' lives. Pray for the unreached peoples of the world. (5 minutes)

2. **Discuss the questions in the workbook.** Allow everyone who wants to contribute to do so. Be careful to keep track of time, however. With eight to 11 questions in each chapter, only five to seven minutes can be allotted to each one. (60 minutes)

3. **Review the Action Plan Assignment.** The Action Plan Assignment is designed to help evaluate and stimulate each student through application of the material within the context of the course. Review progress and clarify expectations regarding each question. Encourage each student to thoughtfully complete these assignments. These assignments will form the foundation for the long-term Personal Action Plan, as charted in Appendix A. (20 minutes)

4. Close the session. Preview the next chapter by skimming the introduction, headings, subheadings, and summary. Close in prayer, asking the Holy Spirit to help each individual *absorb* and *apply* what is relevant. (5 minutes)

Student Guidelines

As with most courses, what you get out of this course correlates directly with what you put into it. If you are truly interested in serving as a tentmaker, this course can help you achieve your goal—but you will need to apply yourself. Preparing for each group session requires that you read the material, thoughtfully answer the questions in the text, and follow through on the Action Plan Assignment. This can take two to three hours each week or longer. If you don't have the time to do the preparation, the course may not accomplish its purpose for you.

If you are taking the course as a church missions administrator or as a missions committee member, put yourself in the "shoes" of the tentmakers. Work with the tentmaker candidates in the study group. Only in this way can you achieve mutual understanding and match expectations.

When preparing for each session, follow these steps:

1. Examine. Resist the temptation to plunge right in with the reading. First examine the Action Plan Assignment. Then read the introductory and summary sections. Consider each heading and subheading. Read the questions interspersed throughout the chapter. Finally, skim quickly through the entire text. This overview should take only a few minutes, but it will greatly increase your understanding of the material and of what is expected from you.

2. Read. Begin reading for comprehension. Anticipate questions and try to grasp the issues being discussed. Mark significant phrases and ideas in the text. Make notes of key points.

3. Questions. After reading, go back and answer the questions in the text. It may not be possible to fit complete answers into the space provided. Make notes to yourself to share in the discussion sessions. If you want to write out complete answers, do so in a separate notebook.

4. Action Plan Assignment. Complete the Action Plan Assignment. The questions in this section usually require you to evaluate an area of your life, investigate a topic or tool, and articulate your findings.

5. Action Plan Goals. This section is intended to convert your reflection into action. Use the Personal Action Plan in Appendix A to record your specific goals, when you will complete them, and to whom you will report when the task is finished. This chart will be your long-term plan for success!

Becoming a tentmaking Great Commission soldier presents one of the greatest challenges anyone can face. We are confident, however, that our Commander in Chief will supply all that is needed, as long as we are willing to respond to His magnificent calling to reach the nations with the good news of Jesus Christ (Phil. 4:19).

CHAPTER 1

Planning for Success

Tentmakers are playing an increasingly critical role in completing the Great Commission mandate. Tens of thousands of these kinds of witnesses are needed to finish the task. The challenge of tentmaking, however, is enormous. Getting a job overseas is relatively easy—there are millions of Christians who currently work in foreign contexts—but the reasons most of these individuals leave home to take jobs usually have little to do with spreading the gospel. Consequently, most workers in foreign countries have little impact for Christ.

Becoming an *effective* tentmaker calls for individuals who are well-trained in *both* vocational and ministerial abilities. They must have relational skills, must be mature, and must be sensitive to the Holy Spirit. Perseverance and personal discipline are also indispensable.

Preparing the way to a tentmaking ministry through careful planning will help tentmakers develop the skills, character qualities, and maturity needed to be successful. In the following article, Don Hamilton speaks to this issue from a heart fully committed to tentmaking and from his 30 years of experience in the corporate world.

❏ *So You Want to Be a Tentmaker?*

Don Hamilton *

I was sitting in an airport a few years ago, when a man came up to me as I was working on my manuscript for *Tentmakers Speak*. "What are you writing about?" the man asked. He glanced at my notes and caught the word "tentmaker." "Oh! Tentmaking!" he said. "You mean like the

---

* Don Hamilton worked for 30 years in the corporate sector before switching in order to encourage tentmakers. In 1985, he founded TMQ Research in Duarte, California, and he conducted an extensive survey of over 800 tentmakers. From this work, the book *Tentmakers Speak* (1987, Ventura, CA: Regal Press) was written, and the Tentmaker Research Evaluation Profile (TREP) was developed.

Apostle Paul?" Without another clue, the man knew exactly what I was talking about.

Tentmaking—the concept is so well-known, it hardly seems to require explanation. In Acts 18:3, we read that Paul made tents for a living while he preached the gospel. Drawing on his example, the word has come to describe anyone who, like Paul, works at a secular job in order to support his or her Christian witness. Some suggest that all Christians who work at secular jobs are tentmakers. "You don't have to be an evangelist, and you certainly don't have to live overseas," they say. "As long as you're living for Christ and earning your own living rather than being supported, then you're a tentmaker."

There is probably some value to a loose definition like this. By and large, however, such a definition tends to confuse rather than clarify the concept. I by no means want to detract from the importance of people who live for Christ on the job. They are probably the best candidates for tentmaking. For our purposes, however, the following definition applies: *A "tentmaker" is a Christian who works in a cross-cultural situation, is recognized by members of the host culture as something other than a "religious professional," and yet, in terms of his or her commitment, calling, motivation, and training, is a "missionary" in every way.*

Tentmakers are people who cross cultural barriers. They are legally recognized by their visas and government documents as something other than ministers or missionaries. They validate their presence in their host culture through interests, skills, or products other than religion, though they openly admit to holding strong religious interests and convictions.

> *Tentmakers are strategic resources to be used for accomplishing God's purposes—purposes that might not otherwise be fulfilled.*

Tentmakers are not evangelical Christians who happen to live overseas. Preaching the gospel is not their "sideline." Tentmakers have a missionary purpose, calling, and training. They are strategic resources to be used for accomplishing God's purposes—purposes that might not otherwise be fulfilled. Biblical evidence and the testimony of countless tentmaking missionaries over the years make one realize that tentmaking is far more than a second-best option in places where career missionaries are unable to gain access.

1. Why is it necessary to bring precision to the definition of "tentmaking"?

_____

_____

Characteristic weaknesses

Despite the many advantages a tentmaking strategy can offer, both tentmakers and traditional career missionaries have noted several areas in which those who call themselves tentmakers appear to be weak. These weaknesses have tended to nullify the potential effectiveness of tentmakers, have created negative

stereotypes, and have damaged the overall credibility of the movement.

1. Tentmakers tend to be "mavericks" or "lone rangers." They have their own ideas and seldom think to link up with ministries already in place on the field. They tend to function with no support team, no report-

ing structure, no accountability, and no consultation with or authorization from anyone but themselves. They are often culturally inexperienced and lack a long-term strategy other than what they can achieve on their own. They tend to accomplish little in the way of measurable positive ends and may even create problems for themselves and other Christians in the area.

2. Tentmakers tend to go to the field biblically and spiritually ill-equipped. They lack the training, background, or other resources to handle the spiritual issues with which they are confronted.

3. Tentmakers often place a low priority on adapting to the culture or learning to use the local language.

4. Tentmakers' jobs take so much of their time and energy that their ministries are subverted.

These are serious problems, but they should not belong to tentmakers in our definition. These weaknesses may be endemic to the average evangelical who gets a job overseas, but they must not characterize a true tentmaker. Remember, tentmakers are missionaries. Most

> *Like other missionaries, tentmakers must equip themselves fully to become the most effective cross-cultural ministers they can be.*

missionaries are not mavericks, lone rangers, without reporting structure, without accountability, ill-equipped biblically and spiritually, or without commitment to adapt to the culture and learn the local language. Like other missionaries, tentmakers must equip themselves fully to become the most effective cross-cultural ministers they can be.

2. *What is your initial response to the weaknesses the author has listed? Do you agree they are "weaknesses"? Why or why not?*

_____

_____

_____

Getting off to a good start

Ahimaaz was the faster runner. He outran Cushi to bring news to King David about the crucial battle that was going on (2 Sam. 18:19-33). It was important that King David receive up-to-date information—but it had to be the right information. David wanted specific information about his son Absalom. Ahimaaz left the battle scene too soon. When he reported to King David, he didn't know the final outcome of the battle. He was told to stand aside until Cushi arrived. Cushi had the complete information, and although it was not the information David wanted to hear, it was accurate and complete. How sad that Ahimaaz was told to

stand aside! He was zealous. He was an excellent runner. He just didn't have the right information.

Many people today are highly skilled in running. They may have great zeal to be involved in a tentmaking ministry. Too bad that they are often only partially prepared! The Apostle Paul's admonition to young Timothy was that, as a man of God, he should be "thoroughly equipped for every good work" (2 Tim. 3:17). That's especially good advice for a prospective tentmaker.

3. *What are possible ways that people get out ahead of themselves in becoming tentmakers?*

Planning for Preparation

In relation to preparation for tentmaker service, five elements come into play:

- Evaluation
- Priorities
- Discipline
- Goals
- Accountability

Evaluation

Evaluation is not a popular word. Most people resist being evaluated. It's too threatening. However, before individuals can proceed in preparation for any worthwhile endeavor, they must know where they stand.

There are several approaches to evaluation. The simplest is self-evaluation using a rating form similar to the ones found in this study. If a person is truly objective, self-evaluation can be very effective. Such objectivity, however, is seldom the case. When the evaluation can also

> **Getting another's perspective on our strengths and weaknesses will help us get a more accurate picture of ourselves.**

be conducted by someone who knows us well, the result is likely to be more accurate. Bobby Burns, the Scottish poet, wrote:

> Oh, would that some power
> the gift give us
> To see ourselves as others see us!
> It would from many a blunder free us.

WELL-PREPARED

10
9
8
7
6
5
4
3
2
1

This is poignantly true of tentmakers whose potential for cross-cultural blunders is all too probable! Getting another's perspective on our strengths and weaknesses will help us get a more accurate picture of ourselves.

Where possible, evaluation against a known standard is the best means of achieving an accurate appraisal. In this kind of testing, a standardized form is used by each candidate, and the ensuing "score" is compared to the scores of hundreds or thousands of others who have taken the evaluation. This method eliminates most of the subjectivity and compares each area against proven, tested criteria. Based on extensive research, I have developed a test for the specific purpose of evaluating tentmaker readiness, known as the Tentmaker

Research Evaluation Profile (TREP).* Even when using such a tool, though, it is best to work with someone who can help you interpret the results and utilize the information to help equip you for the field.

Priorities

When lists of recommended qualifications for tentmaking are gathered from several sources, as they are in this course, it is inevitable that the candidate will be faced with a long list of "must," "important," and "should" items. It can be quite overwhelming for a potential tentmaker to try to face such a list all at once. We all have limitations on our time and energy. There needs to be some way to create a sense of priority. Evaluation instruments help us determine how we are doing in these different areas. If we are weak in an area that is classified as a "must," this takes top priority. As time and energy permit, we can work on "important" areas, as well as the "shoulds." Items I consider to be "musts" are summarized on pages 1-9 through 1-12 under the heading "Accepting the Challenge."

4. How do evaluations and setting priorities work together in determining a course of action?

_____

_____

_____

Discipline

In the title of this manual, *Working Your Way to the Nations*, "working" takes on a double meaning. The most obvious meaning is using your work skills as the means of entry and support as you go to serve as a tentmaker. The term also implies that proper preparation is

> **If anything, tentmaking is more difficult than conventional missionary service, and it requires more thorough preparation.**

hard work. Preparation covers many disciplines and requires much time and energy. Those who think tentmaking is an easy alternative to conventional missionary service need to rethink their philosophy of ministry. If anything, tentmaking is more difficult than con-ventional missionary service, and it requires more thorough preparation. Working your way through the requirements for tentmaking takes real discipline over a prolonged period of time.

Goals

No plan can be created without stated goals. Before a specific program for preparation can be drawn up, however, there needs to be a good understanding of the term "goals." There is much unclear thinking about this subject, especially among Christians. "I want to be more like Christ" is a fine objective, but it is not a goal. Goals are specific. "I will be spending at least 20 minutes each day in personal Bible study by the end of this month" is a goal leading to the objective of "being more like Christ." It is a *valid* goal because it is *Significant, Achievable, Measurable*, and *Manageable*—"SAMM"! Let's examine each of these qualities of valid goals.

* The TREP is available for $20.00, post-paid, from Don Hamilton, TMQ Research, 312 Melcanyon Road, Duarte, CA 91010.

Significant

In most cases, to say, "My goal is to get out of bed in the morning," is not very significant. However, for someone who does not regularly share his or her faith, to say, "I will learn how to share my faith and will speak to someone who needs Christ by December 31 of this year," is significant, especially if the person is preparing to be a tentmaker.

Achievable

Stating that your goal is to move the sun back 10 degrees is certainly significant, but it is not achievable. Be sure your goals can actually be done. The goal, "I will speak to someone who needs Christ by December 31 of this year," is both significant and achievable.

Measurable

Goals must be measurable to be valid. "I will memorize more Scripture" is not a valid goal. It is not measurable. To state this goal in valid terms, we need to add a quantity. "I will memorize 50 new verses by the end of this year" is measurable. If, however, the goal is not set until December 1, the goal may not be achievable, and thus, it is invalid.

For any goal to be realistically measurable, checkpoints or milestones need to be present along the way. A mentor can help here. If the date when the goal is set is June 1, instead of December 1, that works out to learning two verses a week. That is achievable, but we should set some milestones. By September 30, we should have memorized 25 verses. Waiting until December 31 to measure progress is not responsible. In addition, dimensions need to be put on "memorize." Does this mean "word perfect," or is a "paraphrase" enough? Do the references also need to be memorized? The more precise we are in our wording, the clearer the goal becomes.

Returning to our original example, "I will speak to someone who needs Christ by December 31 of this year" is significant, achievable, and measurable.

Manageable

Here is where most goal setting fails. What do we mean by "manageable"? Simply stated, manageable means that some specific person *owns* the goal, and that person has the resources—time, money, and opportunity—to accomplish the goal.

How manageable is our stated goal, "I will speak to someone who needs Christ by December 31 of this year"? The word "I" indicates ownership. Do you have the resources to carry out this goal? If not, you might need to obtain some training in this area. Have you been witnessing to others? Possibly this is too large

> *In general, we tend to set goals that are unrealistically high for the short term and too low for the long term.*

a goal for you for this year. A better goal might be, "I will take training in leading someone to personal faith in Christ by December 31 of this year." That is a significant, achievable, measurable, and manageable goal. SAMM!

In general, we tend to set goals that are unrealistically high for the short term and too low for the long term. Applying the SAMM criteria to goal setting should help considerably in correcting this tendency.

---

5. Why is understanding proper goal setting important in the achievement of our plans?

Accountability

No servant of God is going to be totally successful unless there is an accountability structure. Ultimate accountability, of course, is to God, but ongoing evaluation and counseling from others need to occur as well. God has placed His servants in positions where they can exercise authority over you. Submitting to these individuals takes humility.

In most cases, the best accountability structure for spiritual and ministerial growth and development is the local church where you are serving. Ideally, you will have one or more counselors who will work with you in your spiritual development, as well as in other aspects of your social and personal growth.

You will also need a *mentor*—someone who will make a special commitment to your development *as a tentmaker*. While discipling is a component of mentoring, the relationship goes beyond this. The ideal mentor is someone who is or has been involved in tentmaking or who has, over the course of time, mentored enough tentmakers to understand the dynamics involved in their preparation and placement. The mentor is ultimately committed to the success of his or her protégé.*

Walt Shearer of International Interns is such a person. He is continuously mentoring tentmaker candidates. He has also developed a program to help churches form a broad-based mentor structure of their own. This kind of structure in local churches is absolutely essential to the massive worldwide mobilization of effective tentmakers.

There are millions of potential tentmaker mentors in our churches today. While many of these are deacons, elders, and missions committee personnel, the greatest numeric potential lies in mature Christian lay people who may not have any official responsibility in the church. They understand what is needed to succeed as Christians in the workplace. As they are linked up with individuals (perhaps in their own vocations) who are preparing as tentmakers, they can make an invaluable contribution by providing wisdom and an accountability relationship.**

Another structure for accountability is a peer-level group like the one with which you may be involved in taking this course. People of a similar age and motivation can help advise and guide you through the years of preparation. When group members have a common goal—becoming tentmakers—this encouragement can be significant. There are some limitations, however. The peer group may be lacking in

> *In most cases, the best accountability structure for spiritual and ministerial growth and development is the local church where you are serving.*

long-term commitment and/or the specific experience and counseling background needed for difficult situations. The work of counselors or of a mentor should thus complement this group structure.

Mission agencies also provide strong accountability structures. Once you've found an agency, they can guide you in the proper preparation. On the field, agencies can provide the on-site support all missionaries need. Not all mission agencies, however, are prepared to

---

* The dynamic involved in the tentmaker relationship is illustrated in chapter 3 of this manual.

** Information on how to develop tentmaker mentors in the local church is available from Walt Shearer, International Interns, P.O. Box 133, San Dimas, CA 91773; telephone (818) 335-6749.

work with tentmakers or are working in the part of the world to which you feel called. When you find a suitable agency, a *site agreement* between you, the agency, and your local church should be written to clarify issues of authority and responsibility. Again, mentors can play an important role in "negotiating" these agreements.*

6. How do self-discipline and accountability work together to achieve the best results?

Working Your Way Through This Course

The author has detailed the elements involved in preparation for tentmaking. Following are some specifics related to taking this course.

Working Your Way to the Nations is designed to help you (or a person you are mentoring) become a tentmaker. The first step is to reflect on the issues which are discussed in each chapter. The questions interspersed throughout the material and the discussion generated by these questions will help you in your reflection.

The second step is to do the Action Plan Assignment at the end of each chapter. Many of these assignments will help you evaluate your readiness for tentmaking. Other assignments ask you to define or articulate your own thinking in a particular area. Under most circumstances, these assignments can be completed during the course of study, if you have committed time between group sessions to do them.

The third step—and one which is essential to your success—is to write goal statements in the Personal Action Plan in Appendix A. These goal statements will move you concretely towards developing the relationships, knowledge, and skills you will need to succeed as a tentmaker. The suggested actions in the Personal Action Plan are keyed to the Action Plan Assignments. Some of these tasks can be completed during the week. Others may require additional steps which may take months or years to complete. When finished, the Personal Action Plan becomes your personal road map to fulfilling your objective of becoming a successful tentmaker.

---

* Chapter 4 of this study develops the concept of a site agreement more fully. Chapter 7 provides a selected list of agencies working with tentmakers.

Working with the Personal Action Plan in Appendix A

The Personal Action Plan moves you from analytic and reflective procedures in the Action Plan Assignment at the end of each chapter, to outlining specific action steps in your development as a tentmaker. The chart is a transition from thinking to doing.

If you are already competent in a listed action, you will not need to outline steps required on your part to complete that action. For example, Action 2-1 in the Personal Action Plan in Appendix A calls for you to memorize Matthew 28:18-20. If you have already memorized this text, you don't need to formulate an action plan to accomplish this task. However, evaluating your competence or faithfulness in a particular area should not be a "solo" call. A mentor will fill a crucial role in helping you determine where you should be placing most of your time and effort in preparation.

Many of the assignments are aimed at helping you to express your thoughts and convictions to others. These assignments will sharpen your own thinking and will also help the people to whom you speak to understand the dynamics of tentmaking. In some cases, these contacts may become fruitful relationships, as the Lord uses this dialogue to create an interest in your preparation and future ministry.

7. *Examine the "action" statements in the Personal Action Plan in Appendix A. From the statements themselves, which imply the longest time commitment from you in order to complete your preparation for tentmaking?*

_____

_____

_____

8. *Why is it important for tentmaker candidates to be able to express themselves articulately to others regarding the rationale for tentmaking and their personal commitment to such a ministry?*

_____

_____

_____

Accepting the Challenge

Tentmaking is not for everyone. Certainly, it is no easy alternative to being a conventional missionary. Being a successful tentmaker is one of the hardest jobs ever, but the rewards that come from being used by God to help others know Him are worth all the effort, pain, and frustration. First, settle in your mind why you want to be a tentmaker; then, diligently pursue an understanding of God's will in the matter.

Tentmaking can be a wonderful way of sharing the gospel naturally, positively, and with the respect and trust of the people with whom you work. Tentmaking is not what we usually think

> **Tentmaking can be a wonderful way of sharing the gospel naturally, positively, and with the respect and trust of the people with whom you work.**

of when we think of missions, but it is a very important kind of missionary endeavor. It is often the only form of missions permitted in many areas, cultures, and countries.

Be prepared

Accept the challenge and prepare yourself adequately for your new career. Commit yourself to an orderly, self-disciplined plan of fulfilling your preparation as a tentmaker. If you take one step at a time, the job won't seem nearly so intimidating.

Develop a strong support group for prayer and encouragement, and go for God's best in your life. The best support group is your own local church. Get involved there, and become submissive and accountable to the leadership.

If you should find that your interest in tentmaking wanes over time, step back. There's nothing wrong with admitting that your first enthusiasm had no roots in God's will and that God actually has other plans for you. You don't have to be a tentmaker to serve God. If He wants you someplace else, don't go against His will—you'll end up as a poor tentmaker, a poor Christian, and a lonely individual.

Spiritual preparation

1. Home support

Within your support structure, find a group of Christians who will pledge to support you on the field with prayer, letters, and encouragement in the faith. Find

someone, such as a mentor, to whom you can be accountable for your spiritual life.

2. Learn the Bible

Become a student of the Word. Try to schedule at least a year of Bible school in your plans. It won't be wasted. Study the Bible on your own and in group Bible studies. You can't get too much of God's Word. Become immersed in the Scriptures and let them infuse every aspect of your life.

3. Learn to pray

Begin (if you haven't already) to pray regularly each day. Be consistent. Pray every day, even—or especially—when you don't feel like it. Don't forget to pray for the Holy Spirit's protection from spiritual wickedness, as well as for life's ordinary problems.

4. Learn evangelism

Have you ever shared the gospel openly with someone? Learn to do it now, or you're unlikely to succeed in another culture. Have you ever prayed with someone to become a Christian? That is one of the highest joys any Christian can have. Learn how now, so that your efforts in the field will be practiced, natural, and honoring to the Lord.

5. Learn discipleship

Learning discipleship presupposes that you have been discipled by someone yourself, and hence have gained experience in teaching and discipling others. Those are large presuppositions! Perhaps your first steps should be to discuss with your mentor how you can become a disciple of Christ. Through that process, you can then learn to disciple others. Some of the classic books on discipleship illuminate the process of both becoming a disciple and discipling others.

Cultural preparation

1. Learn the language

Commit yourself to learning the local language wherever God sends you. Knowing the host culture's language is always necessary for successful evangelism. You show respect for the people and their heritage, and you become able to communicate with their hearts, not just their heads. Don't worry about mistakes. Even mistakes can be opportunities for friendly conversation with those whose language you are trying to learn.

2. Learn the culture

Don't present your own culture as your gospel. The message will only be heard and respected if it is presented in a manner that is acceptable within the context of the host culture. You will have to devote great effort and sensitivity to learn the culture. Showing deep respect for the people and a hunger to learn about their culture is a good place to start.

Professional preparation

1. Learn to be the best

Your credibility as a Christian will be strongly tied to how well you do the job you are hired to do. It doesn't say much for the excellence of your faith if your job performance is mediocre. Learn to be the best engineer, language teacher, doctor, or printer you can be. If you try to slide by in your profession with the thought that you're doing God a favor by serving as a tentmaker, your coworkers will find you out and lose respect for you at the same time they lose respect for God.

2. Learn how to integrate your work and your ministry

Right here at home is the best place to learn that your whole life is ministry. Your working hours, your breaks, your lunchtimes, your evenings, and your weekends are all part of your ministry. Being a Christian involves 100 percent of your time. You really need to work on this area in your home country, or you will suffer frustration on the field because you don't have time to do "missionary" work.

3. Become involved at home

Wherever you are going to serve as a tentmaker, you will need cross-cultural experience. Get involved now in an ethnic neighborhood or with inner-city work. Work with international students. Get experience as a short-term missionary. Join the Peace Corps. There are lots of opportunities.

4. Read some good books

The bibliography for this course has an excellent listing of books that bear directly on tentmaking. Those marked with an asterisk are "must" reading. They are available in your local Christian bookstore, a seminary library nearby, or directly from the publisher.

Serving God

As a tentmaker, you have the rare privilege of being on the front lines of God's war against sin, of being in the vanguard of Christian missions today. Be proud to be a tentmaker. Rejoice that God has chosen you to be a part of fulfilling the Great Commission!

So you want to be a tentmaker? Be a good one!

Summary

Tentmaking means different things to different people. The term can be used broadly to identify anyone who is an active witness for Christ in the workplace. For our purposes, a tentmaker is *a Christian who works in a cross-cultural situation, is recognized by members of the host culture as something other than a "religious professional," and yet, in terms of his or her commitment, calling, motivation, and training, is a "missionary" in every way.* When this definition is applied, the primary weaknesses identified in tentmakers can be avoided through adequate orientation, equipping, and accountability.

In order to become a well-equipped tentmaker, candidates must first evaluate their readiness, establish a set of priorities in preparation, and embark on a disciplined, goal-oriented plan for becoming equipped. The "SAMM" approach to goals establishes guidelines for creating valid goals. Such goals are significant, achievable, measurable, and manageable. The Action Plan Assignment at the end of each chapter and the Personal Action Plan in Appendix A are intended to help tentmaker candidates create a goal-driven plan for becoming effective tentmakers.

An essential component for godly service is accountability. Ultimate accountability is to God, but God uses others in our lives to counsel us and keep us from stumbling. The local church is the best place for tentmaker candidates to establish accountability relationships. In addition to those who may help candidates develop spiritually and socially, tentmakers need a mentor—a person with a special commitment to help tentmakers succeed in their calling. Other accountability structures include peer groups and the mission agency. Without accountability, it is unlikely that tentmakers will succeed in their preparation or ministry.

Action Plan Assignment

Every chapter in this manual has an Action Plan Assignment. These tasks are given to help you begin dealing with the issues related to tentmaking. If you complete these assignments, when you finish the course you should have a good idea of what it will take to prepare yourself to serve as a tentmaker. Use the Personal Action Plan in Appendix A to help you implement each Action Plan Assignment.

1. *Tentmakers are often independent-minded people. They are full of initiative and feel they hold the keys to their own destiny. These qualities can be viewed as strengths, but they can become tentmakers' primary area of weakness if not harnessed within the bounds of accountability structures. "Mavericks" and "lone rangers" often do more harm than good. Submission to authority and going through "channels," however, can be difficult and, at times, risky. It's hard to put our lives in the hands of others. It's equally hard for others to accept that responsibility. Trust is a fundamental issue.*

   Write out a clear statement which expresses your commitment to developing trusting accountability relationships in becoming a tentmaker.

2. *Planning does not come naturally to all of us. It may be difficult for you to create a Personal Action Plan, as suggested in this course. While planning is only part of God's process for leading us, it is a valuable exercise. Some of the Proverbs speak directly to this issue. Examine Proverbs 15:22, 16:3, and 16:9. Plan your way to the nations. As you*

do, the "SAMM" approach to goal setting can be a blessing to you. Memorize its components and apply it to goal setting in your Personal Action Plan.

3. *There is no doubt that a mentor can make all the difference in your ultimate success as a tentmaker. Someone who identifies with you and shares the excitement and responsibility of your preparation and ministry will be a continual encouragement and strength. It is not easy, however, to find such a person. Mentoring is not a widespread practice in churches today. Finding someone who is willing to commit to such a relationship may take time and prayer. Following are some of the qualities of an "ideal" mentor.*

Qualities of an "Ideal" Mentor

An "ideal" mentor:

1. Is a mature Christian.

2. Is a committed member of a church (preferably your own).

3. Is successful in his or her vocational field (preferably your own field as well).

4. Is a successful witness in his or her work.

5. Has cross-cultural experience (preferably as a tentmaker).

6. Knows you and will commit the time necessary to see you through the process of preparation and placement as a tentmaker.

Figure 1-1

This list represents an ideal. Seldom, if ever, will you find someone with all of the above qualities. Point number 6 is probably the most important.

Mentoring is a growth experience in itself. The mentor and protégé will be growing together in their abilities and experience. Expectations should be realistic on both sides. As in any relationship, there will be failures. Learn to work through these.

Review the above list and use it in identifying persons you know who could possibly serve as your mentor. Write down their names. Discuss these individuals with those in missions leadership in your church. Begin praying that the Lord will lead you to the right mentor.

CHAPTER 2

Getting Perspective

Becoming an effective tentmaker begins with a broad understanding of the mission enterprise. Although God's mission purpose can be traced throughout the entire Bible, Jesus Christ's Great Commission gave the task of reaching the whole world the force of a mandate for the apostles and the church. The command, "Go therefore and make disciples of all the nations..." (Matt. 28:19) was meant to be obeyed by Christ's true followers until His return.

Many centuries after this command was issued, the church has yet to complete the task. While the regular Protestant missionary task force has done a remarkable job of spreading the good news during the past two centuries, two billion people today live beyond the reach of a living gospel witness. Most of these *unreached peoples* are in countries where regular missionaries are prohibited. These are *creative access* countries, where Great Commission Christians must use indirect means to introduce the kingdom of God.

Radio, videos, cassettes, and literature are excellent means of offering the *message* to unreached peoples. However, *living witnesses*, embodying the grace and work of Jesus Christ, are the essential catalysts which are needed to establish disciples of Jesus Christ in these regions.

To enter creative access countries, Christian witnesses must use *tentmaking* strategies. This term is borrowed from the Apostle Paul's practice of exercising his trade of making tents while involved in mission work. Paul had a number of reasons for working with his hands as he witnessed for the Lord; self-support, avoidance of criticism, and providing an example are three of the most prominent. These reasons are still valid for today's tentmakers. We add to them the critically important aspect of entry into creative access countries.

J. Christy Wilson, Jr., was of the first generation of writers to bring into prominence the discussion of tentmaking. In this chapter of our study, Dr. Wilson establishes the basis of tentmaking from biblical, historical, and strategic perspectives.

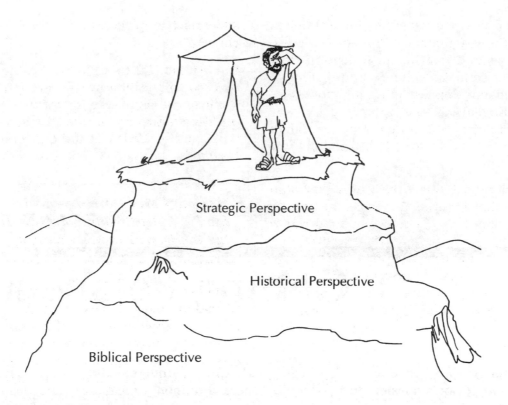

Strategic Perspective

Historical Perspective

Biblical Perspective

❏ *Witness While You Work*

J. Christy Wilson, Jr. *

When I went to Afghanistan as an English teacher in 1951—even though the country is the size of the state of Texas, or larger than France, or twice the land area of the Philippines—there was not one Afghan Christian in that whole nation. It was completely unevangelized. Later on, we found that there were 51 different languages spoken in that country and over 120 different unreached people groups.

My parents were missionaries in the province of Azerbaijan in northwestern Iran for 20 years, from 1919 to 1939. Thus, I was born in Iran. As a boy, I heard my parents and other Iranian believers praying for a nation to the east which did not have one Christian. When my national pastor asked me what I wanted to do when I grew up, my mother told me that I replied that I wanted to be a missionary to Afghanistan. He stated, "But missionaries are not allowed there!" I answered, "That is why I want to be one there."

* Dr. J. Christy Wilson, Jr., was born of missionary parents in Iran. In 1951, he went to Afghanistan, where he served as a teacher, public school administrator, and eventually pastor to the expatriate community in Kabul. Mrs. Wilson served to start braille education for the blind in that country. In 1966, Dr. Wilson became Executive Director of the International Afghan Mission, and in 1970 he supervised the construction of the first Christian church on Afghan soil (destroyed by a hostile Muslim government in 1973). The Wilsons returned to their home in the U.S. in 1974, where he has served as Professor of World Mission at Gordon-Conwell Theological Seminary. Dr. Wilson's books include *Today's Tentmakers: An Alternative Model for World Evangelization* (1979, Wheaton: Tyndale), *Afghanistan: The Forbidden Harvest* (1981, Elgin, IL: David C. Cook), *Bringing Christ to the World* (1988, South Hamilton, MA: Gordon-Conwell), and *More to Be Desired Than Gold* (1992, South Hamilton, MA: GCTS Book Center).

When I had finished my educational training, Afghanistan still did not allow missionaries. But they wanted instructors to help in their government schools. Thus, I applied through the Afghanistan embassy in Washington, D.C., to teach English in that nation. After I was accepted, I signed a contract, and the Afghan government paid my way to Kabul and gave me a small salary.

It was only after I had arrived in Afghanistan that I saw that this was just what the Apostle Paul had done. As a *tentmaker*, Paul was a self-supporting missionary. I too realized that I was earning my own way as a teacher and, like Paul, my main purpose was to be a witness for Christ. I then saw that this was a means for creative access to areas that were closed to regular missionaries, which could help evangelize the whole world and complete our Lord's Great Commission. This is the reason I wrote the book *Today's Tentmakers: An Alternative Model for World Evangelization*, which is based on our experience in Afghanistan.

The Great Commission

William Carey, an English lay pastor during the late 18th century, was attending a ministers meeting. He stood up and asked a question regarding what the group was going to do about the hundreds of millions of people who as yet had not heard the gospel. The moderator said, "Young man, sit down. When God wants to save the heathen, He will do it in His own way, without your help or mine." The general idea among Christians of that time was that the Great Commission applied only to the apostles, to whom Christ had given the command in the Gospels, and therefore it was not addressed to believers after the first century church.

But William Carey answered this false interpretation of the Bible by showing that the Great Commission applied to every Christian. In his booklet *An Enquiry into the Obligation of Christians to Use Means in the Conversion of the Heathens*, he pointed out that if our Lord's

> *William Carey started a revolution in the Protestant world, which resulted in the modern missionary movement.*

mandate applied only to the apostles, then Christians did not have the right to baptize, since the mandate for baptism was given right along with the command to evangelize or make disciples of every people group. Carey quoted Matthew 28:18-19, "Then Jesus came to them and said, 'All authority in heaven and on earth has been given to Me. Therefore go and make disciples of all nations, baptizing them in the name of the Father and of the Son and of the Holy Spirit.'"

Next, Carey went on to show that Christ added the promise, "'And surely I will be with you always, to the very end of the age'" (Matt. 28:20). He argued that since the apostles did not live until the end of the age, Christ must have been speaking to every believer down through church history. Thus, the Great Commission applied to every Christian. Carey not only started a revolution in the Protestant world, which resulted in the modern missionary movement, but he himself formed a missionary society and obeyed his Lord by going to India with his family in 1793.

---

1. *Why was it important for William Carey to establish the validity of the Great Commission (Matt. 28:18-20) for believers of all times?*

Today's unreached

In William Carey's day, there were hundreds of millions of people who had not heard the gospel. Today there are over two billion unreached people, who are living in approximately 11,000 people groups. The goal is to seek to plant evangelical churches in each of these unevangelized mosaics of society, which then in turn could reach out with the gospel to those in their own culture. In this way, the world can be evangelized according to the command of Christ. As Dr. Adoniram Judson Gordon said, "Our responsibility is not to bring the whole world to Christ, but it is assuredly that of bringing Christ to the whole world."

Dr. Tetsunao Yamamori points out that a majority of the unreached people in the world today are in areas which do not allow regular missionaries.* Thus, if these people are to be evangelized, it will have to be done by tentmakers (missionaries who enter these countries as laborers, tradesmen, students, technicians, professionals, and businessmen). Most of these unreached people groups are in the region known as the *10/40 window*, which is 10 degrees to 40 degrees above the equator and extends from North Africa to East Asia. This region includes peoples who make up the Muslim, Jewish, Hindu, Buddhist, and Animist blocs.

Creative Access Countries in the 10/40 Window

Afghanistan	Djibouti	Iran	Macau	Portugal	Turkmenistan
Algeria	Egypt	Iraq	Mali	Qatar	United Arab
Bahrain	Ethiopia	Israel	Malta	Saudi Arabia	Emirates
Bangladesh	Gambia	Japan	Mauritania	Senegal	Vietnam
Benin	Gaza Strip	Jordan	Morocco	Sudan	West Bank
Bhutan	Gibraltar	Korea, North	Myanmar	Syria	Western
Burkina Faso	Greece	Korea, South	Nepal	Taiwan	Sahara
Cambodia	Guinea	Kuwait	Niger	Tajikistan	Yemen
Chad	Guinea-Bissau	Laos	Oman	Thailand	
China	Hong Kong	Lebanon	Pakistan	Tunisia	
Cyprus	India	Libya	Philippines	Turkey	

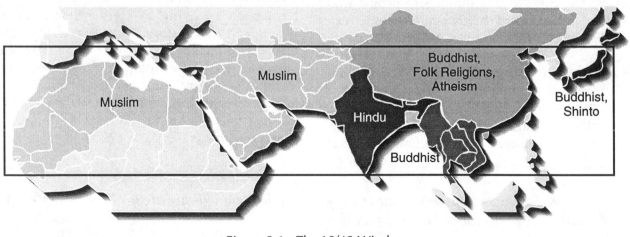

Figure 2-1. The 10/40 Window

---

* See Yamamori, T. (1993). *Penetrating missions' final frontier: A new strategy for unreached peoples.* Downers Grove, IL: InterVarsity Press.

2. *What is the difference between a reached people group and an unreached people group?*

_____

_____

Tentmaking Missionaries

The Lord has done much to help further the evangelization of the world through fully supported missionaries. For example, largely through the work of such missionaries, there are now more people who call themselves Christians in the southern hemisphere than in the northern hemisphere. But if the Great Commission according to Christ's command is to be fulfilled, both tentmakers and regular career missionaries (those who are fully dedicated to and supported through Christian work) are needed and must be mobilized, trained, and sent.

Ford Madison, who has been a tentmaker in Central America, has said, "Just as in the first reformation the common people were given the *Word* of God, so we need a second reformation when the common people are given the *work* of God." During the Protestant Reformation, the false dichotomy within the church between the clergy and the laity was discovered in the biblical truth of "the priesthood of the believers." But this truth really has not been put into practice. Many Christians still follow the medieval heresy that the pastor should do all the work for the local church and that the fully supported missionary should be responsible for evangelizing the world.

The concept of tentmaking thus is of the utmost strategic importance if Christ's commission of world evangelization is to be fulfilled. Mildred Cable, who was an outstanding missionary with the former China Inland Mission in the Gobi Desert, wrote, "No place is closed to God. If the front door is closed, we should try the back door." Tentmaking is God's way of getting in through the back door to areas which do not allow regular missionaries. However, we still need many more fully supported witnesses to go to those areas which do allow them.

> **Tentmaking is God's way of getting in through the back door to areas which do not allow regular missionaries.**

Thus, the Christian church must mobilize an army of self-supported witnesses or tentmakers, along with regular missionaries, if the world is to be evangelized for Christ. These tentmakers and regular missionaries are to go from all nations to all nations, so that the whole church can take the whole gospel to the whole world.

3. *Why are both tentmakers and regular career missionaries needed to complete the Great Commission?*

_____

_____

_____

Biblical basis of tentmaking

The main biblical model we have for tentmaking is the Apostle Paul. We read in Acts 18:1-4, "Paul left Athens and went to Corinth. There he met a Jew named Aquila... with his wife Priscilla.... Paul went to see them, and because he was a tentmaker as they were, he stayed and worked with them. Every Sabbath day he reasoned in the synagogue, trying to persuade Jews and Greeks."

When we look at the concept of tentmaking in the Scriptures, we see that most of the men and women in the Bible worked and were self-supporting. Even our Lord for most of His life was a carpenter in Nazareth. But for the three-plus years of His ministry, He was fully supported, especially by women believers. We read in Luke 8:1-3, "Jesus traveled about from one town and village to another, proclaiming the good news of the kingdom of God. The Twelve were with Him, and also some women who had been cured of evil spirits and diseases: Mary (called Magdalene) from whom seven demons had come out, Joanna the wife of Cuza, the manager of Herod's household, Susanna, and many others. These women were helping to support them out of their own means."

The Apostle Paul in 1 Corinthians 9:4-23 gives the reasons for his being a tentmaker. He first states that full support is biblical, as he makes the statement in 9:14, "The Lord has commanded that those who preach the gospel should receive their living from the gospel." But then he goes on to reveal the reasons that he chose to be a self-supporting tentmaker.

> **Most of the men and women in the Bible worked and were self-supporting.**

One reason was the rabbinic custom of not taking any money for teaching the Word of God. This was the reason that rabbis used to have another profession from which to gain their support, and then they could offer their services free for instructing people in the Scriptures. Thus the Apostle Paul in being a tentmaker was following a well-established Jewish custom, which made it possible for rabbis to

minister to small groups of Jews who were scattered around the world in the *Diaspora.*

It was during the Counter-Reformation in the 16th century, when Jews fled from Europe to North Africa, that the rabbis, because of their poverty, first started to get paid for their services, as many are today. For example, the rabbi I knew who was the head of the small synagogue in Kabul, Afghanistan, supported himself by being a money changer with a banking business.

Paul kept the tradition of self-support so that he could make the preaching of the gospel free. He expresses this idea in 1 Corinthians 9:16-18, "Woe to me if I do not preach the gospel! If I preach voluntarily, I have a reward; if not voluntarily, I am simply discharging the trust committed to me. What then is my reward? Just this: that in preaching the gospel, I may offer it free of charge."

There was another purpose to Paul's tentmaking profession. He believed that by being self-supporting he could not only make the gospel free, but also win more people for Christ. He states, "I make myself a slave to everyone, to win as many as possible" (1 Cor. 9:19). Many non-Christians today think that all preachers, pastors, evangelists, and missionaries are in their professions to make money. For example, Billy Graham is often accused of making a fortune as a television evangelist. This allega-

tion is false, but people still use it as an excuse for not accepting the gospel. Paul, by being self-supporting, made the preaching of the gospel free and thus avoided this common criticism. He was more effective than he might have been otherwise, since unbelievers could not excuse themselves simply by saying that Paul had the making of money as his motive.

> *Paul believed that by being self-supporting he could not only make the gospel free, but also win more people for Christ.*

By being a tentmaker, Paul also identified with others who were in his trade. This was the way he won Aquila and Priscilla to Christ while he made tents with them. In 1 Corinthians 9:20-22, he expresses this principle of reaching the mosaics of society through identifying with them, in order to contextualize the gospel: "To the Jews I became like a Jew, to win the Jews. To those under the law I became like one under the law... so as to win those under the law. To those not having the law I became like one not having the law... so as to win those not having the law. To the weak I became weak, to win the weak. I have become all things to all people so that by all possible means I might save some."

4. From 1 Corinthians 9:4-23, what are the advantages to gospel witness that Paul derived from being a tentmaker rather than a fully supported Christian worker?

_____

_____

_____

_____

Like Paul, tentmakers today avoid the criticism leveled at fully supported Christian workers, and they can be more effective in reaching those to whom a salary is a stumbling block.

They also have ready access to others who are in their same occupation and can bring them to Christ, using their understanding and affinity of interests as a bridge.

Another aspect of Paul's tentmaking ministry was an accountability structure. Since Paul and Barnabas were sent out by the church in Antioch, they then reported back to that congregation. It is important that tentmakers today have accountability with a local church.

> **When possible, tentmakers should line up with mission agencies, which are able to help them in many ways.**

Furthermore, as a mission team Paul and Barnabas were accountable to one another. Paul was also a *mentor* to Timothy, Titus, Aquila, Priscilla, Lydia, and many others who were on his teams and thus, as we see through his epistles, they were accountable to him. Today, it is important to have tentmaking teams which can be of mutual assistance and which can be more effective than "lone rangers."

When possible, tentmakers should line up with mission agencies, which are able to help them with language orientation, preparation for culture shock, fellowship on the field, assistance in establishing converts in local churches, and the stress of reentry when they return home. The mission structure can often provide an accountability structure where the sending church cannot. The Holy Spirit, speaking to the church in Antioch, called and sent out Barnabas and Saul. The Lord Jesus said, "I will build My church" (Matt. 16:18), and He used the church to equip and send these missionaries. The Holy Spirit, through Paul, also initiated the mission team (structure) which functioned in relation to the church in Antioch (Acts 13:2-4). If the world is to be evangelized according to the command of Christ, the local church needs to work in partnership with mission agencies.

5. *What advantages and disadvantages are there to tentmakers' working through a mission agency rather than being sent solely by their church?*

_____

_____

_____

_____

Tentmakers Are Real People

Most Christians earn a living in secular occupations and have the potential for becoming self-supporting tentmakers. This principle of self-support was true in the Old Testament as well as in the New. All of the patriarchs, as well as most of the prophets, worked for their own living. It was only the Levitical priests who were to be supported by other people. Even our Lord Jesus Christ, as we have seen, was a carpenter for most of His life.

6. *What other concrete examples of tentmakers can you find in the Old Testament? How did God use these people?*

_____

_____

_____

_____

The Swiss Basel missionaries

God has also used tentmaking to reach un-reached people groups throughout church history. For example, the Swiss Basel missionaries introduced self-supporting methods for

> **In church history, tentmaking has been a method whereby the national converts can become self-supporting and thus have healthy churches that don't depend on foreign money.**

their converts on the mission fields. In India they started textile mills. One of these Swiss missionaries invented the dye for khaki, which is now used all over the world, especially by the military. Lord Roberts, the British general over the army in India, visited this missionary-sponsored industry. When he saw the khaki dye (*khaki* means "the color of dirt" in Persian), he said that this was the cloth he needed to help his soldiers be better camouflaged. Thus, the British army uniform was changed from red coats, which made the soldiers targets of the Afghan sharpshooters, to the khaki uniforms of today.

In 1889, the Swiss Basel missionaries in Ghana introduced the cocoa bean into that country. (Cocoa originally came from tropical America.) The missionaries did this to give the national Christians a means to become financially self-sufficient. Within 20 years, by 1909, Ghana was producing more than half of the world's cocoa crop. The missionaries also supplied ships to export the production to Europe, which resulted in the Swiss chocolate business. Thus, in church history, tentmaking has not only been a means for missionaries to support themselves, but has also been a method whereby the national converts can also become self-supporting and thus have healthy churches that don't depend on foreign money.

The Apostle Paul

In 2 Thessalonians 3:7-9, the Apostle Paul states the importance of his being a self-supporting tentmaker. He also shows that he expected his converts to carry out this practice as well. "You ought to follow our example," he urges the Thessalonian believers. "We were not idle when we were with you, nor did we eat anyone's food without paying for it. On the contrary, we worked day and night, laboring and toiling so that we would not be a burden to any of you. We did this, not because we do not have the right to such help, but in order to make ourselves a model for you to follow."

7. *Potentially, how can the benefits of tentmaking extend to the population that is targeted for evangelization? How relevant is this concept for today?*

_____

_____

_____

_____

The Moravians

Another historical example is the Moravians. After their 1727 revival at Herrnhut in Germany, they sent missionaries all over the world who were self-supporting tentmakers. These missionaries took their trades as artisans with them and thus not only paid their own expenses through this means, but also taught national converts these skills. They did these things in Africa, Greenland, North America, Central America, and South America, as well as in other parts of the world. The biblical basis for their actions was 1 Timothy 4:8b, "Godliness is profitable for all things, having promise for both the present life and the life to come."

The Moravians saw tentmaking as a means of making profit for the Lord. They also established businesses, which not only supplied funds for their missionary work, but also employed national Christians. In their factories, they had devotions from the Bible for the whole staff. They also established medical insurance plans for their workers. Thus, the Moravians employed tentmaking as an effective way of continuing the evangelization of the world through self-supporting missionaries and as a means of assisting their converts financially.

William Carey

William Carey planned to go to India as a fully supported missionary. However, Dr. Thomas, who was a Christian physician on his team, turned out to be a spendthrift and squandered in a few days all the money they had for their first year. It would have taken five months to get word that they needed money back to England by sailing ship, which was the fastest means of communication of the day. Then after the funds had been collected, it would have taken five months to send the money back to India, making the total time about a year. Therefore, William Carey got a job as head of an indigo factory. From then on, he was a self-supporting tentmaker. Toward the end of his life, he said that wherever possible, missionaries should be completely or partially self-supporting. Then the churches could send out more witnesses to help complete Christ's commission.

> *William Carey said that wherever possible, missionaries should be completely or partially self-supporting. Then the churches could send out more witnesses to help complete Christ's commission.*

Some potential tentmakers wonder whether they will have time to witness and plant churches if they are employed in a secular job. The Apostle Paul evangelized practically the whole Roman world as a tentmaker. William Carey, who started the modern missionary movement, was not only self-supporting, but also did extensive translation work. He translated the whole Bible into six languages, the New Testament into 23 others, and parts of the Scriptures into 11 other tongues, including Chinese. These two outstanding missionaries demonstrate that it is possible to be a tentmaker and still be a very effective missionary.

8. *What elements of Paul's background allowed him to be a successful evangelist and church planter while supporting himself (and others) with a secular job?*

_____

_____

_____

House churches

Aquila's and Priscilla's tentmaking business led to the establishment of a house church. We read in Romans 16:3-5, "Greet Prisca and Aquila, my fellow workers in Christ Jesus. They risked their lives for me. Not only I but all the churches of the Gentiles are grateful for them. Greet also the church that meets in their house."

The chief goal of tentmaking witness should be to plant a local church and help it grow. This is especially true if unreached people groups are to be evangelized. In the Great Commission, our Lord commanded not only that Christians are to make disciples from among all people groups, but also that they are to baptize converts in the name of the Father, the Son, and the Holy Spirit and teach these new believers to obey everything that He had commanded

(Matt. 28:19-20). Carrying out this commission necessitates the planting of churches.

It is ideal to use the "house church" model for this task. When my wife and I first went to Afghanistan in 1951, we along with other

> **The chief goal of tentmaking witness should be to plant a local church and help it grow.**

Christian tentmakers were able to establish such a church in our home. This house church later developed into a base for Christian ministries to the people of that country, as well as being a worshiping and witnessing congregation for the international community.

9. *Why does Dr. Wilson suggest that a "house church" model may be the ideal for tentmakers?*

_____

_____

Tentmaking is not a new idea. It is as old as the Scriptures. There is no need to argue whether it is a better or worse method of sending Christian missionaries than other approaches. Both fully supported career missionaries and tentmakers are biblical models and are urgently needed if the task of world evangelization is to be completed. It is true, however, that unless tentmakers are prepared and

sent into unreached areas of the world, these regions which are restricted to access by career missionaries will be isolated from Christian witness. Christ said, "Go and make disciples of all nations...." Until that task is finished, we must use all means at our disposal to penetrate the last missions frontiers and place tentmaking missionaries among the unreached peoples of the world.

Summary

The Great Commission (Matt. 28:18-20) is not an option. It was given to all believers "to the end of the age." Missiologists see the world in terms of a mosaic of peoples. Perhaps 11,000 of these groups—more than two billion people in all—are unreached with the gospel message. Most of these people live in the 10/40 window, a region encompassing countries which are restricted to access by regular career missionaries. In many cases, sending out tentmaker missionaries is the only means of placing Christian witnesses among these unreached peoples. Thus, the mobilization of a vast army of tentmaking missionaries is of utmost strategic importance to the completion of the Great Commission.

The concept of tentmaking is well supported in Scripture. The term *tentmaker* is derived from the fact that the Apostle Paul exercised his trade of making tents in order to support himself during his missionary journeys. By earning his own keep, Paul disarmed critics who might accuse him of preaching for money; thus, he avoided being a stumbling block to the gospel and was able to be more effective with people. He was also able to minister to those of his own trade by identifying with them. Like regular career missionaries, tentmakers should be under the authority of their church. In many cases, it is also helpful for them to work under the accountability structure of an established mission agency.

There are many examples of tentmakers in both the Old and the New Testaments. The patriarchs, prophets, and even Jesus Himself supported themselves through their occupations, at least for a time. Historically, tentmaking has also played a great part not only in sending and supporting missionaries, but also in benefiting the national people with a means of livelihood. In spite of demands on their time by their secular occupations, men such as the Apostle Paul and William Carey have demonstrated that tentmakers can be extremely effective. It is important to keep in mind that tentmakers work toward the establishment of the church, wherever they serve. In many cases, the house church model may be the most effective.

Action Plan Assignment

1. *If you haven't done so already, memorize the Great Commission in Matthew 28:18-20.*

2. *The reasons for tentmaking aren't obvious to everyone. Prepare an outline of a clear rationale for tentmakers as an indispensable missionary component, using evidence from the biblical, historical, and strategic perspectives. Then share these thoughts with at least three other people.*

3. *Is tentmaking a strategic component of your church's missions policy? Find out by examining a copy of the written policy or talking to someone in missions leadership.*

CHAPTER 3

Cross-Cultural Servants

Completing the Great Commission is not an option for the church: it is a command. Without tentmaking missionaries, it is unlikely that the church will be able to finish the task. Most of the hundreds of millions of people beyond the reach of the gospel live in countries where creative access for missionaries is required. If these needed workers are to be raised up, where will they come from? One of the primary sources will be the eager young people of this generation who, early on, have captured the Great Commission call and a vision for the unreached nations of the world. What will it take to bring this commitment to a point of mature involvement as tentmaker missionaries? Dr. David Tai-Woong Lee has counseled and trained many young people who desire to go into missionary service. In the following article, he describes the process of converting youthful enthusiasm into readiness for the challenge of cross-cultural ministry.

❑ *Spiritual Readiness for Cross-Cultural Ministry*

David Tai-Woong Lee *

Kim, a young man in his early 20's, came to talk to me. He had been a Christian for about a year and a half. In that time, his missionary vision had grown remarkably. He was now at a place where he felt he needed to make a decision about becoming a tentmaker in one of the world's creative access countries. "What should I do? What steps do I have to take to become a tentmaker?" he asked. As I looked at the young man, I saw his sincerity and zeal. In his earnestness, he seemed ready to die for the Lord's sake; but was he ready to *live for Him as a cross-cultural servant*? How should I advise him? I knew there were areas he should de-

---

* Dr. David Tai-Woong Lee is the director of the Global Ministry Training Center in Seoul, Korea. The center's programs encompass training for both regular and tentmaking missionaries. Dr. Lee also serves on the World Evangelical Fellowship Missions Commission and is considered one of the primary mission leaders of Korea.

velop and be tested in before he ever put his foot on a mission field.

Mission leaders, especially those who lack experience in administrative roles, often make a serious mistake at this point. When they see such a fresh and dedicated person, their first thought is to place the new missionary among one of the unreached people groups as soon as possible. Yet time and again, we have witnessed that these untrained individuals not only jeopardize their own security, but also have the potential of destroying the patient work that others have done over the years. This is particularly true for those who are placed in creative access nations.

People have false assumptions about tentmakers. They think that since they are not career missionaries, they can probably go to the field with little or no training. The truth is that while career missionaries usually have a good support system on the field, many tentmakers have to depend on their own resources. It is essential, therefore, to evaluate potential tentmakers in a number of areas.

1. *In what ways might an untrained or spiritually immature person hinder God's work in a creative access country rather than help it?*

_____

_____

_____

Examining your motives

"Kim, besides your obvious love for the Lord and desire to serve Him, why do you think you want to become a tentmaker?"

"Since I became a Christian, I've had a growing dissatisfaction with my job here in Korea. I know that there are opportunities elsewhere for people with my skills. It's a good time for me to make a change. I'd like to travel and see the world. I know the Lord needs people in the mission field, and I'm willing and able to go."

2. *List the reasons Kim wanted to become a tentmaker. Can you list some additional reasons individuals might consider tentmaking? What are your own reasons for this interest?*

_____

_____

_____

_____

_____

Individuals express a desire to become tentmakers for a number of reasons. As in Kim's case, they may have mixed motives. Kim's stated reasons are not evil as such. Yet his answer was missing an essential ingredient to successful tentmaking—the clear call of God to missionary service. Without this calling, Kim might accomplish his other objectives, but his effectiveness for Christ as a tentmaker was in doubt.

> **The tentmaker is like any other of God's envoys. He should be a tentmaker because of a clear calling to a cross-cultural ministry.**

As I looked at Kim sitting across from me, my heart went out to him. He was not unlike many other young people I have counseled, with a bright, fresh enthusiasm for mission. Was his attraction to tentmaking an adventure? Was it an escape? Or was God beginning to speak to someone He had called for the challenging task of communicating His love cross-culturally?

"The tentmaker," I began tentatively, "is like any other of God's envoys. He should be a tentmaker because of a clear calling to a cross-cultural ministry. He should be concerned about obeying the Great Commission, glorifying the Lord, and wanting to obey Him at all costs. Kim, you have experienced the love of God, and you want to preach and witness to the lost. You are on the right track. Try to lay aside other motivations which are drawing you to tentmaking, and begin pursuing a knowledge of God's calling on your life. If He is calling you to become a cross-cultural witness, He will confirm that call."

Sensing my genuine concern for him, Kim showed by his next question that he had received well my gentle rebuke. "If it's true I should have a call to cross-cultural ministry, how do I receive that call? How can I know for sure that God is calling me to this kind of ministry?" With great care, I began to outline for him how he might come to a clearer under-standing of God's will for him regarding cross-cultural service.

Examining your call

"God's call comes differently to different people. There is no one situation where God limits Himself in issuing a call. Nevertheless, there are two extremes to avoid. One is basing one's call on purely personal feelings without solid facts. The other is relying only on facts without any subjective reality and conviction. A call, if it is a healthy one, must lie in the continuum between these two extremes (see Figure 3-1). There must be both the subjective and objective aspects to a call. If you lack objectivity, it may be wise to seek more information. Conversely, if you lack subjective convictions, you should pray and even fast to see what God is telling you, on the basis of the knowledge that you already have about mission needs and tentmaker opportunities.

"If you want some concrete results in determining the nature of your call, follow these practical steps. Although we cannot put God into a box, this is a time-proven process. First, pray with the Scriptures open. Look at some of the most important missionary calls and visions of mission in Scriptures, such as Ephesians 3:1-13, the book of Acts, and the Great Commission passages. Second, listen to the Holy Spirit. Ask Him to lead you as you read through the Scriptures with an open mind. Third, consult missionary biographies, statistics, information on countries, and whatever resources you can get hold of. Fourth, pray specifically for clarity and depth of conviction regarding God's call.

"When all of these elements are factored together, you should, in time, arrive at a sound

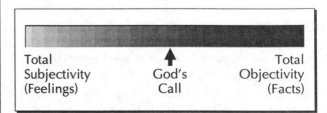

Total Subjectivity (Feelings) — God's Call — Total Objectivity (Facts)

Figure 3-1. God's Call Must Lie on the Continuum Between Feelings and Facts

decision. If you feel the Lord is calling you into cross-cultural ministry, then pray, 'Here I am. I am willing to take a step forward. Show me the way!' If it is the will of God, you should experience His peace in the decision. After you have made the decision and confirmed it in your heart, then begin to take whatever steps are necessary to follow your call. This is a good time to approach a mission leader as well as your pastor. They should be able to counsel and guide you in this process."

3. Read Ephesians 3:1-13. What guiding principles regarding God's calling do you find in this passage?

_____

_____

_____

4. What other passages can you think of which might be important to consider prayerfully as you examine a calling to tentmaking?

_____

_____

_____

Steps to maturity

Kim had listened attentively as I explained to him the way to pursue the confirmation of God's calling on his life. As I finished, he spoke up. "I feel I've done much of what you're suggesting. I've prayed a lot and even fasted. I

> **A call usually comes when you are experiencing spiritual growth and are actively engaged in ministry.**

admit I don't know much about tentmaking, but I've been reading about the Middle East and the great spiritual needs there. I can't say for sure whether I should go there, but it seems that just praying about it isn't giving me the confirmation I'm seeking. I see that I need to become more knowledgeable about Muslim ministries. Is there anything else I can do?"

"A call seldom occurs in a vacuum," I explained. "It usually comes when you are experiencing spiritual growth and are actively engaged in ministry to the best of your ability, regardless of your training; you are serving in a church, witnessing to friends, and praying for the world. To start with, I'd like you to rate yourself on how you are doing in terms of your own spiritual growth." I pulled a sheet of paper from a file and handed it to Kim (see Figure 3-5 on page 3-14). "This is a list of some of the ingredients which should be evident in a person who is growing spiritually. Take some time and rate yourself using a 10-point scale. The higher the number, the greater the level of maturity you've reached. For the sake of convenience, the rating scale is divided into two sections: your relationship with God and your ministry skills."

As Kim glanced down at the list, I continued with my instructions. "This list is for your own use. Be as honest as you can with yourself. You might want to have your pastor or someone who knows you well rate you, too. When you feel you have an accurate assessment, use the same list to make goal projections for the next six months. Whatever ratings you may have given yourself as your current status, set a goal two to three numbers higher as your growth objective."

> **Spiritual growth takes place best when it is nurtured simultaneously by two spheres: a corporate framework and an individual program.**

Kim's eager look encouraged me to continue helping him understand how spiritual growth is achieved. "Spiritual growth takes place best when it is nurtured simultaneously by two spheres: a corporate framework and an individual program. The corporate framework has to do with the spiritual climate of the church you attend, while the individual side has to do with a tailor-made discipleship plan you go through" (Figure 3-2).

I again went to my file drawer and pulled out a couple of diagrams. "Kim, let me show you what I mean graphically. Through *worship, fellowship, preaching, service, training,* and *education,* the church can provide a favorable climate for spiritual growth. Assuming that you are in a healthy church, you still need to be nurtured individually in a number of essential areas in order to grow into a mature tentmaker.

"The arrow in this first diagram shows how your self-directed program for growth is intended to achieve certain objectives. First, you need to learn to feed on the Word of God without the help of others. This is probably the most important growth factor when it is coupled with prayer. When you do both of these regularly in a quiet place, you establish a 'quiet time' in which to develop your communication with the Lord.

"Second, you need to ground your spiritual life solidly by studying such books as Romans, Ephesians, and the Gospels. These books will give you a firm biblical and theological foundation. It is wise to have a solid grasp not only of the content of these books, but also of important topics, such as being justified by faith (Rom. 1-5), overcoming sinful desires and re-

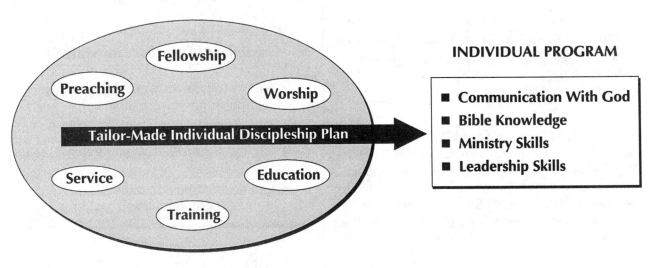

Figure 3-2. Favorable Climate for Spiritual Growth

Leadership Skills

Ministry Skills

Bible Knowledge

Communication With God

Repentance and Faith

Figure 3-3. The Basis for a
Global Vision for World Mission

lying on the power of the resurrected life of Jesus (Rom. 6-8), understanding the future plan of God for the universe (Rom. 9-11), and living a life of servanthood in ministry to others (Rom. 12-16).

"Third, you need to learn ministry skills, such as personal evangelism, how to nurture others, and discipleship training principles.

"Fourth, you must cultivate leadership skills. All of these must be integrated into a global vision for world mission.

"As you pursue your personal growth plan, you will begin developing the essential elements for becoming an effective tentmaker. This second diagram (Figure 3-3) illustrates how this process builds towards a personalized global vision for world mission."

As I finished, I sensed that I had overwhelmed Kim. "Wow, I had no idea so much was involved in reaching spiritual maturity!" he groaned. "How mature do I have to be before I can become a tentmaker? It could take years for me to achieve what you are suggesting. I feel like

I'd have to become a spiritual giant just to get to the field!"

I almost chuckled at Kim's response. Enthusiasm is often daunted by the prospect of hard work and patient waiting. God's call, however, is strengthened and nurtured by the same process. Kim needed to hear this firm word. He needed to let the Lord begin to work in his heart.

"How mature must you be before you can be a tentmaker? There is no hard and fast rule on this matter," I answered cautiously. "Nevertheless, I'd like to suggest the following four minimal guidelines. First, you must be able to nurture yourself spiritually in a context in which you may not receive much spiritual or emotional support from others. Second, you must be competent in your chosen vocation. Third, you must be able to adjust emotionally to the stress of living in your host culture. Fourth, you must have practiced skills in witnessing to other individuals and nurturing them in their spiritual growth."

A few moments passed before Kim spoke. "I can see that there is a lot more to this tentmaking than meets the eye."

"Why don't you take some time to think and pray about these matters?" I suggested. "Come and see me again if you feel the Lord is confirming a real sense of calling in you to serve Him as a cross-cultural servant."

Guidelines for Measuring Maturity

- Ability to nourish yourself spiritually without support from others.
- Competency in your chosen vocation.
- Ability to adjust emotionally to the host culture.
- Ability to witness to others and nurture them in their spiritual growth.

Figure 3-4

5. *Are the minimal guidelines for maturity which the author sets forth reasonable? Why or why not?*

_____

_____

_____

The Tentmaker and Others

Nearly seven months went by before I saw Kim again. When he called on me late one afternoon, I could see in his facial expression that he was eager to share with me what had transpired since we last met. God had been dealing in his life and had caused him to face many issues squarely. Kim's flight of enthusiasm was being converted into a measured walk with God as he disciplined himself through his daily quiet time. He had also been studying. Shaping theology didn't come easily, but Kim was motivated by a new understanding of the importance of being able to feed himself from the Word.

The Lord had also spoken to Kim about his calling to cross-cultural mission. His conviction about serving in a creative access country had grown. As he had read about the deep spiritual and physical needs in many of the Muslim nations, his heart had been drawn towards serving among these unreached people. He was troubled, however, in thinking about how they might be converted to Christ in countries where public proclamation of the gospel was prohibited. "How am I to be a witness under such circumstances?" Kim queried.

"Under these conditions, your only means of witness may be your life itself. Outspoken verbal witness may jeopardize not only your own security, but also the security of coworkers. Therefore, one of the best ways to magnify Jesus as a tentmaker is with a servant attitude. This can be so powerful that people will end up asking you the reasons and resources which enable you to be so different from others. This will present a wonderful opportunity to introduce Jesus."

"I can understand that in theory," replied Kim, "but it seems like a very hard thing to practice over the long run."

> *One of the best ways to magnify Jesus as a tentmaker is with a servant attitude.*

"A servant attitude is not easy to develop," I responded. "For a short while you could wear a facade. As pressure builds up and time wears on, such artificial attitudes will wear out, and you are bound to reveal your real self. The only way to achieve a servant attitude is to change from within. Change comes as you experience Jesus in your life, particularly His servant attitude. Cultivate the humility of Jesus Christ as seen in Philippians 2:5-11. You will soon understand that humility is a by-product of a life which is crucified with Christ. Such a person draws from the Lord the power to deny himself daily, and he clothes himself with other virtues such as compassion, kindness, humility, gentleness, and patience (Col. 3:12). If tentmakers will indeed be servants, not only will their lives speak, but the words of their testimony will be powerful—so powerful that people will be converted!"

6. *Consider Philippians 2:5-11. In most societies, a servant is used by others and is often despised. Why is it important for tentmakers to act as servants? What can tentmakers expect if true, God-enabled spiritual servanthood is achieved?*

_____

_____

_____

Communication skills

"I think I'm beginning to understand how a servant attitude will open doors for witness," Kim said. "But isn't it just as important to be able to communicate the gospel once that door has been opened? I would think that we have to be able to communicate with the people."

"You're right, Kim. Communication is a key to many things in life. Certainly it is a key to successful marriage, team ministry, friendship, cross-cultural witness, and life. For cross-cultural tentmakers, good communication skills are crucial. First, they will prevent many misunderstandings and unnecessary personal conflicts, both with the nationals and with fellow tentmakers. Second, they will enhance the development of sound relationships and friendships. Often these are the channels through which the gospel is being communicated. Third, and above all, they can be used for effective witnessing. Once you are fluent in the language, prime opportunities will come to communicate the gospel. After all, this is the real reason that people become tentmakers.

"We know from communications theory that not only are words important, but you, the messenger, are a key part of that message. This means that if you display humility and a servant's attitude, you will have a better chance of effectively communicating the true gospel. When you demonstrate a haughty and proud attitude, you will present a distorted message. It is essential for us as tentmakers not only to have communication skills, but also to become the kind of people who match the content of the gospel message. Only in this way will we communicate Christ and His power to change lives."

7. What is the main point Dr. Lee is making regarding the interrelationship between a servant's attitude and true communication?

_____

_____

_____

Relational skills

"I think I'm beginning to see," said Kim pensively. "If I'm going to be an effective witness to my host culture, it has to come from the heart. It's going to be tough for me, but it makes sense. I have a lot to learn about communication skills, too. But if I'm to be a servant to the people, does it mean I can't stand up for what I believe, for my own convictions?"

"That's a good question, Kim. Many people sacrifice their own convictions to gain acceptance, but there is no substitute for possessing genuine Christian character in relationships. Exercising relational skills without personal credibility will corrupt the effectiveness of your witness in the long run. Let's suppose you are going to China. Even a hardline communist will favor a person with genuine Christian convictions above an atheist who has both vocational skills and relational skills, yet lacks integrity. So before we discuss developing relational skills, we need to affirm the need for integrity and love. If these are already in place, there are some learned skills which will enhance relationship building.

"One of these skills is the ability to make friends. Dr. Phil Parshall shares his story of befriending a number of Muslim intellectuals. Some of these became permanent friends and often functioned in bridging obstacles to the gospel. For some, making friends is as natural as breathing. If you are in this category of people, you already have overcome a big hurdle. The majority of us need to *learn* how to make friends. This is particularly true when you are in a foreign culture."

"Yes," admitted Kim, "it's very difficult for me to make friends. It just seems that I don't have much in common with a lot of people, especially those who don't love the Lord."

"Building relationships is not really an option for tentmakers. There are several natural ways to meet people and begin building friendships. Demonstrating a genuine interest in learning from others is one way. I was once on a train heading for Kuala Lumpur from Singapore. I sat next to a Malay Muslim girl, wondering how

> **Exercising relational skills without personal credibility will corrupt the effectiveness of your witness in the long run.**

I could engage her in conversation. I pondered for about an hour before an idea came to me. Using simple vocabulary, I carefully began to ask her about Malay culture. By the time we reached our destination, I was able to have an in-depth conversation. I not only shared my testimony with her, but was also able to hear her tell her story as a Muslim. Out of curiosity, I asked why she, as a Muslim girl, was not offended talking to a Christian man. She said simply, 'Because you wanted to learn about our customs.' Showing a genuine interest in others—their lives, beliefs, countries, and culture—is a key to establishing relationships.

"Learning to enjoy sports with others is another easy way to build relationships. In fact, any special interest or talent, such as playing a musical instrument, can be a key to relationship building. Beyond these simple paths to friendship, basic knowledge in understanding others through psychology, cultural anthropology, and cross-cultural communication will be very helpful."

8. An old proverb says, "In order for a man to have friends, he must show himself friendly." How do you make friends? Analyze your strengths and weaknesses in this area.

_____

_____

_____

_____

The Tentmaker and His Work

"Making friends sounds simple as you explain it. I guess part of my problem is that I'm pretty preoccupied with myself. I haven't really shown myself to be very friendly, even to those I work with. In fact, this is really a problem for me. I don't really like my job. There's a lot of stress where I work, and it makes me edgy. I'm afraid I've offended a few people. Maybe if I go overseas I can get a fresh start. But what I really would like to do is quit my profession and be a full-time worker for the Lord. I guess I'll have to put up with a job, though, if I'm going to be a tentmaker."

> **A tentmaker who just does a job to get into a country finds himself very frustrated.**

"I think I can sympathize with what you are feeling, Kim. A lot of people seem to have the same problem, and it really frustrates them. But a tentmaker who just does a job to get into a country also finds himself very frustrated. Working overseas isn't going to erase the fundamental problem of how you view your work. As a tentmaker, your work *is* your ministry. Let me illustrate this important principle.

"Dick is a professor of economics serving in one of the creative access countries; it is a comparatively open Muslim society. He teaches in one of the universities and has wonderful opportunities to meet Muslim university students in his classroom. As these students witness Dick's life, many are drawn to him. Dick now has several Bible study groups. He often meets with students who come for personal counseling. He advises them on a wide range of matters, from marriage problems to spiritual concerns. How did these opportunities come about? In this case, it was Dick's classes in economics that opened up an avenue of witness. Dick pours himself into his work. Day after day he shares with his students his mind and his heart. He is an excellent professor, and he shows genuine interest in his students and their lives. Students can feel this man's uniqueness. As Dick opens up to them, they see Jesus. For Dick, his work is intricately tied to his ministry. His work *is* his ministry!"

9. *Do you feel that your work is (or could be) your ministry, as in Dick's case? Why or why not?*

_____

_____

_____

Pursuing excellence

"Wow, that's a great testimony! I guess Dick is one of those lucky guys who likes his work. Frankly, I just do what I need to get by, so that I can get out of there and witness for the Lord. Is there anything I can do to help make my work a base for witnessing?"

"Yes, there are at least two areas to consider. First of these is pursuing excellence in your own area of expertise. The higher the achievement level you have attained in your own area, the more likely you will win genuine respect and acceptance. In Dick's case, he demonstrated himself to be an excellent teacher. The students' respect and acceptance became his opportunity to witness for the Lord. If his performance had been careless, he would have quickly lost his audience.

"There is also excellence in the area of personal integrity. Suppose you are a professor, but you don't keep your word. You don't show genuine care and love for your students. You are mostly preoccupied with your own interests. You don't treat your students with respect. The outcome is obvious. Your words of testimony will have little power. Your students will discredit the gospel, along with you as a teacher.

"The Bible commands us that anything we do, we should do heartily, as unto the Lord. This demands that we pursue excellence in our own area, whether we are teaching, working as a

> *People need to notice a difference in us. Our work is the most obvious and public display of our lives.*

technician, involved in business, or even serving as a full-time Christian worker! People need to notice a difference in us. Our work is the most obvious and public display of our lives.

"Tentmakers also need to seek excellence in areas which are useful to the host country. They should study and analyze beforehand the area where they are going to serve. They must learn what the marketable skills or trades are for that area. Then they should concentrate on developing these skills and becoming an expert. They may even need to acquire a high academic degree in a specific discipline or a degree in business administration, urban planning, or computer programming. This requires long-term planning, especially if tentmakers want to gain an appropriate amount of work experience in their field before going overseas."

10. *What occupation are you involved in? Are you pursuing excellence in your field? How could you improve in this area?*

_____

_____

_____

_____

The road to spiritual maturity

Kim let out a long sigh. "I can see I have a long way to go," he said. "But I'm not discouraged. I see now that tentmaking is not just a way to get into a country to witness for the Lord. It is a way of life, a mindset. I really need to change some of my attitudes towards my work and begin to pursue excellence in a number of areas."

> **Tentmaking is not just a way to get into a country to witness for the Lord. It is a way of life, a mindset.**

I smiled at Kim's new-found sobriety. "You've already come a long way, my friend. The road ahead is a long one, but our Lord has promised to accompany us along the whole length of it. Many so-called tentmakers have gone to the field with attitudes which were similar to yours when you first came to me. Most of those individuals have failed to accomplish significant spiritual ends. Lest you feel you have arrived at a complete understanding, let me say that I have painted for you a broad picture regarding spiritual maturity, personal relationships, and the life and work of a tentmaker. This is not exhaustive. You have a long way to go in terms of attaining excellence in each of the three areas mentioned. Yet, you have made a good start.

"As we all endeavor to grow more in each area, may God give us grace upon grace, counsel upon counsel, encouragement upon encouragement, love upon love, faith upon faith, as He brings us to maturity. There will always be higher ground to conquer. As Paul so aptly puts it in Philippians 3:12-14, 'Not that I have already obtained all this, or have already been made perfect, but I press on to take hold of that for which Christ Jesus took hold of me. Brothers, I do not consider myself yet to have taken hold of it. But one thing I do: forgetting what is behind and straining toward what is ahead, I press on toward the goal to win the prize for which God has called me heavenward in Christ Jesus.'"

Summary

Not all those who feel drawn to tentmaking are suited to the task. Motives must be examined and spiritual readiness evaluated. Unless tentmakers are relatively mature and know how to sustain themselves spiritually, their mission is not likely to succeed. Fundamental to the whole process is a clear sense of calling to cross-cultural mission. Spiritual growth occurs best when it takes place in the nurturing context of a church and is paralleled by a personal program focused on developing one's knowledge of God and the Scriptures. Once this base is established, it is important to learn ministry skills—especially how to lead others to Christ and disciple them.

Tentmakers must be able to be witnesses. Because of security conditions in many of the creative access countries, the lives of tentmakers may be the primary means of communicating the gospel message. Portraying a true servant's attitude is the best way to model the gospel message. People must be able to notice a difference in tentmakers. Beyond this, transmitting the message verbally when the opportunities arise is also critical. Building relationships is not an option for tentmakers. Friendships can be started if tentmakers show genuine interest in other people and also through affinity with some activity. These friendships will provide bridges to gospel witness.

Tentmakers must also seek excellence in their work if they are to gain a hearing. In many cases, work is the most public expression of Christians' faith. Work is ministry in this context. A positive attitude and a striving for excellence are the best ways to gain genuine respect.

Action Plan Assignment

1. *Have you pursued a clear understanding of God's calling on your life for cross-cultural service? Write out an explanation of your calling as clearly as you understand it. Share this information with at least one person in missions leadership in your church.*

2. *Rate your calling on the subjectivity/objectivity continuum that Dr. Lee talks about on page 3-3. Is your calling in balance? If not, what do you need to do to bring it into balance? List action steps that you can take to correct any imbalance that exists.*

3. *Rate yourself using the Spiritual Life Rating Scale found on the following page. Read the Scripture passage for each point if you feel you need clarification for the item. You may want to write your answers on a separate piece of paper and use the chart in your book to make a photocopy for your pastor, spouse, or close friend who can also help you arrive at an honest rating. When you are through rating yourself, prayerfully consider which areas you will purpose to improve in over the next few months, and mark where you want to be able to rate yourself at the end of that time.*

Spiritual Life Rating Scale

My Relationship With God	No or Never									Yes or Always

My Relationship With God

| | | No or
Never | | | | | | | | | Yes or
Always |

1. I am a Christian and am fully assured of my salvation in Christ Jesus (1 John 1).   1 2 3 4 5 6 7 8 9 10

2. I acknowledge the Lordship of Jesus Christ in my life through word and deed (Phil. 3:7-14).   1 2 3 4 5 6 7 8 9 10

3. I am experiencing the fullness of the Holy Spirit (Eph. 5:18-20).   1 2 3 4 5 6 7 8 9 10

4. I am guided by the Holy Spirit (John 16:13-15).   1 2 3 4 5 6 7 8 9 10

5. My convictions about truth and reality are based on the Bible and its teachings (2 Tim. 3:14-17).   1 2 3 4 5 6 7 8 9 10

6. I demonstrate Christian character (Gal. 5:22-26).   1 2 3 4 5 6 7 8 9 10

7. I have a regular quiet time.   1 2 3 4 5 6 7 8 9 10

8. I am experiencing the significance of corporate life and worship.   1 2 3 4 5 6 7 8 9 10

My Relationship With Others

1. I conduct myself with maturity and humility towards others (Phil. 2:1-8).   1 2 3 4 5 6 7 8 9 10

2. Witnessing to others is a way of life for me (2 Tim. 4:1-5).   1 2 3 4 5 6 7 8 9 10

3. I know my spiritual gift and am serving the church with it (Rom. 12:1-8).   1 2 3 4 5 6 7 8 9 10

4. I am helping nurture other young Christians in their spiritual growth (2 Tim. 2:1-2).   1 2 3 4 5 6 7 8 9 10

5. I am helping others with their physical and financial needs (Jam. 2:14-18).   1 2 3 4 5 6 7 8 9 10

6. I am demonstrating leadership qualities (1 Tim. 3:1-13).   1 2 3 4 5 6 7 8 9 10

Figure 3-5

CHAPTER 4

The Crucial Role of the Local Church

In this chapter, we will examine what the home church and the tentmaker need and expect from each other. We will move outward from the biblical example to explore attitudes, programs, and actions for both churches and tentmakers.

Those in leadership in many churches are still suspicious of tentmaking. They may wonder about the effectiveness of sending people overseas who will have to spend most of their time at a secular job. They don't have a vision for witness in the workplace and perhaps don't understand the dynamic of Christian mission in creative access countries. Other church leaders may be sympathetic to the cause, but they don't know how to respond to tentmakers. Regular career missionaries are a known entity, but how do we deal with this new breed? Tentmakers aren't even in the missions policy!

The responsibility for creating an atmosphere of understanding and support doesn't fall entirely into the hands of church leadership: it is the duty of tentmakers as well. Many tentmakers will have to sow faithfully and lovingly to create the understanding they need. A great deal of hard work may also be required. In the following article, Pastor Derek Christensen provides an excellent orientation both for tentmakers and for the leadership of their local churches. As we work our way through this chapter, we want to look at two churches. The first is our biblical model, the sending church at Antioch. The second is *your* church. The questions interspersed throughout this chapter will help you think about how things are at your church, and how they might be....

❑ *The Story of Two Churches*

Derek Christensen *

John and Mary are a good, keen, Christian couple, with excellent job skills and work experience, a deep interest in missions, and a longing to do something for God.

The door never opened for them to go into career missionary service... it wasn't possible for them to go to Bible school... yet in their hearts, John and Mary truly feel called to serve in Christ's global cause. Unfortunately, there never seemed to be a way for their bodies to follow their hearts.

It was sad, really, because John and Mary made a significant impact in their jobs with their hard work, their compassion, and their honesty... sad, too, because in their church they were greatly valued, leading a home group, discipling new Christians, and generally being an encouragement to their pastor. They should have felt satisfied with their service, but they weren't.

They went to their pastor, and he smiled warmly and prayed with them.

They went to their missions committee, but they did not fit the missions policy.

They went to their home group, who loved and affirmed them and were glad to have them still anchored at home.

John and Mary are frustrated tentmakers.

---

1. Were the responses of the pastor, the missions committee, and the home group to this couple appropriate? Why or why not?

_____

_____

_____

_____

---

* Derek Christensen is the pastor of a church in Pakuranga, Auckland, New Zealand. He has been involved in preparing and supervising the work of tentmaker missionaries in Papua New Guinea. He currently directs the work of Marketplacers International, a tentmaking organization in New Zealand.

We would like to suggest that a church which is functioning as it should would respond differently to this situation. Ideally, there should be a climate of belief and practice in the church, out of which people naturally emerge for all types of missionary endeavors, including tentmaking. Let's rewrite John's and Mary's story, finding ways that a church—perhaps even your church—can become a healthier place for potential tentmakers.

The role of the local church in mission

The first church in our story is the well-known biblical example of the congregation in Antioch. When examining this sending church, we usually focus on the first three verses in Acts 13. If we add references from Acts 11, 14, 15, and 18, we get a far richer picture of the mutual relationship between the home church and its missionaries.

Figure 4-1 lists the roles of the sending church, based on the example set by the church in Antioch. The list is divided into two parts: (a) tasks relating to preparing and sending out workers and (b) tasks focusing on maintaining relationships with those workers. Let's examine each of these tasks.

Preparing and Sending Out Workers

Making disciples

In the Great Commission, Jesus told His followers to *go and make disciples* (Matt. 28:18-20). The local church is in the business of making true disciples. To make disciples, all mission workers, including tentmakers, must first be disciples themselves. We have to plan for this to happen. So often we are enthusiastic

Roles of the Sending Church		
TASKS	**ANTIOCH CHURCH**	**OTHER REFERENCES**
PREPARING AND SENDING OUT WORKERS		
Making disciples	Acts 11:26	Eph. 4:11-13 1 Cor. 3:1-15
Recognizing gifts	Acts 13:1-2	Rom. 12:4-8
Training, equipping, and testing	Acts 15:32	Eph. 4:11-13
Discerning the call	Acts 18:24-28	
Commissioning to service	Acts 13:3	Acts 6:1-6
MAINTAINING RELATIONSHIPS		
Praying	Acts 13:3	Phil. 1:19
Providing fellowship, nurture, and support	Acts 11:26-30	Phil. 4:10-20
Holding accountable, understanding	Acts 14:26-28	

Figure 4-1

about new Christians, but we are haphazard in maturing them. We forget that Jesus had to grow *in wisdom and maturity, in fellowship with God and with man* (Luke 2:52). The local church needs a deliberate and systematic discipling process, ideally one that includes an individual spiritual guide for each new Christian.

2. *Have you been deliberately discipled by a more mature Christian? If so, was your discipleship developed through your local church? If a "systematic discipling process" is not already in place, is it feasible to implement such a concept where you fellowship? Why or why not?*

_____

_____

_____

_____

_____

Spiritual career guidance

An extension of the more traditional discipleship concept is that of *spiritual career guidance*, which is something new in the life of most local churches. There are two phases to this process, involving (a) spiritual career advising and (b) development of mentoring relationships.

> **Too often we let young people make all their own choices and select all their training by themselves.**

Spiritual career advisors are mature Christians who help young people in the church make wise career choices based on spiritual principles. They offer counsel from the time young people begin to make their first choices regarding their future vocations. They also help build strong spiritual foundations into young people's career training. *Mentors* get involved when youths enter the job market. Mentors are mature Christians with experience in careers similar to those of their protégés. Their goal is to help each young person succeed as a Christian in the workplace.

Too often we let young people make all their own choices and select all their training by themselves. Then, if God calls them into tentmaking, we may try to squeeze them back into a suitable spiritual framework and rush them into some catch-up spiritual preparation. It is important to pay special attention to young people starting tertiary education. They have big choices ahead. We need to be there with them so their choices are God's choices.

3. *Pastor Christensen is suggesting a rather radical concept for most churches. How might career guidance be implemented in your church?*

_____

_____

_____

_____

Recognizing gifts

If we disciple well, we will recognize gifts and possibilities within new Christians. Small groups are excellent vehicles for this process of recognition, especially groups that aim to help their members grow to full spiritual potential. Imagine a group which assists its members in identifying their gifts and in which the leaders ask members, every six months, where they are going and how they plan to get there. Such accountability is bound to produce results in people's lives.

Gifts and possibilities, however, do not appear automatically. They show up best in a climate that fosters involvement. In the case of tentmaking, mission awareness and exposure to the task are critical. Churches that expose their people to other cultures, to adventurous evangelism, and to "real life" problem solving allow for rapid identification of the gifts God has given their people. The measure to which

> **The measure to which a church has people engaged in adventurous, cross-cultural mission reflects the measure to which it is engaged in adventurous evangelism in its own setting.**

a church has people engaged in adventurous, cross-cultural mission reflects the measure to which it is engaged in adventurous evangelism in its own setting.

4. *Reflect on Pastor Christensen's last statement. Is your church involved in "adventurous, cross-cultural mission"? Is there a direct correlation with "adventurous evangelism" on the local scene? Explain your answers.*

_____

_____

_____

_____

_____

Training, equipping, and testing

After gifts have been identified, the next step is to train believers in the use of those gifts. Training involves more than just a classroom lecture. Good training informs, inspires, applies, evaluates, encourages, affirms, and is coupled with a good dose of practice. Obviously, not every local church can do all these things by itself. Other institutions, such as Bible schools, mission agencies, and missionary training programs, are often available to help. The local church, though, is responsible to see that its people are nurtured in their gifts and are growing properly.

Some training is general. It equips church members to deal with problems and opportunities in the local setting. Other training is geared specifically towards cross-cultural service. If a person has the gifts, abilities, interest, and perhaps a genuine calling to cross-cultural ministry, the church is responsible for testing that calling. When the call is discerned to be valid, the church then needs to help equip the individual for service.

Discerning the call

One of the discernment tasks of the local church is to help people recognize their call to cross-cultural ministry and evaluate the windows of opportunity which may present themselves. Does this person have a genuine heart for mission? Is he or she called of God to career mission service or a tentmaking role? Is God calling the person to act right now? Is a particular opportunity suitable for this individual? Such discernment is critical. Anyone considering service outside the local church should have the clear commendation of the local church. The church exists in part to test ministry calling in a nurturing and supportive climate.

> *Anyone considering service outside the local church should have the clear commendation of the local church.*

At this point, if the church has been doing its job, discipleship and training should converge with gifting and calling. Enthusiasm for a mission venture is not necessarily a mission calling. A genuine calling squares with observed behavior. Since tentmakers often find their own employment and support themselves, it might be assumed that the church doesn't have much to say about a tentmaker's ministry. This is not true. Discerning counsel should be offered to ensure that new tentmakers will not be expected to do more than they have proved themselves capable of doing at home. We must leave room for the stretching challenge of faith, but we cannot expect an airline ticket to turn a home town spectator into an international achiever.

5. *How do people in your church learn of missions? Are they likely to receive a call to mission service through this program? How is this call evaluated?*

_____

_____

_____

_____

_____

Commissioning to service

Once a call has been confirmed, the church needs to start operating in a sending mode. It must work alongside those who have been called, to help them get from where they are to where they need to be. This assignment is a highly responsible one, which needs to:

- Be clearly defined.
- Have a group to do it.
- Have someone supervising.
- Have a means of keeping the assigned group in touch with the whole church.

In the case of tentmakers, the following questions need to be addressed:

1. Where are the tentmakers going to serve?

2. Do the service opportunities match the vocational skills of interested tentmakers?

3. What further training or experience do tentmakers need in order to take advantage of the opportunities?

4. Will tentmakers go through a regular mission agency? If so, which one? If not, how will the local church provide field support?

5. As a church, can we commend these tentmakers as spiritually mature and able ministers? If not, how can we help them mature and grow in ministry skills?

6. Will the tentmakers need financial support from the church? If so, how much, and how are we to help them raise it?

7. How and when are we going to commission these tentmakers?

In Acts 13, Paul and Barnabas were thoroughly discipled and trained. God's call had been tested. The church members had confidence in these men and were able to commend them. Paul and Barnabas knew the task, had the boat fare, and knew their first destination. They were fit for the sending. So the church fasted and prayed, laid their hands on the pair, and sent them off.

6. *Is there a "sending" group in your church which helps those with a confirmed mission call to prepare themselves to go? If so, how does the group function? If not, how might such a group be organized?*

_____

_____

_____

_____

Maintaining Relationships

Praying and supporting

We hear less of what the church at Antioch did while Paul and Barnabas were away. For his part, Paul kept in touch. In Acts 14:27-28, he reports back to the church and "spent a long time with the disciples" after that first missionary journey. In Acts 18:22-23, we again see Paul taking the opportunity to spend time with his home church. Perhaps the entire process can be summed up as maintaining appropriate communication or making an effort to do what is needed to maintain close ties.

In some ways, Paul was really too large a character to "belong" to one church. We see his relationships expressed through many churches. Paul urges Christians to pray for him. He expresses gratitude to those who supported the team with gifts and who saw themselves as fellow workers in the gospel (Rom. 15:30-32; 2 Cor. 1:11; Phil. 1:4-5, 15-18).

The tentmaker and the local church

What does your home church expect of you as a tentmaker?

1. The church wants to be in the know

The congregation wants to participate in the whole process of your getting to the field. Too many pastors and churches have heard these words from promising and gifted members: "I thought I would let you know I have been accepted for service in Transylvania by the Regions Unimagined Mission Society, and they wanted me to tell you I need $30,000 a year in support."

The church is the body of Christ. The body wants to know what its parts are doing! If God begins to stir your spirit with His call, involve the church in what is happening from the beginning. They will love you for

> *If God begins to stir your spirit with His call, involve the church in what is happening from the beginning.*

it! This is just as vital for tentmakers as for career missionaries. Tell your pastor, missions chairperson, home group leader, or trusted elder. Find out what steps they expect you to take. Read the missions policy. Invite people to pray with you. If you are dialoguing with a mission agency, let the church be part of that communication. This will foster partnership, not rivalry for your loyalty.

If you plan to work in a creative access country, consider security issues. Under these circumstances, you will have to limit publicity in your home church. Work out the details beforehand, not after a crisis!

Plan an appropriate commissioning. What will you be called in terms of your church missions policy? Will there be photos, listing in a newsletter, wall displays of your location?

Some tentmaking agencies recommend a *site agreement*. This is a set of guidelines drawn up by all the parties involved— home church, local Christian community overseas, any sending or mission agency, sometimes the employer, and, of course, the tentmaker. The site agreement sets out lines of communication, job expectations, steps for resolving conflicts, and emergency procedures such as evacuation. If the home church is part of this agreement, they will really feel an investment in you.

7. *How would you go about drawing up a site agreement?*

_____

_____

_____

_____

2. The church wants to know how you are doing "on the job"

Find out how your home church expects you to keep in touch. How often do they expect you to write? What format? Do they want photos, tapes, videos from you, or even a telephone call during a church service? Have you left a detailed information kit telling them where you are and what you are doing? Today it is so easy to keep in touch. Technology is on our side!

3. The church wants to be your spiritual family during home leave

Some missionaries on leave rush through customs and then start a furious round of

> **Be fair to your home church! If they have loved you, prayed for you, and supported you, give them a chance to put their arms around you again, physically and spiritually.**

holidays, visiting, speaking, and fundraising all over the country, calling back at the home church just to say good-bye or pick up a support check! The home church feels cheated, and the same is true for tentmakers. Again, decide ahead of time what each expects of the other. Be fair to your home church! If they have loved you, prayed for you, and supported you, give them a chance to put their arms around you again, physically and spiritually.

What can you expect from your home church in return?

- Open communication.
- Participation in the sending process.
- Partnership in a site agreement.
- Love and fellowship.
- Spiritual covering.

The church should keep you up to date with church news. Tell them what you would like— newsletters, tapes, reports, etc. Remember security! The church could also provide spiritual support packages. Tentmaking can be desperately lonely and spiritually barren. Some churches provide resources to keep their personnel spiritually alive. Packages might contain helpful devotional material, good teaching and worship tapes, magazine articles, and occasionally a helpful book. Such care packages mean people back home are thinking carefully about you as a person and about your spiritual needs.

What about field visits? People travel so much today, it is possible a suitable church member or a pastor can visit you. Regular career missionaries appreciate visits, and so will you as a tentmaker!

8. *What mutually agreed upon expectations exist between your church's tentmakers and those involved in their equipping, sending, and support?*

_____

_____

_____

_____

_____

Acknowledging the church's role and authority

It is important for tentmakers to work out how they fit into the life of their home church. Career missionaries have a well-established pattern of authority, including their local Christian community, their mission organization, and their field council. Tentmakers are often in a far looser arrangement. This is where the idea of a site agreement is useful. If you want the love, support, and prayer of your home church, how do you acknowledge the church's place in your life and work?

Here are some basic principles:

1. Accept your church's discernment of your gifts and readiness for service.

2. Expect the church to provide a reference or letter of commendation that is honest and fair.

3. Give them the right to be part of the team shaping your service. Provide them with all the information they need to make good decisions.

4. Do not make major changes in service or location without involving the church leadership.

> *Tentmakers who have the grace and humility to accept the authority of the home church often make the lasting impact overseas.*

Many tentmakers are strong, adventurous, risk-taking Christians with far more energy and vision than the average church member. Yet in the end, tentmakers who have the grace and humility to accept the authority of the home church often make the lasting impact overseas.

9. *Submission to authority can be a risk to an eager young tentmaker. After all, the church leadership could ask you to stay at home until you fulfill some additional expectations. What good reasons exist for submitting to the authority of church leadership in spite of these risks?*

_____

_____

_____

Working It Out

Balancing responsibility and authority

In the preceding section, the author has discussed the importance of tentmakers' submitting to the authority of the local church. Authority and responsibility go hand in hand. There is a direct correlation between the ownership of responsibility and the amount of authority needed to manage the responsibility. Church leaders vary widely in the amount of responsibility they are willing to accept for tentmakers. Some churches are fully involved in every aspect of preparation, sending, and on-field support. Others prefer to delegate the responsibility to tentmakers and/or to a mission agency. The amount of involvement depends on the church's philosophy in these matters and on its ability to meet the demands that are required by assumed responsibility. A large church with many resources may find it easier to assume full responsibility than a smaller one. Such a church may also want to exercise a greater degree of authority in the ministry of tentmakers.

Conflict can arise when expectations on the part of the church leadership or of tentmakers are unmet. Church leadership may want to exercise full authority over tentmakers' plans and ministries, but they may fail in the responsibility of equipping, sending, or supporting tentmakers. Likewise, tentmakers may have a very defined and independent plan which they may expect the church leadership to accept and implement, but they may not want to submit to the church's counsel and input.

The ideal is a realistic and balanced approach. Those in leadership in the church need to evaluate their resources and their ability to manage responsibility for cross-cultural ministers. Tentmakers need to respond appropriately and trust that God will use their church's leadership in the fulfillment of their calling. Developing this trust relationship is critical.

Responsibility and authority are usually distributed among tentmakers, the church, and the on-field ministry team or mission agency. In almost all cases, church leadership will want to have opportunity for input into tentmakers' plans—particularly the timing of those plans. In addition, churches may want to help tentmakers evaluate their readiness, suggest and/or provide a course of training, and provide a final "approval." A clear understanding of the amount of oversight, financial support, prayer support, and moral support which the church is willing and able to supply is of critical importance. Direct responsibility for tentmakers' ministry on the field may best be handled by a mission agency which is focused on that task.

The important principle to keep in mind is that where responsibility for an area is assumed, the authority needed to carry out that responsibility needs to be present also, whether that authority is exercised by the church, tentmakers, or an agency. Only in this way can churches become prolific seedbeds for tentmakers. In the following sections, Pastor Christensen discusses other areas that churches may want to consider in relation to tentmaking.

The missions committee and its program

How can a church or missions committee establish a tentmaking "track" in the life of the church? Start with the missions committee. For many, the whole idea of tentmaking is fairly new, and it seems a big jump from a traditional missions approach to a more flexible one. In fact, the jump is a small one. Many of the basic ideas in a standard missions policy still apply.

New areas include the following:

1. Write tentmaking into the missions policy as one of the strategies of modern mission. This means the missions committee needs to understand tentmaking and recognize that there is no rivalry between traditional strategies and this reemerging strategy.

2. Help the church learn about tentmaking. For example, some churches include special sessions in a missions conference on tentmaking or even devote their annual event entirely to the subject.

3. Find good resources on tentmaking and introduce them into the life of the church. Today there are many books, articles, and videos on tentmaking. Tentmaking groups produce leaflets and resource kits. Add these to the church library, and give some to the pastor.

4. See if there are church members working overseas who could be equipped for a more intentional tentmaking role. Not every Christian working overseas is a tentmaker. Some, though, may have the gifts and the heart. Work out what additional training these people need and how to establish links and agreements. Nothing increases

> **Never take shortcuts! It is more important to wait for God's chosen tentmaker within your church than to promote someone not quite suitable.**

church interest in a topic like knowing someone involved! Just a little warning, though. Never take shortcuts! It is more important to wait for God's chosen tentmaker within your church than to promote someone not quite suitable, simply to get the attention of the congregation.

10. Which of the preceding suggestions are currently part of your church's tentmaking activities? Which could be incorporated? List any additional ideas you may think of.

_____

_____

_____

_____

The church and its climate

What sort of church produces good tentmakers? Churches that have a healthy view of work and a biblical view of the church! Tentmaking is just marketplace theology in a mission setting. If your church understands the workplace and encourages people to be Christ's

> **When you have been to "church," are you better equipped to face the coming week? Does Sunday have any effect on Monday? If it does, tentmaking will grow!**

ambassadors there, it will also produce tentmakers. One good test is to ask how those in leadership view the membership. Do the people exist to keep the church going, or does the church exist to keep the people going? When you have been to "church," are you better equipped to face the coming week? Does Sunday have any effect on Monday? If it does, tentmaking will grow!

Following are some ideas for promoting a focus on the Christian at work:

1. Hold an annual "work" service when people come to church in their weekday work clothes, school uniform, etc. Invite them to bring an item from their work for a display. Include prayer requests for and testimonies from the workplace.

2. Bring occupational groups together to share what it means to be a Christian in that kind of work. Help them explore ethical issues peculiar to that group.

3. Set up a group for the unemployed so they understand that the church cares about their sense of work loss.

4. Use testimonies, prayers, and illustrations from the workplace in church services. Affirm people in their work. Let them know they are on the cutting edge of evangelism.

5. Preachers, ask some trusted people in the congregation to tell you if your messages include enough help for the workplace.

6. Pastors, try having lunch once a week with a church member at the person's place of work, to discover what the member does and what the workplace looks like.

7. Preach on work and workers. A good resource is Herbert Lockyer's book *All the Trades and Occupations in the Bible*, which lists 207 occupations found in the Bible.*

11. What does "marketplace theology" mean in your own words? What are some practical steps that could be taken to promote this concept in your church?

_____

_____

_____

_____

_____

Going back to the couple described at the beginning of this chapter, how would John and Mary have fared at your church? Would your church be happily planning their commissioning as tentmakers to some darkened corner of the globe, where they might be spiritual lights? May God will that thousands of churches around the world will become nurturing, sending churches with a vision for mobilizing thousands of new laborers into God's harvest. Tentmaking missionaries offer the only solution to evangelizing millions of people living in creative access countries. May local churches wake up to this tremendous challenge and opportunity!

Summary

If we take the Antioch church found in the book of Acts as our ideal sending church, we may discover that our own church does not approach this standard. The roles of the sending church are defined in a process which includes making disciples, recognizing gifts, equipping, discerning the call, and commissioning the missionary. Once missionaries are on the field, the church is involved in praying, supporting, and providing accountability and understanding. The church should provide a healthy climate for the growth of missions and tentmaking through a clear exposition of workplace theology.

Both churches and tentmakers have expectations of each other. The church wants to be informed, desires to share in tentmakers' experiences on the field, and wants to be tentmakers' spiritual family. Tentmakers need to know there are good lines of communication, a church which participates in their sending, a genuine sense of partnership (perhaps expressed in a site agreement), a place for love and fellowship during home leave, and a real spiritual covering.

Working out the accountability relationship requires a balance of authority and responsibility. The more limited a church is in its resources, the more it may need to depend on partnering

---

* Lockyer, H. (1969). *All the trades and occupations in the Bible*. Grand Rapids, MI: Zondervan.

agencies to set up and assume accountability. A site agreement can help all those involved to understand clearly what is expected and where the responsibility lies. Churches which can provide a healthy climate for tentmakers will be making a tremendous contribution to reaching the unreached, particularly in creative access countries.

Action Plan Assignment

1. *Figure 4-1 on page 4-3 lists the roles of the sending church. How closely do these roles match what your own church does to equip and send missionaries? Chances are, there will be areas that can be improved. Discuss these areas with others who are interested in tentmaking. For each area, list at least one thing you can do to help improve this process in your church.*

2. *A site agreement is prepared jointly by those who have a stake in the mission venture. This contract will include at least your church and yourself. It may also include a mission agency, your employer, and the Christian community you will be involved with on the field. It sets out (a) lines of communication, (b) job expectations, (c) steps for resolving conflicts, and (d) emergency procedures such as evacuation. Think through the implications of a site agreement between yourself and your church. Write out your mutual expectations in terms of the listed topics.*

3. *Use the rating scale below to see how well your church and its tentmakers are communicating. What can you do to improve this rating? List steps that can be taken to improve communications.*

Church/Tentmaker Communications Rating Scale

	No or Never ... Yes or Always
1. The church as a whole knows who our tentmakers are, where they are, whom they work with, and what to pray for.	1 2 3 4 5 6 7 8 9 10
2. The pastor and/or missions leadership keeps in touch regularly with our tentmakers.	1 2 3 4 5 6 7 8 9 10
3. The missions committee knows exactly what the current needs are.	1 2 3 4 5 6 7 8 9 10
4. Tentmakers keep in touch with the church, bearing in mind security matters.	1 2 3 4 5 6 7 8 9 10
5. There is a clear policy for "home time" covering rest, reporting, refreshment, and reassessment of the task.	1 2 3 4 5 6 7 8 9 10

Figure 4-2

CHAPTER 5

Critical Considerations of Deployment

Thus far in our study, we have focused on personal issues and on tentmakers' relationship to their local church. With this chapter, we begin to consider some of the logistics of tentmaker placement. Several interrelated issues present themselves as we enter this arena. The first is the *bivocational identity dilemma* which most tentmaker missionaries face, particularly those who go to creative access countries. The second is balancing work with personal time and energy, so as to create a climate for ministry opportunity. Finally, we take a quick look at various tentmaking avenues, together with advantages and disadvantages of each.

❑ *Exploring the Whos and Hows of Tentmaking*

*Jonathan Cortes **

"What's your *real* work here?" the customs official said with a scowl. Bill glanced quickly at what the official was examining. With horror he saw what some well-meaning person from his church had written on his baggage: "For missionary use only."

Bill is a tentmaker. After going through a short course in Teaching English to Speakers of Other Languages (TESOL), he had obtained a job in a creative access country in Asia. What was the official to believe? Was Bill an English teacher or a missionary? In fact, he was both.

The uncomfortable situation in which Bill found himself illustrates the difficulty experienced by churches as they make the transition to sending tentmaker missionaries, who use

---

* Jonathan Cortes is a frontier missions facilitator for The Navigators. Based in Singapore, he is responsible for preparing the way for tentmakers from developed Christian ministries throughout the world to go to the least evangelized and discipled countries of Asia.

lay credentials as a means of serving in countries which restrict access to regular career missionaries. The situation also reflects the dilemma in which these church-sent tentmakers find themselves as they grapple with their own identity under prevailing security measures in restricted situations.

Bivocational Dilemmas

The story of Bill does not end here. Although he eventually got his visa to stay and teach in the country, the questions kept coming. Bill only teaches a couple of hours a week, and outside of his classes he is asked how and why he is living in the country. He is often pressed further with repeated questions of increasing intensity. Although he is on a teaching visa, he knows that he would never have come to this country only to teach English. He is really in the country to be a missionary. He can't say this, however. His evasive answers bother his conscience and create an atmosphere of mistrust, which is hindering his ministry opportunities.

Without much prefield orientation to help him avoid or resolve some of these conflicts beforehand, Bill feels tremendous pressures. These pressures produce stress on his conscience, on his body, on his family (who face the same questions in their everyday lives), on his host organization, on his sending agency, and on the nationals he wants to relate with and serve.

1. Why could the bivocational dilemma of real identity be hard on one's conscience?

_____

_____

_____

Facing the pressures

The author identifies both external and internal pressures that Bill is facing. There is pressure from external sources as the local people try to figure Bill out. Internally, Bill is experiencing pressure from his conscience, which is beginning to accuse him. Like many tentmakers, Bill didn't have to deal with these issues before he left his own country. Now the pressures seem ready to overwhelm him.

The issue of true identity is one of the most critical to a tentmaker's success. Many tentmakers have failed because they have not dealt with this issue before going to the field. When a tentmaker adopts an occupation simply as a cover, there is a lot of pressure from external sources in trying to reconcile what others see as a contradiction. When a tentmaker's position is untenable, suspicion is a natural reaction. A case in point might be a 35-year-old man with a family, who has been enrolled in the local university for years without making much progress towards a degree. Other examples are a businessman who never seems to do business and a teacher who only teaches a few hours a week.

Most of the unreached areas of the world are poor, and many have repressive governments. It doesn't make sense to the people of such a host country for someone to leave a more developed country—leave family, leave freedom, and leave opportunity—to take up residence in their land. This lack of understanding creates a feeling of distrust. When tentmakers can't be completely open and declare their Christian mission, the situation can wear them down psychologically, no matter how dedicated they may be.

Questions come relentlessly. "Why did you come here to work? This is a poor country with few opportunities. Why would you want to live here instead of in your own country, where there is more freedom and it's easier to earn a living? What about your parents and relatives? Don't you miss them? How much do you make? How can you live as well as you do when you only teach a few hours each week? What is your real reason for being here? Are you a spy, a drug dealer, a subversive, a missionary...?"

One obvious way to solve this problem of identity is to make certain that the tentmaking occupation isn't simply fabricated as a cover. When the job is clearly legitimate to everyone who is observing, the pressure tends to ease off. A relatively well-paying or prestigious position helps affirm this sense of authenticity, as does affiliation with a government or with an international agency or company. A real liking for the job and enthusiasm in carrying it out also help affirm the tentmaker's rationale for being in the country.

2. Why is it essential for the successful tentmaker to have a clearly defined, legitimate work role in the host country?

_____

_____

_____

The second kind of pressure Bill is facing is internal. Like many tentmakers, he didn't take time back home to deal with what, once on the field, he began to feel was a dishonest lifestyle. Prompted by his evasive answers to people in the host culture, his conscience accused him of being a fake, a fraud, and un-Christian. How could he live a lie? These accusations involved some real ethical questions. In the following sections, our tentmaker author discusses how to face some of these issues.

Ethical issues

There are ethical issues to consider when entering a country as a tentmaker missionary. These are worth considering:

- Withholding of information.

- Writing down half-truths.

- Concealing the truth.

- Living a double life to some extent.

- Being forced to make other difficult ethical choices.

- Putting the family into difficult circumstances, to their possible detriment.

Being confronted with ethical issues such as these is not something to be taken lightly. Much is at stake for the family, ministry contacts, ministry team, and tentmaker. It is important to discern whether everyone involved can operate in this style of ministry with a clear conscience toward God and men. Many tentmakers have failed because they have not resolved these conflicts in their own minds before going to the field.

3. *What might have been included in Bill's prefield orientation to try to deal with issues of conscience?*

_____

_____

_____

The obligation to witness

The Christian's ultimate authority to be a witness to and of the gospel is derived from Jesus Christ, to whom all authority has been given in heaven and on earth. Because all authority belongs to Him, we cannot accept the concept of a "closed land." Every land is open to Him who holds the key of David, who opens and no one can shut, who shuts and no one can open (Rev. 3:7).

Satan's power, on the other hand, is both limited and derived, and it is subject to Christ's supreme authority. Though Satan uses others to "close" countries, this prohibition is in direct contradiction to and is invalidated by Jesus Christ's commands to "go into all the world" (Mark 16:15) and to "make disciples of all nations" (Matt. 28:18-20). We must obey God's commands above all others (Acts 4:1-20).

We have an obligation, therefore, to be witnesses for our Lord, even when "proselytizing" is forbidden. This is neither easy nor simple. There are some general principles, however, for thought and prayer. These should be considered in the light of the need for discretion, tact, and care, and they should be balanced with Gideon's warning to those who fear: "Whoever is fearful and afraid, let him return and depart early" (Judg. 7:3).

The spoken word of witness was normative in New Testament times. Jesus commissioned His disciples to "herald" the gospel to every creature. This implies spreading the good news by word of mouth. This emphasis links the message with the messenger. God is delighted and honors a witness who says, "I am not ashamed of this message." In fact, most cultures have a deep respect for such an attitude. It is one with which they can identify. The "silent witness" is often despised and at best is misunderstood. As tentmakers invest their lives in the Great Commission, they need to have wisdom and discretion about what they are communicating both verbally and nonverbally.

4. *Look up Romans 1:14-16. What was Paul's basic attitude towards the gospel? Why? How should this mindset be expressed in the tentmaker's life?*

_____

_____

_____

Witnessing without proselytizing

There is no human law that says you cannot be open in your personal belief in Jesus Christ. Jesus Himself said, "I spoke openly to the world" (John 18:20). Paul said, "I kept back nothing that was profitable to you" (Acts 20:20). We are to walk in the light and never lie or deceive. Yet it is also clear in Scripture that not everything needs to be revealed.

The main reason governments officially ban proselytism is that, in the past, proselytism has involved attacking or insulting the country's main religion, leading men astray from their social and religious groupings, polluting their high moral standards, weaning people away from nationalism, or subverting the state by producing a Western subculture. All of these activities can produce social disorder and problems for the government.

It is possible, by God's grace and wisdom, to be a child of God, a worshiper of Christ, and still be a contributing member to the socio-economic welfare of even an atheistic nation.

It is possible to be a servant of Christ and not be a blasphemer of other gods or a traitor to the best interests of another country's government. Indeed, if biblical Christians let the Word become flesh in their lives (John 1:14), if they

> *It is possible, by God's grace and wisdom, to be a child of God, a worshiper of Christ, and still be a contributing member to the socio-economic welfare of even an atheistic nation.*

are able to teach gently as humble servants of Christ (2 Tim. 2:24-26), and if they have a message of *agape* love (John 3:16), they do not come to disrupt the established order. They come to bring Christ, to introduce fellow sinners to a Savior and Redeemer who loves them and who cared enough to die for them.

5. What is the best solution to the external and internal pressures of the bivocational dilemma?

_____

_____

_____

It is not always possible to avoid the bivocational identity dilemma. Therefore, it is important for the tentmaker to study this matter thoroughly before going to the field and to come to a firm conviction in his or her own heart and mind. Advance study may not stop the questions, but it should help relieve the stress. Withstanding external pressures is much easier if the tentmaker's own conscience isn't also producing accusations! The bivocational dilemma can be solved by a legitimate job and a clear conscience regarding witness in a "closed" country. While these are perhaps the most critical issues, there are others which also should be dealt with. Mr. Cortes discusses additional issues related to tentmaking in the sections that follow.

Work/Ministry Mix

Mark had spent a long time in his own country obtaining academic qualifications and the job experience he felt would serve him well in his dream to minister cross-culturally. During the years of preparation, he had married and had two children. He was in his 30's by the time he actually was commissioned by his church and sent to a target country.

> *It became a daily struggle for the whole family not to be sucked into the orbit of the expatriate community at the expense of developing relationships with the people they had come to win.*

The company for which Mark worked had a policy of meeting the educational needs of its employees' children. As a result, Mark and his family were tied to a location near the international school, in a community built to house foreigners. It became a daily struggle for the whole family not to be sucked into the orbit of the expatriate community at the expense of developing relationships with the people they had come to win.

Meanwhile, Mark's wife was complaining that she was having trouble learning the language because of her commitment to raising the children. Cultural adaptation was made more difficult because Mark and his wife, being in their 30's, were fairly well set in their cultural patterns. Mark had numerous responsibilities in setting up operations under difficult prevailing business conditions. Work in the office was hard and often long. After doing a good day's work, Mark felt exhausted and was ready to relax for the rest of the evening.

Mark wasn't the type of person who could switch rapidly from one kind of activity to another. The thought of building relationships for ministry was difficult for him and for his wife as well. As a result, they slowly began to abandon their earlier dreams of developing the same kind of ministry in which they had been involved in their home country.

6. What were the obstacles to effective tentmaking which Mark and his family were experiencing? Were some of these avoidable? If so, how?

Several points are worth observing from Mark's situation. Some people are unable to use their time to maximum advantage. After a day's work, they are exhausted. They don't have the energy to invest in building relationships. This situation raises the question of whether a tentmaker's ministry and work goals are in balance. There are circumstances which will prevent tentmakers from being effective ministerially. Jobs which are too time consuming do not allow tentmakers to be effective ministers. In some cases, tentmakers may have to sign a statement promising that they will not witness. In addition, the company they work for may shield tentmakers from the local people by placing them in a kind of "colony" of expatriates.

Can tentmakers really be effective when they have full-time jobs? Yes, but there must be a healthy dose of realism. One of the greatest barriers to effective tentmaking is "romanticism." People tend to have a romantic picture

> *Entering a country is relatively easy; being effective once there is another matter altogether.*

that all they need to do is obtain their qualifications and fly to a far country to experience instant effectiveness. Entering a country is relatively easy; being effective once there is another matter altogether.

Factors influencing effectiveness

The case studies of Bill and Mark that are presented by the author illustrate the fact that positioning oneself vocationally for effective tentmaking is more complex than might appear initially. On one end of the spectrum is a tentmaker whose reason for being in the country doesn't make much sense to the nationals and who is ineffective as a result of the ensuing mistrust. On the other end of the scale is a tentmaker who has a good job with plenty of credibility, but who doesn't have much time for ministry. Somewhere between these two extremes is a range in which a tentmaker can be most effective. Vocational legitimacy plus time and energy for ministry create the best climate for ministry opportunities.

Figure 5-1 on the next page demonstrates this principle. The vertical scale represents time and energy for ministry. The horizontal scale represents vocational legitimacy. The shaded lines divide the graph into four quadrants. When both vocational legitimacy and time and energy for ministry are rated 5 or higher, the tentmaker will function in a climate in which ministry opportunities are readily available.

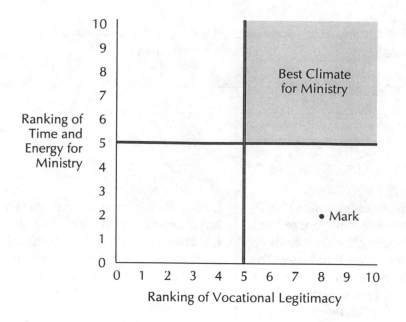

Figure 5-1. The Best Climate for Ministry

Let's rate Mark on this graph. His vocational legitimacy is pretty high, so we'll give him an 8. Regarding time and energy for ministry, however, he rates rather low, perhaps a 2. The coordinates (8,2) put Mark in the lower right-hand quadrant. He could be worse off, but ideally, his placement should be in the upper right-hand quadrant if he is interested in ministry opportunities.

Beyond this consideration, there are other factors which contribute to the effectiveness of a tentmaker. These include the level of spiritual maturity and ministry skills achieved before going to the field, as discussed in chapter 3. In the following sections, Mr. Cortes examines some of the personal qualities needed as well as the experience and skills required to juggle work and ministry effectively.

The "ideal" tentmaker

There are a host of recommendations and suggestions about what vocational and ministry qualifications an "ideal" tentmaker should possess. These recommendations imply setting standards, which further suggests a process of training, evaluation, and selection—elements quite new to most churches. Yet careful training and assessment are important. Mission agencies and boards can testify to the "casualty rate" of missionaries and tentmakers who are unable to adjust to their assignments and who are forced to leave the field for various reasons. There are major costs involved when missionaries are compelled to return home.

What are some of these costs?

- There are personal costs to tentmakers and their families in terms of lost years, readjustments to home, starting another assignment, or finding a new job. Tentmakers also have to deal with feelings of personal failure.

- There are costs the field will have to bear. The work suffers a setback, as it usually takes months or years to find a replacement. When one is found, it takes time for that individual to adjust to the field. Sometimes, negative public relations caused by an insensitive tentmaker may take years to heal. People who have been hurt need restoration.

- There is a cost involved for leaders and coworkers at home and on the field. Financial costs are also involved.

7. *Considering the costs of failure, does the local church have the responsibility of trying to detain a tentmaker who is not adequately prepared for cross-cultural service? Why or why not?*

_____

_____

_____

Evaluating the tentmaker's readiness

The primary evaluator of a tentmaker's readiness for service is often the tentmaker himself or herself. The decision to become a tentmaker

> **Since tentmaking involves other people, it is recommended that evaluations come from both sending and receiving ends of the cross-cultural endeavor.**

should be bathed in prayer. Since tentmaking involves other people, it is recommended that evaluations come from both sending and receiving ends of the cross-cultural endeavor. Pastors and other missions leaders in the church should get involved in this process. Evaluators should assess the whole person. They should look to see whether notable weaknesses are balanced by compensating strengths. The resulting blend of qualities must give confidence to those who make the final selection of personnel that the tentmaker can fulfill the job.

In the case of a couple, it is recommended that both spouses be measured by the same criteria. An exception might be ministry gifts and experiences, which should be evaluated in accordance with the demands of the expected ministry.

Figures 5-2, 5-3, and 5-4, on pages 5-15 through 5-19, can be used as evaluation tools, either by tentmakers themselves or by others who know them well, or both. Such evaluation instruments are valuable tools for those who are planning training and orientation programs for potential tentmakers. Specific problem areas and weaknesses can be worked on directly by each candidate. Although individuals cannot be expected to become perfect through these efforts, a conscious awareness of problem areas is important in order to understand team dynamics and to detect early warning signs of problems on the field.

Vocational Paths and Models

There are many paths to tentmaking. Not all of these apply to every country. For example, it is a common misconception that a medical doctor can get into a country easily if there is a severe lack of medical personnel in the target nation. Most countries have legislation which heavily protects their professional classes, small as these may be. Such laws make it very difficult for foreign doctors, engineers, architects, and other professionals to practice in these countries. Notable exceptions are teachers of English or other foreign languages and professors of technical and scientific subjects. Tentmakers should investigate each situation thoroughly before committing themselves to a particular tentmaking path. In the following section, our author describes several kinds of tentmaking occupations and lists their advantages and disadvantages.

The contract worker, technician, and professional employee

Working as a tentmaking employee of a foreign company or institution presents both benefits and challenges. Some benefits are:

- Full salary support.

- Legitimate local identity as part of a registered firm.

- Housing and children's education often included in an incentives package.

- Round-trip travel usually provided.

- Language study may be provided by the firm.

- Career path improvement as one transitions home.

- Excellent opportunities for focused witness in context of work relationships.

Some challenges are:

- The job may be isolated, with little opportunity to interact with or develop good relationships with nationals outside work, either for witnessing or Christian fellowship.

- Language study, if not provided for, may be limited because of work constraints.

- Companies may make employees sign a statement not to witness regarding their faith.

- Time demands may be so stringent that it may be very difficult to develop a ministry.

- Too little room may be allowed for vocational flexibility.

Some jobs can be quite demanding and can restrict ministry expectations. Diplomats, middle managers, and most medical personnel have jobs which fall into this category. On the other hand, teachers, journalists, writers, secretaries, research workers, etc., generally have more flexibility.

The representative of a foreign company

The world of business is truly international, with many companies, large and small, exporting products to other countries. These businesses often send representatives overseas to open markets for them. This process entails working with government authorities, prospective partners, representatives from related enterprises, buyers and sellers, etc. These activities require a great deal of representation, research and development, administration, and communication. Beyond being able to build relationships, one must also be a good administrator, since most of the work is self-directed. Advantages and disadvantages are similar to those of being an employee. More control over one's own time may be an advantage of this kind of activity.

The entrepreneur

Starting a small business overseas is another tentmaking path, especially for those who are entrepreneurs by nature. Some of the most tried avenues are the import/export business, business consulting, and small scale manufacturing. The concept of business ministry enables ordinary, everyday Christians to scatter to various parts of the world as witnesses for our Lord in the marketplace. Christian entrepreneurs should be well-trained and qualified in business or international trade, spiritually mature, and culturally sensitive. One advantage of small businesses is that the business may provide job opportunities and a chance to teach nationals to live by Christian values and principles. Small businesses are definitely a way of helping Christians in other lands to become influential leaders within their communities.

There are some pitfalls, however. Involvement in making the business successful can lead Christian entrepreneurs to an overemphasis on this aspect of their work. This in turn may lead to neglecting the totality of their life ministry, which involves their marriage and family life, their personal walk with God, and ministry to nationals.

> **The concept of business ministry enables ordinary, everyday Christians to scatter to various parts of the world as witnesses for our Lord in the marketplace.**

Starting a business can be particularly stressful where the infrastructure support of the host country (banking and finance, communications, transportation, and legal and government regulations, or the absence thereof) may not be as developed as in the tentmaker's own economy. As with all business ventures, the cost of building the necessary infrastructure, both material as well as human, may be much greater than anticipated, and if one does not have enough financial backing, the business will fail. The business may also fail if it is neglected due to an overemphasis on ministry. As in all tentmaking activities, balance is important.

Relief and development

One of the most used paths for Christian involvement in restricted contexts is along the lines of relief and development. This avenue provides an excellent way to build redemptive relationships through service and meeting felt needs of the people. It is an excellent vehicle to model the Christian value of service to like-minded nationals or organizations. It is also a golden opportunity to reproduce the value of ministry to those who are vulnerable and needy, through local disciples.

Many international relief and development organizations already exist. The raising and management of funds, as well as sensitivity in

relating to governments, are perennial issues which must be dealt with by these organizations. Agencies like these must model good organizational and financial capabilities because the needs, tremendous as they often are, can overwhelm any administrative structure if it is not well managed and planned.

The necessity of relating with government structures is an excellent opportunity for witness, as well as an area which needs wisdom. Skilled diplomacy is often necessary. Being able to maintain steadfast biblical principles in management and delivery of services is strategic to the economic and sociopolitical needs, which often go hand in hand in these contexts. Diplomacy is also important to the long-term prospects of staying as a viable entity within the country and modeling Christian love.

8. *Several paths to tentmaking have been mentioned. Which path are you thinking about? What are the advantages and disadvantages of using this particular approach in tentmaking?*

_____

_____

_____

_____

Looking for a Job Opportunity

Each prospective tentmaker is set in a context of vision, calling, training, skills, experience, personal circumstances, and opportunities. Conversely, each area of the world which is targeted for tentmaking ministries also has its peculiarities and specific vocational opportunities. Matching tentmakers with opportunities isn't always easy. A number of Christian organizations are rising to this challenge. Some are databank services, which for a small fee provide individuals with a listing of job leads by their vocation and/or country of interest. Others are tentmaker placement services, which are country-specific and are more thorough in screening and placing applicants.

Tentmakers can inquire directly for job opportunities through embassies and trade associations. Newspapers often advertise for foreign employment, and in some countries there are specialized secular services which advertise foreign job openings. Trade journals often advertise for overseas positions. In all cases, the challenge is to find the right match between the tentmaker and the opportunity. In all these efforts, we must rely heavily on the Holy Spirit's guidance.

Throughout our previous discussion, we are assuming that the tentmaker is acting in a fairly independent fashion. Some mission strategists, however, are beginning to understand the dynamic of planning for team ventures. These enterprises recruit, train, and often initiate ventures in a target area and feed tentmakers into the project. The ventures usually involve some kind of business: running a manufacturing plant, setting up a consulting firm, establishing a language school, opening an agro-business, etc. In today's climate of international trade, almost every region of the world is open to some kind of "foreign investment" which will also allow a specific group of tentmakers to participate directly and obtain residence.

There are advantages and disadvantages to this approach. These ventures usually need to be organized and funded by sympathetic businessmen who possess a good deal of experience and substantial financial resources. Once established, however, the business can provide a channel for dozens of tentmakers. Because a team is used, some of the members can concentrate on ministry, while others focus on the business. Beyond a significant spiritual impact, some of the more established of these ventures have received official national recognition and have been looked on as model businesses. Both the church and the host country have been built up. This is a win/win situation which is ideal for tentmaking enterprises.

Summary

Tentmakers are faced with pressures from both external and internal sources. Living in a repressive climate where Christian witness isn't allowed can compound these issues. Those who assume untenable work roles are subject to suspicion and distrust. Evasive answers to probing questions begin to wear on sensitive consciences, and questions about the ethical nature of tentmakers' mission may be raised. Developing firm convictions about the legitimacy of one's witness, as well as entering the country with an authentic and rational occupation, will help mitigate the effects of the bivocational dilemma.

Beyond these issues, tentmakers must seek a balance between work and ministry. Work which is all-consuming and leaves no time for ministry will frustrate ministry-minded tentmakers. Some occupations are more prone to this difficulty than others. Other barriers to effective witness may be restrictive measures on witness which the company may place on its employees and/or limited exposure to the people of the host culture.

There are many paths to tentmaking ministry—almost as many as there are legitimate occupations. Generally, we classify tentmakers as employees of companies or governments, representatives of foreign companies, business entrepreneurs, and relief and development workers. Each category has advantages and disadvantages. Choosing a particular path also involves understanding the opportunities which may exist in the target country. Making a match isn't always easy. The process requires much research, thought, and prayer.

Action Plan Assignment

1. *How do you feel about the ethics of going to a country which prohibits evangelism and conversion of its people? Write your position as best as you can, supporting your statements with Scripture. Share your thoughts with at least three other Christians who are not doing this assignment.*

2. *Take some time to use the evaluation scales in Figures 5-2, 5-3, and 5-4 (pages 5-15 through 5-19). Have someone who is close to you also evaluate you in these areas. Counsel with your mentor and/or a mature, trusted Christian about areas of weakness which you've identified.*

3. *Which path are you thinking of choosing as a tentmaker? Some skills lend themselves to a number of approaches. The decision about which path to follow will also be influenced by the opportunities available in a given country. Discuss your options with someone who is sharing the responsibility for your decision. Then outline the research and other steps you need to take in order to decide firmly which vocational path to take.*

Personal Qualities Rating Scale

	No or Weak									Yes or Strong

1. **Emotional maturity.** Able to handle stress. Having no hidden strongholds or resentments.

   1 2 3 4 5 6 7 8 9 10

2. **General flexibility.** Socially and culturally tolerant, especially of others' doctrinal views. Able to switch rapidly from one activity to another. Sensitive to environmental factors and able to adapt accordingly. (Culture shock and stress can be severe for an inflexible person.)

   1 2 3 4 5 6 7 8 9 10

3. **Physical and emotional capacity.** Having no acute or chronic disorders which require constant medical attention. (Stresses on the field are demanding, and fatigue sets in even for the strong.)

   1 2 3 4 5 6 7 8 9 10

4. **Sensitivity.** Able to understand both verbal and nonverbal cues which communicate how other people are feeling and what they are really saying or thinking. (This quality usually stems from a strong identity in Christ.)

   1 2 3 4 5 6 7 8 9 10

5. **Social adaptability.** Reasonably comfortable with people or social changes. Able to relate to all kinds of people.

   1 2 3 4 5 6 7 8 9 10

6. **Friendliness.** Genuine and sincere in building relationships. Keen in developing new relationships.

   1 2 3 4 5 6 7 8 9 10

7. **Language aptitude.** Committed to gaining an appropriate level of fluency in the host language. Determined to understand the cultural conditioning of the gospel and to learn ways of communicating the message in the cultural context. (Having an "ear" for tones in the language is advantageous.)

   1 2 3 4 5 6 7 8 9 10

(Continued on next page)

Figure 5-2

Personal Qualities Rating Scale (cont.)

	No or Weak	Yes or Strong

8. **Vocational flexibility.** Determined to choose the job opportunity which is the most strategic in relation to one's mission in the country. Willing to adapt as needed. 1 2 3 4 5 6 7 8 9 10

9. **Good stewardship of resources.** Ultimately dependent upon the Lord for financial resources, whether they should come totally through secular employment and self-support, or partially through friends, a church, or a mission agency. 1 2 3 4 5 6 7 8 9 10

10. **Humility and teachableness.** Having the mind of Christ and being a servant for His sake. Being a keen learner with a teachable and gracious attitude. (Humility is a quality prized highly in most cultures.) 1 2 3 4 5 6 7 8 9 10

11. **Love for others.** Having a strong manifestation of Christ's love in one's life. Accepting other people and their culture. Having no racial prejudice or pride. Showing love for co-workers so others may know the unity that exists in Christ. 1 2 3 4 5 6 7 8 9 10

12. **Good marriage and family relationships.** Committed to spouse and children, in Christ. Stable as a couple before leaving for the field, since wives face similar pressures on the field as their husbands. Having a strong enough family unit so that the family will not become a hindrance to the ministry. 1 2 3 4 5 6 7 8 9 10

Figure 5-2 (cont.)

Bivocational Skills and Experience Rating Scale

	No or Weak									Yes or Strong

1. **Commitment to God's calling and gifting.** Having a conviction of one's role in the total ministry of the church and in fulfilling the Great Commission. Viewing a cross-cultural ministry as a vital component of this calling.

   1 2 3 4 5 6 7 8 9 10

2. **Ability to witness to others.** Exhibiting spontaneity and creativity in sharing the gospel and one's own testimony. Trained to reach people in a variety of situations.

   1 2 3 4 5 6 7 8 9 10

3. **Ability to follow up individuals in the basics of discipleship.** Practicing the same disciplines oneself. Continuously learning in order to be proficient in the use of Scriptures. Able to communicate Bible truth.

   1 2 3 4 5 6 7 8 9 10

4. **Gifts/strengths which contribute to the team and its equipping of others.** Committed to the team concept of ministry. Able to discern with initiative where one can fit.

   1 2 3 4 5 6 7 8 9 10

5. **Ability to work harmoniously with others.** Possessing a sober assessment of one's own strengths and weaknesses. Aware of strengths and weaknesses in others. Having a strong sense of assurance and identity in Christ. Committed to working as a team.

   1 2 3 4 5 6 7 8 9 10

6. **Adequate professional or academic qualifications to match openings in the host country.** Possessing the necessary qualifications (background experience, training, and expertise) to contribute effectively in the work openings related to one's background.

   1 2 3 4 5 6 7 8 9 10

(Continued on next page)

Figure 5-3

Bivocational Skills and Experience (cont.)

	No or Weak		Yes or Strong

7. **Mindset of application to the host culture.** Ready to transfer one's knowledge and skills within the language and culture, using the resources of the host country. Having a vision of developing and enabling local leaders to continue the work in the lay ministry.

1 2 3 4 5 6 7 8 9 10

8. **Sense of time management.** Knowing how to maximize one's time with initiative and creativity to achieve personal goals.

1 2 3 4 5 6 7 8 9 10

9. **Accountability in relationships.** Holding oneself accountable to the Lord. Having a healthy respect and accountability with the civil authority of both passport and visa governments, with other team members and supporting agencies, with employers or teachers, with one's home church and the local church, and with professional colleagues.

1 2 3 4 5 6 7 8 9 10

10. **Adequate training for cross-cultural ministry.** Possessing relevant professional expertise and Bible or theological competency. Able to communicate and adapt cross-culturally. Able to handle ethical and security situations and manage stress. (Family members should also get involved in the training process.)

1 2 3 4 5 6 7 8 9 10

11. **Biblical perspective on work and ethics.** Having a biblical view on key issues relating to work, working relationships, wealth, and possessions. Having convictions concerning ethical and moral values in order to handle situations in which compromises may be expected.

1 2 3 4 5 6 7 8 9 10

Figure 5-3 (cont.)

Negative Factors Rating Scale

	Major Problem								Not a Problem

1. Unresolved relationship problems:

    - With parents and family.   1 2 3 4 5 6 7 8 9 10
    - With present and past leaders.   1 2 3 4 5 6 7 8 9 10
    - With others.   1 2 3 4 5 6 7 8 9 10

2. Overbearing leadership style (usually an indicator of hidden insecurities).   1 2 3 4 5 6 7 8 9 10

3. Excessive dependence on spouse or others (another indicator of hidden insecurities).   1 2 3 4 5 6 7 8 9 10

4. Serious health problems (good medical facilities are rare on the field).   1 2 3 4 5 6 7 8 9 10

5. Obligations to elderly parents or other family at home (a source of ongoing concern and stress).   1 2 3 4 5 6 7 8 9 10

6. Financial obligations (another source of worry).   1 2 3 4 5 6 7 8 9 10

7. Besetting sin patterns (a stronghold for the enemy; Satan can really take advantage of these on the field).   1 2 3 4 5 6 7 8 9 10

Figure 5-4

CHAPTER 6

Biblical and Doctrinal Foundations

In the previous chapter, we explored some of the issues surrounding the identity of tentmakers and the viability of their ministry on the field. Because tentmakers' agendas also include witnessing and leading others to Christ, their activities may not always be sanctioned by the host government. To reduce stress on the field, tentmakers should deal with this area of conflict before embarking on an overseas assignment.

This chapter more thoroughly addresses the issue of beliefs. The creative access countries are no place to send those who are unsure of their doctrine. At a recent conference on training in Brazil, the sad account of a young Brazilian missionary was related. He was serving as a tentmaker in a North African country and was challenged by a Muslim religious leader to a spiritual duel. "Let's spend a day in prayer and discussion," the Muslim suggested. "I'll pray to Allah, and you pray to your God. We will pray that the truth will be revealed." By the end of the day, the young man had become a Muslim.

Many Christians are like this young man—sustained in their faith through enthusiastic participation with other believers in their home church, but lacking solid, personal Bible knowledge and convictions about what the Bible teaches. While this spiritual state is never healthy, a church can provide a sense of security for such individuals as they adhere in general to what the leadership espouses. Nevertheless, as the above incident demonstrates, it is dangerous to send this kind of individual to an environment in which it is likely that personal beliefs will be attacked by those who are specifically trained to demolish weak Christians.

In the following article, Dr. Joshua Ogawa outlines for us the biblical and doctrinal foundations essential to successful cross-cultural ministry. He also provides a good orientation in how to approach others who adhere to differing religious systems.

❑ *Know Before You Go*

Joshua K. Ogawa *

"'You did not choose Me, but I chose you and appointed you to go and bear fruit—fruit that will last'" (John 15:16).

"Miss Ando was killed in a car accident! She has gone to be with the Lord!" I was stunned by the shocking news. Miss Eido Ando, a Japanese tentmaker, was on her way to Pontianak, West Kalimantan, Indonesia, when she was tragically killed. It was indeed sad news to us who knew her personally.

We were all left with the question of God's timing. "Why did she have to die in the middle of her productive life?" She had served as a tentmaker only four years. As we meditated on the Word of God, we were reminded that God's plan is different from ours. "'For My thoughts are not your thoughts, neither are your ways My ways,' declares the Lord. 'As the heavens are higher than the earth, so are My ways higher than your ways and My thoughts than your thoughts'" (Is. 55:8-9).

What made Miss Ando such an outstanding tentmaker? First, she was a skilled nurse and midwife. Using her vocation as a base, she humbly and quietly sought opportunities to serve those needy people in the villages of Kalimantan. All her training, talents, and gifts were meant for both the physical and the spiritual needs of the people. For this purpose, she was patiently learning the language and culture. Miss Ando was loved by people back home and by those on the field. Above all, she was loved by God. Her fruit still remains.

We do not know why God took Miss Ando, but she has left a beautiful model of a tentmaker through her life and example. She will be remembered as a woman of the Bible and of prayer. Her diary was full of Scripture and of specific prayers. Her biblical and theological training gave her command of her beliefs. A good grasp of the doctrines of God, the universe, man, Christ, the Holy Spirit, salvation, the church, and the end times helped her understand herself and the world around her. She was solid in her convictions, and this quality enabled her to express her commitment to God and His purposes as an effective tentmaker.

Believing the Bible

An effective tentmaker must first believe that the Bible, both the Old and New Testaments, is the *inspired Word of God*, which is both *inerrant* and *infallible* in all that it affirms. In

> *An effective tentmaker must first believe that the Bible, both the Old and New Testaments, is the inspired Word of God, which is both inerrant and infallible in all that it affirms.*

the Bible, God has given the complete revelation of His will for the salvation of men. The Bible is also the *divine and final authority* for Christian faith, life, and service. Let's examine each of these concepts individually.

The inspired Word of God

The words of the Bible were *inspired* by God or "God breathed" (2 Tim. 3:16). The writers of the Bible were "moved by the Holy Spirit" (2 Pet. 1:21). It is not that they were used by God

---

* Born in Japan and trained in physics, theology, and mission, Joshua K. Ogawa served as a missionary in Indonesia and in Singapore from 1973 to 1989 with Overseas Missionary Fellowship. He is the founding dean of the Asian Missionary Training Institute (now known as ACTI) in Singapore. Since 1990 he has been the first General Secretary of the Evangelical Free Church of Japan.

mechanically as His robots or word processing operators. Nor does the inspiration of the Bible mean that only the words of Jesus are inspired, or that only the thoughts but not the words of the Bible are inspired. We must also reject the idea that the Bible becomes God's Word only when one has a subjective experience of encountering God while reading the Scriptures. The Bible, written by men moved by the Holy Spirit, is the eternal Word of God.

Inerrant and infallible

Since the Bible is the inspired Word of God, it is inerrant and infallible. *Inerrant* means that the Bible does not have errors. *Infallible* means that the Bible is incapable of containing error. This does not mean that everything in the Bible is affirmed as true and correct. For example, a phrase of Psalm 14:1 states, "There is no God." The context of this statement allows us to understand that the Bible here does not affirm atheism, but rather the folly of atheism.

1. *Why is it important for successful tentmakers to act on the firm conviction that the Bible is the inspired, inerrant, and infallible Word of God?*

_____

_____

_____

_____

Our final authority

There is a logical process of reasoning: Because the Bible is the inspired Word of God, it is also inerrant and infallible. Because of these attributes, the Bible is our final *authority* in matters of faith, life, and service.

Within Christianity, churches have different confessions, statements of faith, creeds, traditions, and practices. There is a danger of elevating these secondary rules governing Christian life and service. The Bible, however, is the only infallible and authoritative rule. Jesus Himself, in His controversy with the

Pharisees, made it clear that human traditions must always be examined in the light of the Bible (Mark 7:1-13).

Authority is different from power. While authority is used always in close connection with what is right and lawful, power emphasizes ability, without having anything to do with what is right or lawful. Today, many people are seeking power. Authority—particularly biblical authority—has largely been ignored, forsaken, or rejected.

2. *How does a firm conviction regarding the final authority of Scripture strengthen cross-cultural Christian witness?*

_____

_____

_____

The Word and missionary service

"The Holy Scriptures... are able to make you wise unto salvation through faith in Jesus Christ" (2 Tim. 3:14-15).

First of all, the Bible is a witness to God's enduring purpose of leading men and women to salvation through Jesus Christ. This is the focal point of the entire Bible. Its message is the gospel of the Lord Jesus Christ. Without the Bible, we cannot know what to share with people so that they may be saved.

The gospel of the Lord Jesus Christ is something very simple in its basic content. "...By this gospel you are saved, if you hold firmly to the word I preached to you... that Christ died for our sins according to the Scriptures, that He was buried, that He was raised on the third day according to the Scriptures, and that He appeared to Peter and then to the Twelve..." (1 Cor. 15:1-5). At the same time, the gospel is presented in the Bible as something very rich in its content because Christ Himself is rich. "In Christ are hidden all the treasures of wisdom and knowledge" (Col. 2:3). Without the Bible, we could never come to know the richness of the gospel to be shared with others. The Bible is central in all missionary endeavors.

Secondly, the Bible instructs believers in Christian faith. This is again another important area of missionary service. We should be able to provide instruction to those who have come to trust in Jesus Christ as their personal Savior, so that they may know how to live good and useful lives that will please God and advance His kingdom. "All Scripture is divinely breathed and profitable for teaching, for reproof, for correction, for instruction in righteousness, that the man of God may be adequate, equipped for every good work" (2 Tim. 3:16-17). Thus, the Bible is indispensable for all missionary endeavors.

Thirdly, the Bible gives us the missionary mandate, as well as the divine power and the ways to carry out the mandate. Both the Old and New Testaments reveal the mandate. God called Abraham and made a covenant with him, saying, "'I will make you into a great nation and I will bless you... and all peoples on earth will be blessed through you'" (Gen. 12:1-3). When Jesus Christ came, He fulfilled the promise given to Abraham and gave the Great Commission to the church. "'All authority in heaven and on earth has been given to Me. Therefore go and make disciples of all nations, baptizing them in the name of the Father and of the Son and of the Holy Spirit, and teaching them to obey everything I have commanded you. And surely I am with you always, to the very end of the age'" (Matt. 28:19-20).

It is impossible to carry out the Great Commission simply using human resources. When divine power comes to us from the Word of God and through the preaching of the gospel, we will be able to fulfill the task. As Paul affirmed, "I am not ashamed of the gospel, because it is the power of God..." (Rom. 1:16).

> *It is impossible to carry out the Great Commission simply using human resources. When divine power comes to us from the Word of God and through the preaching of the gospel, we will be able to fulfill the task.*

The Bible provides many models and examples for carrying out the missionary mandate, such as the disciples and the Apostle Paul. Our Lord Jesus Christ was the perfect model. "Jesus Christ, being in very nature God, did not consider equality with God something to be grasped, but made Himself nothing, taking the very nature of a servant, being made in human likeness, and being found in appearance as a man, He humbled Himself and became obedient to death, even death on a cross!" (Phil. 2:6-8).

3. In what ways is a thorough understanding of the Bible essential to effective tentmaking?

_____

_____

_____

Dependence on the Holy Spirit

The Bible was produced by the Holy Spirit—He *inspired* it. The Bible is the means by which the Lord Jesus Christ, through the Holy Spirit, provides salvation, instruction, and guidance. He illumines the minds and hearts of those who hear the Word of God so that they can understand the true meaning to be applied in their life and ministry (John 16:7-11). Readiness to practice or apply the teaching of the Bible in our daily lives is the key to understanding the real meaning of the Scriptures. The Holy Spirit instructs us and prompts us to obedience (1 Cor. 2:12-13). This is the way the Spirit works.

How do we cultivate our dependence upon the Holy Spirit? First, we must be rightly related to Him. The Word commands us to "be filled with the Spirit" (Eph. 5:18), or more precisely, *being filled continually* with the Spirit. In other words, we are to be in perpetual communion with Him.

We break this communion when we *grieve* the Holy Spirit (Eph. 4:30) through sin. As soon as we become aware that we have grieved Him, we should immediately confess our sin so as to be restored to our unchanging privilege, as believers, of fellowship with God.

We should also be aware of the fact that we may *quench* the Spirit (1 Thess. 5:19). We do this through disobedience to God's express will. We must seek to know His will and yield our lives to it. A sacrificial life is required in order to do the will of the Father. Jesus Christ is the pattern for us in this endeavor.

When we are in communion with the Holy Spirit, we *walk* in the Spirit (Gal. 5:16). This signifies an unbroken reliance upon the Spirit to do His will. Only thus can we resist fleshly desires and Satan's power, which cause confusion in our lives. When we walk in the Spirit, we experience the victory of grace.

> **Christians and churches must depend on the missionary Spirit in order to be renewed and strengthened in the ministry of the gospel.**

The Bible reveals that the Holy Spirit is the missionary Spirit. "'Not by might nor by power, but by My Spirit,' says the Lord Almighty" (Zech. 4:6). "'But you will receive power when the Holy Spirit comes on you; and you will be My witnesses in Jerusalem, and in all Judea and Samaria, and to the ends of the earth'" (Acts 1:8). Christians and churches must depend on the missionary Spirit in order to be renewed and strengthened in the ministry of the gospel.

4. Why is it essential for tentmakers to cultivate their relationship with the Holy Spirit?

Doctrinal Stability

Today, religious pluralism* is prominent. We must be willing to understand the faith of the people with whom we share the gospel. We need to take time to read through their teachings and to appreciate what and how they believe. We must take note of their vocabulary and patterns of thought. If we really love others, this is the least we should do, for love demands that we appreciate what is precious to those whom we love.

The so-called "Christian" cults—Christian Science, Kimbaguism, Jehovah's Witnesses, Iglesian ni Cristo, Mormonism, the Unification Church, and others—claim different Christs. Founders of new religions claim that they have received new revelations.

Traditional religions continue to make very different claims about the nature of deity and mankind's relation to deity. Theravada Buddhists disregard the religious ultimate; Jodoshinshu Buddhists maintain that the experience of salvation/enlightenment is possible simply through exercising faith in the Amida Buddha and through recitation of the *nembutsu*; Zen monks believe that *satori* (enlightenment) is attained only through self-discipline. Moreover, the non-Christian religions are not merely sets of concepts about the religious ultimate and man's destiny. They include systems of culture, society, and the government, as well as the religious foundation. They are all-inclusive ways of life.

---

* Religious pluralism is the proliferation and general acceptance of multiple religious systems.

Christianity has a unique understanding of God and man, which results in two characteristic approaches to non-Christian religions. One approach affirms other religions with an emphatic "yes," because God is a God of reconciliation in Christ, who claims the world He loves. The other approach proclaims a strong "no," because God is a God of absolute judgment upon sinful man and the world.

During 25 years of Christian ministry—regardless of whether I was in Japan, Indonesia, Singapore, or other countries—I have observed that missionaries and missions have said (or have meant to say) an emphatic "no" too quickly to things that are foreign or unknown to them. Missionary sensitivity to people requires first a strong "yes" to their very being. It seeks to understand and appreciate what they

> *Missionary sensitivity to people requires first a strong "yes" to their very being. It seeks to understand and appreciate what they have believed so far.*

have believed so far. Only after that does it bring a "no" to their non-Christian way of life—but with love and sensitivity.

5. Why is it important for tentmakers to respect the religious convictions of others if they are to be effective in witnessing to them of God's love and forgiveness in Christ?

_____

_____

_____

_____

The proclamation of the uniqueness of Christ

In the midst of religious pluralism, Christian mission must begin with the firm belief in the Bible as the inspired Word of God. The Bible is the only authoritative revelation of our infinite creator God. The Christ and His uniqueness which we proclaim must be the biblical Jesus in whom God has revealed Himself through *the* Incarnation. This Jesus Christ died on the cross to redeem our sins, rose from the dead, ascended into heaven, and is coming back to this world again. Convictions and experiences in the Spirit which we share with others must be based on the written Word of God.

The uniqueness of Christ contains within itself a strong "no" to all non-Christian religions. When this characteristic isn't evident, syncretism results.* Syncretism uncritically adopts cultural terms and forms which do not truly reflect biblical concepts. Worldviews, along with religious ideas and practices which are incompatible with the gospel, are often blended into Christianity. As a result, some elements that are essential to the gospel are left out.

Syncretism changes the content of the unique Christian message as revealed in the Word by

---

* Syncretism is the blending of any religion with any similar or alien elements from other religions.

God Himself. Christian cults and liberal contextual theories show these syncretistic features. Syncretism may take place even among so-called Christians when they cease to live under the authority of the Word, the Lordship of Christ, and the guidance of the Holy Spirit.

The value system of such individuals is no longer Christian but that of this world. They are lovers of self, lovers of money, and lovers of pleasure, rather than lovers of God (2 Tim. 3:2-4). They lose their burden for missions.

6. How do a strong "yes" and a strong "no" interact for effective witness?

_____

_____

_____

In the presentation of the unique salvation of Christ in religiously and culturally plural societies in the world, the critical points of contact are the Christian communicator's disposition and attitude. Tentmakers must live under the Lordship of Christ and be guided by the Spirit. Only in this way can they be sensitive to the felt need of the people and address others through Christ's love.

Knowledge of Doctrine

Dr. Ogawa has emphasized the need for a solid doctrinal foundation. Unfortunately, many Christians don't have much use for doctrine. It's enough to know that we *do* believe. We're not particularly interested in knowing *why* we believe, nor do we want to be able to articulate our beliefs. Tentmakers, however, cannot afford to disregard this discipline. Muslims are trained to attack simplistic Christian beliefs. Hindu pantheism can absorb a naive presentation of the gospel into its "many gods" worldview, leaving the Christian witness perplexed and frustrated. Buddhist indifference to the Christian message is a challenge even for those with the best of theological backgrounds. Tribal spirit worshipers may have a more accurate perception of spiritual realities than most Christians. Spiritual encounters in this context have left a good number of missionaries confused and even frightened.

Good doctrinal understanding begins with a thorough knowledge of the Word of God. Doctrinal error usually involves something which is added to Scripture or taken out of context. Knowing the Word thoroughly helps us to recognize instantly when someone gets off on an extra-biblical tangent. It also helps us to defend Christian practice and beliefs. When we know the Bible, the Holy Spirit easily brings to mind passages applicable to discussions or to issues being faced. Knowing the Bible also gives us confidence to enter into any dialogue on spiritual matters.

Theologians have taken this body of innate knowledge gained through Bible study and reading and have organized it topically into a systematic Christian worldview. Thus, beliefs regarding God, Christ, the Holy Spirit, man, salvation, the church, angels, demons, the end times, and a number of other topics have been articulated and compiled systematically into Christian doctrine.

In the following sections, Dr. Ogawa outlines some of the basic doctrinal areas which are important for tentmakers to understand. He emphasizes the need to know the worldview and religious system of the people being reached. As with culture, understanding other people's religious beliefs involves first a thorough knowledge of one's own Christian doctrine. With an adequate base, tentmakers can then go on to study more profoundly certain doctrines which relate most directly to the context in which they serve. They can also understand how other belief systems differ from their own.

Key doctrines

In order to identify the key doctrines for tentmakers, it is important to understand the worldview of a people. One of the most direct ways to do this is to learn how people understand deity (God or gods), man, and nature. Their concept of time may also be important for a clearer understanding of their worldview. As tentmakers enter the host culture, they immediately encounter different ways of perceiving and doing things. Gradually, a biblical reconsideration of their own ways of thinking and doing things begins to take place.

God, man, creation, the universe, history

Tentmakers should be well grounded in a biblical worldview of God, man, creation, the universe, and history. Christians believe in the one eternal God, who is both Creator and Judge of all men. He is a God who not only creates, but also governs all things. He is thus Lord of history and brings judgment at the end of history. He is one God, but He exists in three persons: Father, Son, and Holy Spirit.

Mankind was created in the image of God. All human beings therefore possess dignity and equality. Because of this dignity and equality, anyone—regardless of race, religion, color, culture, class, sex, or age—should be loved and served.

Christ, Holy Spirit, sin, salvation

Though created in God's image, man rebelled against God and fell in sin—and death entered the world. Therefore, the doctrine of salvation and redemption in the Lord Jesus Christ and the doctrine of the Holy Spirit become crucial.

Here is a model of doctrines of Christ and the Holy Spirit for tentmakers:

We believe that Jesus Christ is true God and true man, having been conceived of the Holy Spirit and born of the Virgin Mary. He died on the cross, a sacrifice for our sins, according to the Scriptures. Further, He arose bodily from the dead, ascended into heaven, where at the right hand of the Majesty on High, He now is our High Priest and Advocate.

We believe that the ministry of the Holy Spirit is to glorify the Lord Jesus Christ, and during this age to convict men, regenerate the believing sinner, indwell, guide, instruct, and empower the believer for godly living and service.

We believe that man was created in the image of God but fell into sin and is therefore lost, and only through regeneration by the Holy Spirit can salvation and spiritual life be obtained.

We believe that the shed blood of Jesus Christ and His resurrection provide the only ground for justification and salvation for all who believe, and only such as receive Jesus Christ are born of the Holy Spirit, and thus become children of God.*

Christian church, eschatology

The doctrines of the Christian church, ordinances, and eschatology may vary even among

---

* Doctrinal position of the Evangelical Free Church, Statement of Faith, Articles III, IV, V, VI.

evangelical churches and denominations. But from the perspective of evangelism and mission, the doctrines of the church and of the return of Christ are vitally important for tentmakers. The following statements are taken from the Lausanne Covenant*:

> We affirm that Christ sends His redeemed people into the world as the Father sent Him, and that this calls for a similar deep and costly penetration of

> *In the church's mission of sacrificial service, evangelism is primary. World evangelization requires the whole church to take the whole gospel to the whole world.*

the world. We need to break out of our ecclesiastical ghettos and permeate non-Christian society. In the church's mission of sacrificial service, evangelism is primary. World evangelization requires the whole church to take the whole Gospel to the whole world. The church is at the very center of God's cosmic purpose and is His appointed means of spreading the Gospel. But a church which preaches the Cross must itself be marked by the Cross. It becomes a stumbling block to evangelism when it betrays the Gospel or lacks a living faith in God,

a genuine love for people, or scrupulous honesty in all things, including promotion and finance. The church is the community of God's people rather than an institution, and must not be identified with any particular culture, social or political system, or human ideology.

We believe that Jesus Christ will return personally and visibly, in power and glory, to consummate His salvation and His judgment. This promise of His coming is a further spur to our evangelism, for we remember His words that the Gospel must first be preached to all nations. We believe that the interim period between Christ's ascension and return is to be filled with the mission of the people of God, who have no liberty to stop before the End. We also remember His warning that false Christs and false prophets will arise as precursors of the final antichrist. We therefore reject as a proud, self-confident dream the notion that man can ever build a utopia on earth. Our Christian confidence is that God will perfect His kingdom, and we look forward with eager anticipation to that day, and to the new heaven and earth in which righteousness will dwell and God will reign forever. Meanwhile, we rededicate ourselves to the service of Christ and of men in joyful submission to His authority over the whole of our lives.

7. *In what ways can knowledge of doctrinal statements (such as the ones the author has quoted) help tentmakers in their witness?*

_____

_____

_____

_____

* The Lausanne Covenant is the doctrinal statement of the worldwide evangelical leaders who gathered together for the International Congress on World Evangelization held in Lausanne, Switzerland, in 1974.

Spirituality

Among Christians, spiritual development is assumed to come almost automatically, as a by-product when a person is saved. Such development is regarded only as a matter of information and is not considered a critical component of a believer's life. In any Christian ministry, however, the spiritual aspect must be the central focus from beginning to end. In fact, in the history of missions, developing Christian spirituality has always been the key to an effective proclamation of the gospel.

As we look at the contemporary spiritual state of the world where the gospel needs to be preached, we see that the influence of secularism, materialism, and other religions, both old and new, has been growing stronger. People have different understandings of spirituality. Tentmakers should understand the biblical meaning of spirituality and the major schools of thought regarding this subject.

Christians are called to offer their bodies as living sacrifices, holy and pleasing to God, which is their spiritual act of worship (Rom. 12:1). They are also called to be a holy priesthood, offering spiritual sacrifices acceptable to God through Jesus Christ (1 Pet. 2:5). Biblical spirituality can be understood from at least four perspectives: (1) God's creation of man; (2) man's fall and God's judgment; (3) man's

redemption in Christ; and (4) man's service to God in the power of the Spirit.

In the history of the Christian church, there have been at least three distinctive schools of thought regarding spirituality. The first is personal; it emphasizes being in the presence of God, the love of God, devotion, and prayer. The second school of thought is conceptual and dogmatic, emphasizing knowledge of the Bible and God, particularly God's holiness. The third school focuses on doing things for God and on God's justice.

> *Missionary movements from the West have tended to define Christian spirituality in terms of either "knowing" or "doing," while in non-Western countries the "being" perception may predominate.*

As far as my observation goes, missionary movements from the West have tended to define Christian spirituality in terms of either "knowing" or "doing," while in non-Western countries the "being" perception may predominate. Indeed, any group of people—whether national, ethnic, religious, or social—has its

own understanding, expectation, and felt need as to spirituality. This is an area in which tentmakers need to be trained in order to become effective witnesses for Christ.

Demonology, spiritual warfare

Spiritual warfare is another area in which tentmakers should be well-informed and trained. "For our struggle is not against flesh and blood, but against the rulers, against the authorities, against the powers of the dark world, and against the spiritual forces of evil in the heavenly realms" (Eph. 6:12).

Tentmakers must understand the reality of the devil and his demons. The devil has many names, such as Satan, destroyer, Beelzebub, serpent, dragon, and prince of this world. He is mighty and violent. He is very intelligent. He is a liar. He can oppress, obsess, indwell, and even possess humans. The devil discredits the life-giving message of the gospel. He keeps Christians silent. He causes pride, lust, doubts, and fear. The devil works through the world, the flesh, demoniacs, and even Christians!

Tentmakers must be equipped with the power of the Word, the Holy Spirit, and all the other spiritual weapons that are available. Through Jesus' death and resurrection, victory over the power and work of the devil has been won. Christians must remain in Christ in order to gain victory over the devil as well.

> **Tentmakers must understand the reality of the devil and his demons.**

Sometimes a "power encounter" is necessary in spiritual warfare. The devil and his minions must be challenged by claiming the Lordship of Jesus Christ and His all-encompassing authority. Such spiritual warfare is a necessary component in successful evangelism and church planting.

8. In what ways is a weak understanding of Satan and his work a potential danger to tentmakers?

_____

_____

_____

Achieving Biblical and Doctrinal Competence

Christians must grow in the knowledge of the Lord Jesus Christ. This growth is achieved in part through a daily time when we meet with God personally. It is a time to listen to God speaking to us individually through the Bible. Through devotions and Bible study, our hearts can be comforted, our minds cleared, our souls refreshed, our strength renewed, and our faith fortified. We can find forgiveness and the assurance of pardoned sin.

"'If My people would but listen to Me, if Israel would follow My ways...'" (Ps. 81:13). God is willing to speak to us. He desires it so that His people can live lives pleasing to Him. "Your word is a lamp to my feet and a light to my path" (Ps. 119:105). God will lead us in the way He wants us to walk. "'If you remain in Me and My words remain in you, ask whatever you wish, and it will be given you'" (John 15:7). We remain in Jesus Christ when His word remains in us. "All Scripture is God-breathed and is useful for teaching, rebuking, correcting, and training in righteousness, so that the man of God may be thoroughly equipped for every good work" (2 Tim. 3:16-17). As God's Word works in us, we grow in Him and become mature Christians.

There is danger in placing too much emphasis on activistic work for God. God wants us to maintain our fellowship with Him and to know His will through personal devotion and Bible study. If we do not seek His will, our work for Him will be according to our own will and could be unacceptable and fruitless. If we know His will and plan, we can work confidently and bear much fruit for His kingdom.

9. *Why is the discipline of a personal, daily time with God so important to the effectiveness of tentmakers?*

_____

_____

_____

Formal biblical studies

It is essential that all tentmakers be students of the Bible through their own personal discipline and devotions. In some cases, however, it may be advisable for tentmakers to pursue formal study which leads to a certificate or degree. There may exist one or more of the following compelling reasons:

- If the prospective tentmaker has a serious lack in biblical and theological knowledge (as may be the case with a new believer), a formal course of study may be an efficient and thorough way of pursuing general knowledge. This is no substitute, however, for developing a lifelong commitment to personal Bible study.

- If the target people expect the tentmaker to have formal biblical studies, it is desirable to complete them before proceeding to the field.

- If coworkers or the mission organization expect the tentmaker to have formal biblical studies, it may be necessary to meet this expectation.

- If one's own ministry expectations (perhaps ordination) require formal studies or a degree from a Bible school, it may be wise to pursue this course.

If one or more of these compelling reasons exist, and if tentmakers have the time, financial resources, and opportunity to enter a Bible college or seminary, it may be beneficial to pursue such training.

Other alternatives exist, however. These will vary. Today, quite a few correspondence courses on the Bible and theology have been developed at Bible colleges, seminaries, and missionary training centers in many different countries. Extension programs, both national and international, are also available.

On an informal level, biblical and theological books are accessible almost anywhere for personal studies. Churches and mission organizations often conduct seminars on varying themes. Tentmakers should make the best use of these opportunities.

Even if tentmakers cannot pursue formal biblical studies before going to the field, they may be able to study while they are living and serving in the host country. Studying the Bible may be even more beneficial if it is done in the cultural and ministry context where tentmakers serve. Another alternative may be to postpone formal study until returning home after an initial period of service overseas.

"I thank my God every time I remember you. In all my prayers for all of you, I always pray with joy because of your partnership in the gospel from the first day until now, being confident of this, that He who began a good work in you will carry it on to completion until the day of Christ" (Phil. 1:3-6).

10. What are the most important factors to consider in determining the role of formal Bible/theology study in a tentmaker's preparation?

_____

_____

_____

Summary

Too much is at stake for tentmakers to be unsure of their own biblical and doctrinal foundations. Building this base begins with a firm conviction regarding the Bible as the inspired, infallible, and inerrant Word of God. The Bible gives us the message of salvation and instructs us how to walk in Christian faith. This faith is cultivated through personal dedication to Bible study and obedience to the will of God as it is revealed through His Word. The Holy Spirit illumines our minds to understand Scripture and prompts us to obedience. By walking in the Spirit, we resist Satan and the desires of the flesh.

We live in a world of religious pluralism. This fact compels us to understand the uniqueness of Christ and His message of salvation. To approach men and women of other faiths and beliefs, tentmakers must combine a firm conviction regarding the Christian message with sensitivity and respect for these individuals and their beliefs. Tentmakers must also have a thorough knowledge of Christian doctrine. Major doctrines include beliefs about God, man, creation, the universe, history, Christ, the Holy Spirit, sin, salvation, and the end times. The concept that spirituality can be influenced greatly by culture is also important, together with sensitivity to the perceptions of others in this regard. Spiritual warfare and the reality of Satan and his demons are other areas to which tentmakers must be alert.

In gaining biblical and doctrinal competence, there is no substitute for personal Bible reading and study. A personal, daily time in the Word is perhaps the best way for most of us to assimilate truth. Through study and communion with God, our hearts can be comforted, our minds cleared, our souls refreshed, our strength renewed, and our faith fortified. In some cases, formal Bible study may also be advisable, if potential tentmakers are seriously lacking in Bible knowledge or if such knowledge is expected by the people tentmakers are going to serve, by the mission society they are associated with, or by other colleagues. Alternatives include Bible institutes, seminaries, correspondence schools, and extension courses. These courses of study might be completed before, during, or after tentmakers go to their field assignment.

Action Plan Assignment

1. *On what foundation have you built your Christian faith? Do you know the Word of God intimately? Evaluate your commitment to knowing the Bible through the following questions:*

   - *Bible knowledge begins with Bible reading. To know the Word of God thoroughly, it is necessary to read the Bible in its entirety. How many times have you read through the entire Bible?*

   - *Participation in personal and small group studies demonstrates a healthy commitment to understand Scripture. How many personal or small group, book or topical Bible studies have you been involved in over the past three years?*

   - *Having acquired (often costly) Bible study resources can indicate motivation towards accurately interpreting the Word of God. How many Bible study resources (concordance, Bible dictionary, commentaries, etc.) have you acquired for your own use?*

   - *Pursuing formal Bible studies may also be a good indicator of a commitment to knowing the Word of God. How much formal or informal training in Bible and doctrine have you pursued?*

   Write out a clear statement of commitment to knowing the Bible intimately. Make this commitment to the Lord.

2. *Evaluate your Bible knowledge using the rating scale on the next page. Specific studies can be undertaken in each of the areas listed. If you rated yourself low in any of these, select one or more that you can plan to study. These studies can be pursued topically with a good concordance, through specially prepared materials, or through courses.*

Bible Knowledge Rating Scale

		Not at All									Very Well

1. I know the books of the Bible, their authors, and what grouping they belong to (historical, poetic, etc.).

   1 2 3 4 5 6 7 8 9 10

2. I know how to study the Bible using sound Bible study principles.

   1 2 3 4 5 6 7 8 9 10

3. I can accurately explain a Scripture passage to someone else.

   1 2 3 4 5 6 7 8 9 10

4. I understand who God is, His character, and His purposes as expressed in Scripture.

   1 2 3 4 5 6 7 8 9 10

5. I understand the life and work of Jesus Christ.

   1 2 3 4 5 6 7 8 9 10

6. I understand the role of the Holy Spirit in my life.

   1 2 3 4 5 6 7 8 9 10

7. I understand the scriptural basis of the church and its role in the world.

   1 2 3 4 5 6 7 8 9 10

8. I understand sin, death, and salvation and how these apply to men everywhere.

   1 2 3 4 5 6 7 8 9 10

Figure 6-1

CHAPTER 7

Personal Readiness

For people living in creative access countries, tentmakers may be the only Christians that unbelievers will ever know. Tentmakers are literally the bearers of the person of Jesus Christ. Bible knowledge and a clear stance on doctrine are essential, but the fragrance of the love of Christ and the manifestation of His character in believers are ultimately what will draw people to the Lord. Only as tentmakers demonstrate the character of Christ will those around them *know* Christ. Eloquent arguments for the rightness of Christianity will accomplish little, if a visible Christ doesn't accompany the message.

The formation of Christian character doesn't happen in a vacuum. Relationships are essential to this development. In the following article, Elizabeth Vance discusses key components of character formation. She also outlines how to utilize each individual's unique gifting, background, and experience in a tentmaking role.

❏ *Growing Into a Unique Tentmaking Role*

Elizabeth Vance *

Julie is a college student who grew up in a good family but who had little personal knowledge of Jesus Christ. "Our family went to church," she recalls, "but we never talked about Jesus at home, and He was never an integral part of our everyday lives." Now, midway through her university studies, Julie is attempting to make decisions about the "will of God" for her life.

---

* Elizabeth Vance spent seven years in the People's Republic of China—five years as a student and two years as a central administrator for a Christian organization that provides professionals with various opportunities within the country. Since leaving China, she has done extensive training and has worked with 15 different organizations that are focused on China. She has also served as a consultant for several organizations, helping them prepare people to be world Christians.

She is slowly coming to grips with the fact that God's will for her is primarily related to her own growth in understanding and displaying the character of Jesus Christ. As she reflects on her everyday life, she realizes that God, as the Creator of the whole world, speaks loudly enough for her to hear. The issue is whether she is willing to listen and obey. Will she walk with God and incline her heart toward her Creator, so that she can be wise in the process of decision making?

As Julie exercises obedience in dealing with life's issues, she begins to understand that part of her walk with God requires the celebration of the creative gifts He has given her. She is interested in serving the Lord with these gifts—perhaps in a less reached part of the world. Julie is not yet sure what her gifts are or how she can best apply them, but she is secure in the knowledge that as she prepares personally and vocationally, God will open up opportunities for her. She is finding that preparation is leading her into an adventure of self-discovery. The more she seeks to know God and understand those around her, the more insight she gains about herself.

1. How does developing Christlike character relate directly to discovering "God's will" for one's life?

_____

_____

_____

Developing Personal Readiness

As Julie is discovering, perhaps the most important aspect of understanding God's direction for our lives is knowing ourselves. God has given us three relationships through which we

> **The most important aspect of understanding God's direction for our lives is knowing ourselves.**

gain wisdom and knowledge about ourselves. These are our relationship with God, our relationship with the communities in which we have been placed, and our relationship with ourselves. Let's examine each of these areas.

Relationship with God

In any relationship, we grow in knowledge of both the other person and ourselves as we spend time together. Our relationship with God is no exception. It is impossible to know ourselves with any degree of honesty without spending regular time cultivating the love relationship God desires with us.

As we read Scripture, we see that one of the major images God uses to portray His relationship with people is that of a lover and husband. To court this marvelous and mysterious relationship, we need to consistently set aside time to worship God. A suggested model for individual and communal worship is outlined below.

"Draw near to God and He will draw near to you" (James 4:8).

1. Praise the Lord.

   • Praise the Creator for who He is.

   • Praise God, remembering the names by which His character is made known to us.

2. Sing to the Lord.

   - "Come before Him with joyful songs" (Ps. 100:2).

   - If you do not enjoy singing, listen to tapes of songs while worshiping.

3. "Be still and know that I am God" (Ps. 46:10).

   - Be silent before God.

   - Relax your whole being.

   - Give God all your tensions and fears.

   - Become aware of God's presence.

   - Rest in God's love.

4. "Enter His gates with thanksgiving" (Ps. 100:4).

   - Be thoughtful and creative as you thank God for the blessings which are yours as a gift from Him.

   - Choose a new theme for which to be thankful each day.

   - Thank God for the spiritual, familial, community, material, physical, cultural, and social blessings which you have received. Perhaps take one of these categories for each day of the week, and then each week concentrate on a new theme.

5. Pray back to God one of the psalms of praise.

   - Psalms 8, 9, 11, 18, 19, 21, 24, 29, 30, 33, 34, 40, 45-48, 61-63, 65-68, 75-77, 89, 91-93, 95-100, 103-105, 108, 110, 111, 113, 116-118, 121, 134-136, 144-150.

6. Confess your sins and forgive those who have offended you.

   - Receive God's forgiveness fully. "The blood of Jesus Christ His Son cleanses us from all sin" (1 John 1:7).

   - Bring your old nature to the cross.

   - Clothe yourself in Jesus (Rom. 13:14).

   - Put on the whole armor of God (Eph. 6:10-18).

7. Meditate each day on a few verses of Scripture.

   - Read through a book of the Bible.

   - Meditate on the passages of Scripture which impress you.

   - As you meditate, feed on the food of the Word.

   - Believe God's character is faithful to you as the Word is revealed to you.

   - Obey God's commands and challenges to you.

8. Wait on the Lord.

   - Once again, *be still* before God.

   - Listen for what may be said or brought to mind.

   - Ask God to bring to your awareness anything which the Spirit would say to you today.

9. Intercede for others.

   - Pray, "Thy kingdom come, Thy will be done."

     – In your own life.

     – In your family.

     – In your church/team.

     – In the lives of fellow personnel.

     – In the lives of your friends.

     – In your city.

     – In your country.

     – In the world.

   - Pray for the nations—one each day.

10. Watch and pray.

    - Think of the crucial issues in the news and intercede for two or three situations, asking God to intervene.

    - Bind the enemy and his activity and pray any Scripture that God brings to mind.

> **There is no shortcut to building our relationship with God. It takes time and the establishment of daily patterns.**

11. Pray for your own needs.

    - Lay this day before God.

    - Pray for the love to serve others.

    - Pray for your outreach, that you might be a witness in life and word.

    - Pray for specific needs.

    - Pray for God's guidance and protection.

12. Love the Lord.

    Prayer is a "love exchange"
    Love the Lord
    Let Him love you

    Praise Him
    Be filled
    with God's joy

    Be filled
    with His Spirit
    Praise Him

There is no shortcut to building our relationship with God. It takes time and the establishment of daily patterns.

2. In what ways, beyond Bible study and prayer, is our relationship with God developed? Why are these other aspects important?

_____

_____

_____

_____

Relationship with communities in which God has placed us

We were not meant to live the Christian life by ourselves. In fact, even before sin came into the world, God said in Genesis 2 that it was not good for a human being to be alone. When Adam first saw Eve, he didn't say, "Wow! That is some woman!" His initial response was,

"Here is another human being—someone like me!" As humans, we need other people. Just as the God we worship is complete in the midst of the love relationship of the Trinity, we are completed through relationships with other people.

Scripture shows that it is in the midst of our relatedness to other people that we manifest the fruit of the Spirit—the character of God. We need to recognize that God has placed us in communities. The first of these communities is our family. Next is a small group of Christians who know us well, then a larger fellowship of believers, and finally the general community. Within the general community, we include relationships with unbelievers—both casual acquaintances and close friendships.

It is in the midst of these communities that our strengths and weaknesses become apparent. The world may judge us by the title or job we have, but as Paul points out in 1 Corinthians 12-14, our gifting counts for nothing if we don't show love in our relationships.

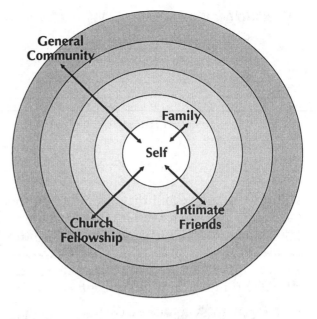

Figure 7-1. Communities

3. In what ways does God use others to help us grow in Christian character?

_____

_____

_____

Being a part of these communities is essential for wise decision making. We need the advice that others can give us as we try to determine God's leading during the various stages of our lives. The book of Acts shows that the church was centrally involved in the call of Paul and Barnabas to their missionary ministry. Unfortunately, many Christians today fail to seek the counsel of their church leadership or other discerning individuals as they plan their futures. Years of wasted effort, along with damaged lives, can result from unwise choices.

Another benefit of these communities is that they can help us learn to *give* and *receive* forgiveness. The words, "I'm sorry, *will you forgive me?*" are rarely spoken. When someone does ask for forgiveness, we often shrug off the offense with, "It's O.K." or, "It doesn't matter," rather than, "Yes, *I forgive you.*" As we seek and offer forgiveness, development of character takes place.

4. *Read Matthew 6:14-15. Why is forgiving others key to our own development in Christian character?*

_____

_____

_____

In *seeking* forgiveness, we admit our guilt. This act reflects a truth that is deeper than simply saying we are sorry for hurting another person. In *offering* forgiveness, we display both humility and mercy. Pride is regarded in Scripture as one of the worst sins. In offering forgiveness, we reject pride as the basis of relationship, and we make humility and mercy central.

To achieve these aspects of character development, we must be involved in relationships with other people. Such relationships inevitably uncover sin—both in ourselves and in others. As we deal with sin, we prove that the gospel we believe is a message not only of redemption, but also of reconciliation.

Relationship with ourselves

The incessant barrage from the media, both print and electronic, has produced a significant impact on today's society. One result is confusion about whom we should esteem. The heroes and heroines who have been lionized by the media leave us questioning Christian values and cause us to judge others by ungodly standards. As a result, both family structure and self-image are destroyed.

Genesis 1:26-31, Psalm 8, and Psalm 139 are three well-known passages of Scripture which reflect how much God values us as His creation. Meditating frequently on these passages can help us avoid being led astray by the world's way of thinking.

To be healthy as individuals, we need to incorporate rhythms and balance into our lives through elements such as daily time spent in the Word of God, regular sleep and exercise, a weekly day of rest, moderation in all things, and relationships marked by mutual submission. There is no easy way to establish these patterns. The fact that God calls us to a life which has balance, however, is affirmed throughout Scripture.

> **To be healthy as individuals, we need to incorporate rhythms and balance into our lives.**

God does not expect us to solve problem areas in our lives by ourselves. Whether we are struggling in our relationships with others or recognizing our own character deficiencies and weak self-image, we need others to help us grow. Becoming vulnerable to others regarding our problems is extremely difficult. However, it is only as we share our struggles that counsel, prayer, and accountability can be brought to bear on situations to help bring about change.

As we spend time with God individually and in community, we will become aware of issues which should be shared with other people. Growth in character results from honest sharing with at least one other person, coupled with time spent studying the Word. A healthy self-image also develops out of a close relationship with God and interpersonal relationships marked by ongoing reconciliation.

5. *How can we combat the influences of the media in learning to value ourselves and our families?*

_____

_____

_____

6. *Where and in what ways does the Bible emphasize balance and moderation in all things?*

_____

_____

_____

7. *How does an accountability structure help bring about change and character development in us?*

_____

_____

_____

Vocational Readiness

Evaluating skills and abilities

Primary to any discussion of skill development in our lives is the question of what energizes us. Where do our real interests lie? Where do we fit? Without doubt, God gifts each of us differently. We tend to overlook this fact, due in part to our formal educational systems and our own fallenness. From a very early age, we tend to compare ourselves with others using common criteria, rather than recognizing that each of us has been *uniquely gifted* to fit a certain role in life.

There is no gifting which cannot ultimately be developed for the sake of the kingdom of God. Among the many skills currently being used in tentmaking situations are graphic arts, teaching of all kinds, legal and medical professions, business abilities, child care responsibilities, establishing kindergartens, agricultural skills,

> **There is no gifting which cannot ultimately be developed for the sake of the kingdom of God.**

theater and drama, international relations, hotel management, and establishing outdoor camping programs. It often helps to ask other people to brainstorm ways that specific gifts could be used.

There are also other areas which can be explored. An exciting new concept in missions utilizes *nonresidential missionaries.** This approach requires the person organizing the mission effort to set forth 100 ways in which

> **Perhaps the most important current efforts aimed at unreached peoples are those which focus on ways and means of placing whole teams in creative access countries through ingenious strategies.**

tentmaking could be carried out in the target area. The lists have included options ranging from teaching to establishing a whitewater rafting tourist industry.

In determining what your skills and abilities are, the primary consideration is not whether those skills are readily marketable. The issue is whether you are prepared to work creatively to use your skills. Perhaps the most important current efforts aimed at unreached peoples are those which focus on ways and means of placing whole teams in creative access countries through ingenious strategies.

8. *How can the biblical assumption that every person is uniquely created and gifted be used dynamically in the discussion of tentmaking strategies?*

_____

_____

_____

_____

* See Garrison, V. D. (1990). An unexpected new strategy: Using nonresidential missions to finish the task. *International Journal of Frontier Missions, 7*(4), 107-115.

Preparing vocationally

A good way to begin vocational preparation for tentmaking is to find out about opportunities for overseas service, through mission organizations that are focused on the area where you are interested in serving. InterVarsity Christian Fellowship publishes a list of over 250 agencies and training institutes. These organizations cover all parts of the world and encompass a diversity of opportunities. Preparing vocationally involves serious research through contacting different marketplace and tentmaking organizations for advice.

Having identified the vocational skill you hope to use as a tentmaker, you may need to acquire additional training and experience in that area. The availability of training may be an issue for some in less developed parts of the world.

However, you can often turn this problem into an opportunity by pursuing studies in the country where you hope to serve. If this is not possible, you may be able to get a job as an

> *Preparing vocationally involves serious research through contacting different marketplace and tentmaking organizations for advice.*

unskilled or semi-skilled laborer in your country of interest. The important thing is to have a clear idea of what opportunities exist in the target area. Then apply yourself creatively to pursue those options.

9. *What advantages are there in identifying work opportunities in the country of interest first, rather than waiting until after personal vocational training has been completed?*

_____

_____

_____

Opportunities

Finding an opportunity

The most critical issue for the majority of potential tentmakers is undertaking the work needed to *find the opportunities*. The opportunities are present, but finding them may require creative thinking and strategizing. This task involves an aggressive pursuit of possible jobs and a readiness to respond quickly to openings. You can generally save time in your search by contacting organizations that train and place tentmakers. One resource that is available is the *Urbana Options Guide*. A listing of some of the organizations presented in this guide can be found in Figure 7-3 on pages 7-13 through 7-16. There are also many other pub-

lications and organizations which can assist you.

You'll need perseverance and creative input from others in order to locate tentmaking opportunities. God does not expect you to find the ideal opportunity on your own. Ask at least five friends to covenant to pray with you about the matter. Keep them in touch with what you are doing. Ask them for ideas and suggestions. Interact with other people as well. Entrepreneurs call this process "networking."

At times, leads may come from unexpected quarters. For example, as I considered entering a restricted country in 1975, I received a post-card in Australia from a man in Denmark whom I did not know, who had heard of my interest. God is able to dovetail all the circumstances of our lives. As you follow up each possibility, sooner or later the right opportunity will present itself.

God has millions of opportunities—as many as there are people. The key to finding them is walking with God, praying, and thinking creatively, with the guidance of others and the help of the organizations that are available.

10. *How do creative thinking, counsel from others, and the resources of organizations contribute to a sense of God's guidance in locating opportunities for tentmaking?*

_____

_____

_____

Research

As you become aware of where you may wish to serve as a tentmaker, it is advisable to do research on that country. Libraries are often a rich source of information. So are mission agencies and Christian student organizations, which can put you in touch with people who can help you. As part of your research, set aside time each week to write letters and read books. Pick up old issues of *National Geographic* and other magazines that feature articles on your country of interest. Information is always available. With perseverance, you should be able to track down a good supply of useful material.

Security issues in creative access countries

If you are planning to go to a part of the world which is hostile to the gospel, you should gain a solid understanding of the history and culture of that country beforehand. For either religious or political reasons (which are based on historical events), many countries today do not want Christians to speak openly about their faith. However, this restriction does not mean that you need to hide the fact that you are a Christian. Preaching on street corners is not appropriate, of course, but there are other ways you can be a witness, even in a restricted area. You need to go into the country ready to serve. As you function in your professional role, opportunities will arise for you to share what is most important in your life. Because of

> **Due to the sensitivity of the area where you will be working, it is important to take time to help people back home understand what they can safely communicate in letters, tapes, and faxes.**

the complexities of each situation, it is wise to get training, if possible, with an organization that knows the country, before you try to engage in ministry.

In addition, due to the sensitivity of the area where you will be working, it is important to take time to help people back home understand what they can safely communicate in letters, tapes, and faxes and what subjects they need to avoid. Often one of the largest problems people in creative access countries face is the mail they receive from home. You may want to consider having someone at home clear your mail before sending it on to you.

11. Why is security an important issue for tentmakers?

_____

_____

_____

To sum up, as you prepare yourself for being a tentmaker, focus on growing in your relationship with God, becoming involved in a home church, developing Christian character, training for employment, carrying out extensive networking to locate opportunities, and amassing as much information as possible about your target country. The process is exciting, sometimes wearisome, and always time-consuming. Pray for creativity, contacts, and perseverance—and have fun pursuing the adventure to which God is calling you. In the midst of everything that God is placing before you to prepare you for service, keep in mind the amazing new worlds which are ahead! They have implications for eternity.

Summary

Determining the will of God for our lives is fairly simple, once we understand that God is primarily interested in our moral development. He uses His Word in our lives, as well as relationships with others, to create Christ's character in us. There are three primary relationships—with God, with others in our communities, and with ourselves.

Our relationship with God goes beyond simply reading the Bible and praying. We need to cultivate a love relationship with the Father through worship and adoration. Our relationships in our communities involve our families, an intimate circle of Christian friends, our church fellowship, and the larger community in which we live. It is only through our relationships with others that we can manifest the fruit of the Spirit. We also learn the importance of reconciliation and of basing our relationships on humility and mercy. In relating to ourselves, we must reject what the world wants us to believe about ourselves and accept God's full love and acceptance. If we are to grow, we also need some framework of accountability.

Vocational preparation involves understanding the kinds of opportunities that may be available in the part of the world in which we feel called to serve. Once an opportunity is identified, training and/or experience may be necessary. Fundamental to our development is the understanding that God has created each of us with unique gifts, background, and interests. We need perseverance to take advantage of an opportunity. Working with organizations which train and place tentmakers is a key to succeeding in this area. Those working imaginatively to form teams and place them in creative access countries may be making the most significant contribution to reaching the unreached.

Action Plan Assignment

1. *Relationships are crucial in tentmaking. The author has suggested that developing and maturing personally involve interplay among our relationship with God, our relationship with others, and our relationship with ourselves. In previous chapters, the relationship with God has been emphasized. Evaluate once again how you are doing in this area. Then evaluate your involvement with the communities around you by rating yourself in the areas listed below in Figure 7-2. Where are you weakest? Many who have been Christians for some time evidence weakness in their relationships with unbelievers. Such relationships are a primary focus of tentmaking. Plan to strengthen this area by developing friendships and seeking to meet unbelievers' needs.*

Community Involvement Rating Scale

	Weak	Strong
1. Family	1 2 3 4 5 6 7 8 9 10	
2. Intimate circle of Christian friends	1 2 3 4 5 6 7 8 9 10	
3. Church fellowship	1 2 3 4 5 6 7 8 9 10	
4. Community at large (including non-Christian friends)	1 2 3 4 5 6 7 8 9 10	

Figure 7-2

2. *A healthy self-image is the key to contentment. As the author points out, television, movies, and other media have sold most of the world a false image of what is ideal. In subtle ways, we have been told what we must be, have, and look like in order to achieve happiness. These values are reflected largely in our lifestyles. It is clear from Scripture that the world's value system is totally contrary to God's (1 John 2:15-17). Christlikeness and worldliness are in direct opposition to each other.*

Many of our personal problems as Christians stem from a false image of who we are in Christ. Who are you in Christ? Have you found contentment in the pursuit of godliness? Can you accept yourself as God accepts you? Can you be content in knowing God and serving Him? Study Genesis 1:26-31, Psalm 8, and Psalm 139. Write out a statement of who you are in Christ. Share these thoughts with three other people.

3. *The author has suggested that contacting organizations involved in tentmaking is important to the process of identifying opportunities. Write to two or three mission organizations. Send them a brief resume of your background and experience. Request information about opportunities for using your chosen vocation or skills in the part of the world you are researching for service.*

Selected Agencies Emphasizing Tentmaking*

	GEOGRAPHIC PREFERENCE															TYPE OF MINISTRY							
	North America	Central America	Caribbean	South America	North Africa	Central Africa	Southern Africa	Middle East	South Asia	East Asia	Southeast Asia	Oceania	Western Europe	Eastern Europe	Former Soviet Union	Agriculture	Business	Data Processing	Education	Engineering	Health	Media	Non-Resident (Research)
Africa Inland Mission International ‡ P.O. Box 178 Pearl River, NY 10965 (914) 735-4014	X				X	X	X									X	X		X	X	X		
Arab World Ministries**‡ P.O. Box 96 Upper Darby, PA 19082 (215) 352-2003					X			X					X				X	X	X	X	X	X	X
CBFMS P.O. Box 5 Wheaton, IL 60189 (708) 665-1200				X	X	X		X	X	X	X		X	X	X								X
Campus Crusade for Christ International 100 Sunport Lane Orlando, FL 32809 (407) 826-2190	X	X	X	X	X	X	X	X	X	X	X	X	X	X	X		X	X	X	X	X		
Christian & Missionary Alliance**‡ P.O. Box 3500 Colorado Springs, CO 80920 (719) 599-5999		X		X		X		X	X	X	X		X	X	X	X	X	X	X	X	X		
Christian Reformed World Mission**‡ 2850 Kalamazoo Ave. S.E. Grand Rapids, MI 49560 (616) 246-0703		X	X							X			X	X					X				
Cooperative Services International-SBC P.O. Box 6841 Richmond, VA 23230 (804) 254-9418	X	X	X	X	X	X	X	X	X	X	X	X	X	X	X	X	X	X	X	X	X	X	X
Educational Resources/Referrals-China 2606 Dwight Way Berkeley, CA 94704 (510) 548-7519										X					X		X	X	X	X			

* This list was compiled from the *Urbana Options Guide*. A complete listing of 250 mission agencies is available from InterVarsity Christian Fellowship, P.O. Box 7895, Madison, WI 53707-7895, telephone (608) 274-9001.
** Has been very active in tentmaker placement.
‡ Also has a Canadian agency listed in the *Urbana Options Guide*.

Figure 7-3

Selected Agencies Emphasizing Tentmaking (cont.)

	GEOGRAPHIC PREFERENCE															TYPE OF MINISTRY							
	North America	Central America	Caribbean	South America	North Africa	Central Africa	Southern Africa	Middle East	South Asia	East Asia	Southeast Asia	Oceania	Western Europe	Eastern Europe	Former Soviet Union	Agriculture	Business	Data Processing	Education	Engineering	Health	Media	Non-Resident (Research)
Educational Services International-ESI 1641 W. Main Street, Suite 401 Alhambra, CA 91801 (818) 284-7955										X				X	X	X	X	X	X				
English Language Institute/China ‡ P.O. Box 265 San Dimas, CA 91773 (800) 366-3542										X						X	X		X	X	X		X
Evangelical Free Church Mission**‡ 901 E. 78th Street Bloomington, MN 55420 (612) 854-1300	X	X		X				X	X	X			X	X	X	X	X	X	X	X	X	X	X
Food for the Hungry, Inc. ‡ 7729 E. Greenway Road Scottsdale, AZ 85260 (602) 998-3100	X	X	X	X	X	X	X		X	X	X			X	X	X	X	X	X	X	X	X	
Friends of Turkey ‡ P.O. Box 3098 Grand Junction, CO 81502 (303) 434-1942								X		X			X	X				X	X				
Frontiers ‡ 325 N. Stapley Drive Mesa, AZ 85203 (602) 834-1500				X				X	X	X	X			X	X	X	X	X	X	X	X	X	X
Global Opportunities 1600 Elizabeth Street Pasadena, CA 91104 (818) 398-2393		X		X	X	X	X	X	X	X	X	X		X	X	X	X	X	X	X	X	X	X
Gospel Missionary Union**‡ 10000 N. Oak Trafficway Kansas City, MO 64155 (816) 734-8500	X	X	X	X	X	X							X	X	X	X				X	X		
International Missions, Inc.**‡ P.O. Box 14866 Reading, PA 19612 (215) 375-0300	X			X	X	X		X	X	X	X		X	X	X	X	X	X	X	X	X		X

Figure 7-3 (cont.)

Selected Agencies Emphasizing Tentmaking (cont.)

	GEOGRAPHIC PREFERENCE															TYPE OF MINISTRY							
	North America	Central America	Caribbean	South America	North Africa	Central Africa	Southern Africa	Middle East	South Asia	East Asia	Southeast Asia	Oceania	Western Europe	Eastern Europe	Former Soviet Union	Agriculture	Business	Data Processing	Education	Engineering	Health	Media	Non-Resident (Research)
International Teams ‡ P.O. Box 203 Prospect Heights, IL 60070 (800) 323-0428	X		X								X		X	X	X	X	X	X					X
InterServe ‡ P.O. Box 418 Upper Darby, PA 19082 (215) 352-0581					X			X	X	X					X		X	X	X	X	X	X	
Issachar P.O. Box 6788 Lynnwood, WA 98036 (206) 744-0400															X	X	X		X	X	X		
Mennonite Board of Missions** P.O. Box 370 Elkhart, IN 46515 (219) 294-7523	X	X		X	X		X	X			X						X	X					
Middle East Christian Outreach ‡ P.O. Box 1008 Moorhead, MN 56561 (218) 236-5963								X								X	X	X	X	X	X	X	X
Mission to Unreached Peoples** P.O. Box 45880 Seattle, WA 98145 (206) 524-4600								X	X	X	X		X	X	X	X	X	X	X	X	X	X	X
Navigators**‡ P.O. Box 6000 Colorado Springs, CO 80934 (719) 598-1212	X		X	X	X	X				X	X			X	X	X	X	X	X	X	X	X	X
Operation Mobilization, Inc.**‡ P.O. Box 444 Tyrone, GA 30290 (404) 631-0432	X			X	X	X	X						X	X	X	X		X	X				
Overseas Missionary Fellowship ‡ 10 W. Dry Creek Circle Littleton, CO 80120 (303) 730-4160								X	X	X						X	X	X	X	X	X		

Figure 7-3 (cont.)

Selected Agencies Emphasizing Tentmaking (cont.)

	GEOGRAPHIC PREFERENCE															TYPE OF MINISTRY							
	North America	Central America	Caribbean	South America	North Africa	Central Africa	Southern Africa	Middle East	South Asia	East Asia	Southeast Asia	Oceania	Western Europe	Eastern Europe	Former Soviet Union	Agriculture	Business	Data Processing	Education	Engineering	Health	Media	Non-Resident (Research)
Pentecostal Assemblies/Canada** 6745 Century Avenue Mississauga, ON CANADA L5N 6P7	X		X					X	X	X	X	X		X	X	X	X		X	X	X	X	X
People International** P.O. Box 2129 Pueblo, CO 81004 (719) 583-0132								X		X				X	X	X	X	X	X	X	X		X
Pioneers P.O. Box 725500 Orlando, FL 32872 (407) 859-3388	X		X	X	X		X	X	X	X	X	X	X	X	X	X	X	X	X	X	X	X	
Tentmaking Franchises 1219 Parsons Trail Denver, NC 28037 (no telephone)										X							X	X		X			
WEC International**‡ P.O. Box 1707 Fort Washington, PA 19034 (215) 646-2322		X	X	X	X	X	X	X	X	X	X	X	X	X	X	X	X	X	X	X	X		X
World Partners/Missionary Church ‡ P.O. Box 9127 Fort Wayne, IN 46899 (219) 747-2027			X	X	X		X		X				X			X	X	X	X	X	X	X	X
World Relief Corporation 450 Gunderson Drive Carol Stream, IL 60188 (708) 665-0235	X	X			X	X				X				X		X	X		X		X		
Wycliffe Bible Translators ‡ P.O. Box 2727 Huntington Beach, CA 92647 (714) 969-4600	X	X		X	X	X	X	X	X	X	X	X	X	X	X			X	X	X		X	
Youth With a Mission International ‡ P.O. Box 55309 Seattle, WA 98155 (206) 363-9844	X	X	X	X	X	X	X	X	X	X	X	X	X	X	X	X	X	X	X	X	X	X	X

Figure 7-3 (cont.)

CHAPTER 8

Two Essential Skills

Tentmakers are often viewed as "spare time" Christian workers. We hope that this study has helped you to dispel that notion. Tentmaking is an opportunity to turn secular work into a vital, strategic ministry for world evangelization. Tentmakers' effectiveness, however, depends largely on their ability to exercise two essential ministry skills—personal evangelism and discipling activities. Full-time Christian workers, even those who are missionaries, are often so caught up in administrating institutions and programs that they log very little time in personal evangelism and discipling. Their work with Christians often insulates them from everyday opportunities for witness. Tentmakers, however, can dedicate ministry time to these vital activities, particularly in settings which are almost totally unevangelized.

Fundamentally, personal evangelism and discipling are relational activities. This is particularly true in creative access countries, where overt proclamation of the gospel and public Christian meetings are prohibited. Under these circumstances, the most proven way to evangelize is through friendships. Discipling, the follow-up activity to evangelism, likewise implies a long-term commitment to individuals. In the following article, Jim Chew explores these two important ministry skills which every tentmaker should be adept in exercising.

❑ *Tentmaking Ministers*

Jim Chew *

Kai became a Christian while doing his engineering studies in an Australasian university. During his freshman year, a fellow student named Bruce befriended him. Bruce presented

---

* Jim and Selene Chew were the first Asian representatives of The Navigators. They initiated the work in Malaysia and served in New Zealand as well. They have also ministered widely in Asia. Mr. Chew works closely with mission agencies and international movements in the area of tentmaking. He is the author of *When You Cross Cultures: Vital Issues Facing Christian Missions* (1990, Singapore: The Navigators).

the gospel and led Kai to Christ. He also helped Kai study the Bible and memorize important Scripture verses. Being a disciplined person, Kai enjoyed studying the Bible systematically and discussing his discoveries with other new believers in the group. Kai was also taught the importance of daily fellowship with God. Soon he began to share his testimony, relating how he had turned to Christ from a background of idol worship. To Kai's surprise, some non-Asian students listened to him and received Christ. Later two of the students whom Kai had influenced became tentmaking missionaries in Asia.

Kai had always had a keen interest in China. After his engineering studies, he returned to his home country for a few years of practical work experience. He continued developing his ministry skills in the context of his home culture. He also learned Mandarin, the language of most people in China. He then went to China, working with an international company.

Kai has now been in China for about 10 years. Through quiet friendships, he has personally led several young men to Christ and has helped them grow spiritually, just as Bruce helped him. These new Chinese believers are now involved in a growing church and are beginning to help others. One of them, a faithful disciple, is now in another city in China and has started to reach out to others needing Christ.

Not many people know about Kai, the tentmaker—only those in his home country who pray for him regularly and friends like me. Other tentmakers who are his close friends also pray for him, and they meet together during specially arranged gatherings to encourage and learn from each other.

1. What factors contributed to Kai's success in ministry as a tentmaker?

_____

_____

_____

_____

The Tentmaker's Foundations

The laying of strong foundations is essential for followers of Christ who desire to serve Him. Whether such individuals later serve on the mission field or at home, these foundations will enable them to remain steadfast and fruitful.

Many books have been written about discipleship training. These resources should be studied and applied carefully. Tentmakers should be reminded that discipleship training is not the work of an institution or a special trainer. Rather, it is accomplished through a nurturing process, which involves:

- God Himself, who establishes and equips believers (Heb. 13:20-21; Phil. 2:13).

- Gifted and trained disciplers, teachers, leaders, and spiritual parents (Matt. 28:19-20; Eph. 4:11-12; 1 Cor. 4:15-16; 2 Tim. 2:2).

- Fellow believers in the body of Christ (Eph. 4:15-16; 1 Thess. 5:11).

- Believers themselves who obey the Word (John 8:31; Col. 2:6-7; Jude 20).

God also uses circumstances in life to cause believers to grow and mature. Character is developed through trials, suffering, and life's pressures.

2. *Why is it important for tentmakers to recognize that becoming a disciple involves a multifaceted nurturing process?*

_____

_____

_____

The tentmaker's call and conviction

Kai had a growing conviction that God was leading him to serve in a special context—China. He was willing to serve God "full time"

> **Tentmakers are people of purpose and usually get to the field through their own initiative.**

and did so for a short time in his home country. Because of his conviction and call to China,

however, he decided to return to his profession as an engineer. Many countries, like China, do not permit traditional missionaries to enter, but these countries welcome professionals who can help meet their needs. Kai held tenaciously to his calling. Tentmakers are people of purpose and usually get to the field through their own initiative.

Skill building for ministry effectiveness

Kai already had the essential skills for being an effective tentmaker. He had professional skills and also spiritual qualities. He had developed ministry skills during his student days. Then, in his home country, he continued learning and developing his walk with God through his disciplines of regular Bible study and prayer and through service in the context of his church and work.

Kai had led others to Christ and had helped them grow spiritually. Successful tentmakers know that it is important to learn to win people to Christ in their home cultures and to establish new believers in a fellowship. They realize it will be more difficult to win and disciple people in a foreign country, where language and culture present barriers.

3. *Why is it important for tentmakers to develop skills in evangelism and discipling in their own culture if they expect to succeed in these activities in another culture?*

_____

_____

_____

Evangelism

Training in evangelism is advisable for any believer who desires to be an effective witness for Christ. For cross-cultural workers, this training is essential. Sadly, there have been many tentmakers who have proven deficient in this most important area. Cross-cultural workers need to be trained in their own culture and then equipped to reach out to others in the new culture.

Training in cross-cultural evangelism includes principles and concepts, as well as skills. Bringing the gospel to another culture is more than a matter of preaching a message. The Apostle Paul recognized that for change to take place, mere words are not enough. He wrote to the Thessalonians, "Our gospel came to you not simply with words, but also with power, with the Holy Spirit, and with deep conviction" (1 Thess. 1:5). Paul continued by describing how he lived among the Thessalonians and worked in their midst. They saw his life. The life and lifestyle of the messenger are extremely important, especially when that messenger first seeks to identify with the people and their culture.

Cross-cultural workers are moving from their own cultural context to another. *Contextuali-*

zation must occur if the workers are to be effective in the new context. What is contextualization? The gospel is universal and is for all people and for every culture on earth. However, the cultural contexts in which God has revealed His message and in which cross-cultural communicators deliver that message are different. In the communication process, contextualization is necessary in order for the

> **In the communication process, contextualization is necessary in order for the message to be clearly understood by the recipients.**

message to be clearly understood by the recipients. This means perceiving the people's *worldview* and subsequently defining, adapting, and applying the message to that context. This is the task of contextualization for cross-cultural communicators.

Contextualization affects three major areas: lifestyle, the message, and the way of doing ministry. The tentmaker's life and lifestyle will either develop rapport with the people or cause them to keep their distance. When Paul went to Thessalonica, his life attracted the people. He could testify, "You know how we lived among you.... You became imitators of us and of the Lord" (1 Thess. 1:5-6).

Paul did not want to burden the people financially. This was his deep conviction. He worked night and day supporting himself. He preached the gospel. He was a tentmaker (1 Thess. 2:9; 1 Cor. 9:6-15; Acts 18:3).

The Thessalonians were willing to hear Paul's message. They understood his message, and it meant to them what it had meant to Paul. In other words, Paul had communicated clearly, to the point that the message was understood and "welcomed with joy" (1 Thess. 1:6). The Holy Spirit brought about conviction. The message was also relevant to the hearers' lives, making its impact. The Thessalonians turned from idols to serve the living God.

Finally, not only had the Thessalonians become part of Paul's life, but Paul had become a part of theirs.*

4. How does Paul's example as a tentmaker in Thessalonica contribute to your understanding of the effective cross-cultural communicator?

_____

_____

_____

_____

Elements of Personal Evangelism

Person-to-person evangelism involves communication through life, word, and deed.

- *Life.* Tentmakers' lives must be exemplary. Like all other believers, tentmakers are to be "salt" and "light" among those who do not know Christ (Matt. 5:13-16).

- *Word.* Tentmakers are always to be ready to witness graciously as opportunities present themselves (Col. 4:6; 1 Pet. 3:15).

- *Deed.* Tentmakers' helpful deeds should pave the way for people to be attracted to Christ (Matt. 5:16; Titus 3:8).

Evangelism should be viewed as a process involving both "sowing" and "reaping" a harvest. The example of Jesus in John 4 is an

> **Training in personal evangelism is best conducted through actual practical situations.**

excellent study of attractive soul-winning. Jesus "reaped" a harvest through the winning of the Samaritan woman, who later witnessed to her whole town.

Training in personal evangelism is best conducted through actual practical situations. It is especially effective if an experienced discipler

---

* For a fuller discussion of this subject, see Chew, J. (1990). *When you cross cultures: Vital issues facing Christian missions.* Singapore: The Navigators.

can teach and observe the disciple over a period of time. I received my early evangelistic training through leaders who were no mere theorists. They were practitioners who were actively engaged in the work of evangelism and discipling.

What are some skills to be learned? Here are several:

- Developing friendships.
- Giving a testimony.
- Leading an investigative Bible study.
- Presenting the gospel.
- Answering questions.

Let's look at each of these.

Developing friendships

Just as Jesus was a friend to many unbelievers, tentmakers also should cultivate such friendships. Unbelievers felt comfortable with Jesus, knowing He was genuinely interested in their welfare. True friendship means accepting people and demonstrating personal interest in them.

In many countries today, using direct approaches in evangelism is not only legally restricted, but also unwise. "Relationship evangelism" is basically the only way to reach people for Christ in these countries. Many tentmakers have found this approach to be fruitful, since people often respond to genuine friendship.

Friendship not only paves the way for natural witness, but also lays a foundation for discipling those who are responsive. This is what Kai did in China. He cultivated friendships with two young men and regularly met with them individually at a park. Over a period of time, they received Christ and were discipled.

Giving a testimony

People almost everywhere are interested in hearing stories. Tentmakers should learn to tell their story. A story about oneself is non-threatening. It is also a means of introducing the gospel in an indirect way. In Acts 22 and 26, we can observe how Paul gave his testimony in a gracious manner. Tentmakers should be prepared to give their testimony briefly or with more detail, as circumstances permit.

Leading an investigative Bible study

An investigative Bible study is particularly effective with those who have inquiring minds and who wish to look more carefully into the

claims of Christ. There are variations in such a study—from exploring key passages to studying a whole book, such as the Gospel of John. A helpful guide can be found in Jim Petersen's book *Evangelism for Our Generation.***

In some cultures, a study on the attributes of God can be relevant. Before non-Christians are introduced to the gospel, their understanding of God often needs clarification.

5. *Why is cultivating friendships important to successful tentmaking?*

_____

_____

_____

6. *What elements do you consider most important in a personal testimony that you intend to share with non-Christians?*

_____

_____

_____

7. *What skills do you think may be required to lead a successful investigative Bible study?*

_____

_____

_____

Presenting the gospel

Christian witnesses need to be alert and ready to present the gospel. Tentmakers should remember, however, that evangelism is a process. They need to major on principles rather than on methods of presenting the gospel. For example, exposing a friend to the Scriptures is a principle. In the parable of the sower (Luke 8), Jesus tells about the seed being sown, what happens to the seed, and why it is sown, but He does not tell how to sow. The "how to" or the method is left to individual believers.

Some Christians have learned to use evangelistic tools such as The Bridge Illustration or The Four Spiritual Laws.** Although these tools may be useful in tentmakers' home contexts, they may not always be appropriate in other cultural contexts. There is a danger in thinking that evangelism has been accom-

---

* Petersen, J. (1985). *Evangelism for our generation.* Colorado Springs, CO: NavPress.

** The Bridge Illustration was developed by The Navigators and The Four Spiritual Laws by Campus Crusade for Christ. Both are tools for presenting the gospel.

plished just because the message has been shared through the use of an illustration.

Cross-cultural evangelism involves understanding the language and culture of the people. In some countries, it is rude to give a negative answer. It is polite to keep on nodding as someone speaks. In some Asian countries, a person's "yes" could mean that he or she believes in Christ as one of many gods. Saying "no" may be an offense in that culture. Therefore, it is essential for cross-cultural witnesses to study the culture of the people they seek to reach. Witness to the gospel always takes place in a cultural context. The Holy Spirit brings conviction as the gospel is communicated in the cultural context of the hearers.

8. Beyond the sharing of the message of salvation in Christ, what has to take place for evangelism to be accomplished?

_____

_____

_____

Answering questions

Tentmakers need to learn to answer questions, including the difficult philosophical ones such as why there is so much suffering. They also need to know the religion of the people they seek to win. In cross-cultural situations, tentmakers will also find new problems and questions seldom encountered in their own culture, such as the worship of ancestors, the spirit world, arranged marriages, polygamy, and many other issues. Sometimes these issues must be resolved before people will believe in Christ. Thus, evangelism is a process of bringing light through the Scriptures. The gospel is still the power of God for salvation to those who believe.

Discipling Skills

Tentmakers desiring to have an effective ministry need to learn to establish and disciple those who are responsive to the gospel. The process often takes longer in cross-cultural situations. Sometimes a family may turn to Christ, and group discipling can be done. The discipling process contributes to the planting of new fellowships and churches or to the growth of existing churches. It is important to

> **New converts should be discipled in their own cultural contexts; they should not be "extracted" from their cultural backgrounds.**

remember that new converts should be discipled in their own cultural contexts; they should not be "extracted" from their cultural backgrounds.

Tentmakers are often part of a team with other coworkers, and the discipling process may be shared by other team members. The goal is to see new believers grow and mature in their own cultures and be effective witnesses among their own families and communities.

9. Why is "group discipling" important to the ultimate goal of establishing churches in unreached areas?

_____

_____

_____

Marks of discipleship

Jesus spoke of the *marks of a disciple*. These may be condensed into three essentials:

- A disciple *identifies* with the person of Christ. This identification means denying self, taking up the cross, and following Christ (Luke 9:23).

- A disciple is *obedient* to the word of Christ. This means faithfully holding to Christ's teaching and applying the teaching to one's life (John 8:31-32). This obedience is costly (Luke 14:26-33).

- A disciple is *fruitful* in the work of Christ. Fruitfulness is seen in the character of the disciple. Disciples love each other with the love of Christ. Their deep relationship with Christ influences others (John 15:8, 16).

Essential aspects of discipling

In discipling others, the following seven aspects are important:

1. The Lordship of Christ

Jesus Christ must truly be Lord of the believer's life. Growing believers must be captivated by the person of Christ. Then they will know what it is to surrender major areas of life to be under Christ's control. These major areas include their careers, marriage plans, families, possessions—yes, their total direction in life will be affected.

2. The intake of the Scriptures

Young believers need to learn to have a systematic intake of the Scriptures—to read and enjoy the Bible, to study the Bible personally and with others in a group, and to memorize meaningful verses. With individual help, young believers soon learn to feed themselves. The process may take a few years.

3. Prayer and devotion to God

Growing Christians need to learn to pray. They can be taught how to have a meaningful "quiet time" as a daily habit. This should not be a daily ritual; instead, worship should be the major motivation. New Christians should also be taught to pray for others. A simple prayer list may help. Confession of sins should be covered specifically, as well as living a life of thanksgiving.

4. Fellowship and the church

Believers grow in the context of fellowship with other believers. New believers need to "belong." They need to learn that the church is their spiritual family. The Bible is full of "one another" passages—Christians are commanded to encourage one another, love one another, bear with one another, instruct one another, etc.

5. Christian character

Paul and his teammates labored hard to "present everyone mature in Christ" (Col. 1:28). Christlikeness was Paul's goal.

Therefore, he wrote extensively about Christlike qualities in his letters. The most essential aspect of discipleship training is the cultivation of Christian

> **The most essential aspect of discipleship training is the cultivation of Christian character.**

character. Although this is a lifelong process, tentmakers can help lay foundations. Paul emphasized the abiding essentials of faith, hope, and love.

A good way of learning about character is to study specific qualities from the Scriptures. Young disciples may want to study the following topics: faithfulness, self-control, purity, servanthood, endurance, and teachability.

6. Relationships

Interpersonal relationships, such as those between husbands and wives, parents and children, employers and employees, and church leaders and members—if they are taught and cultivated early during discipleship training—will stand new believers in good stead in later years. Such lessons are also important for missionary preparation. "One another" exhortations in the Scriptures which apply to all believers need to be taught in practical terms. For example, in what practical ways can believers serve one another or show kindness to one another or bear one another's burdens? When conflicts arise, how can they be resolved biblically? Young believers need to learn scriptural principles and apply them in the context of their own culture.

7. Witnessing

Tentmakers should teach young believers to share their faith with members of their own family and with friends. This is the most fertile soil for ongoing, fruitful evangelism and church planting.

Dependence on the grace of God

Discipleship training exacts energy and effort from trainers and trainees alike. Paul labored hard and was hard on himself. Training in godliness requires disciplined spiritual habits.

One of the dangers facing those in such training is dependence on sheer self-effort to accomplish results. The Bible gives a balanced view, telling believers to work hard, but also giving the assurance that it is God who works in them "to will and to act according to His good purpose" (Phil. 2:12-13). Paul worked very hard, but he acknowledged that his efforts were through the grace of God that was with him (1 Cor. 15:10-11). God's continual work in the lives of believers is a work of grace. Just as tentmakers are recipients of God's grace for salvation, God continues to pour out His grace, unworthy though the recipients are. It is the grace of God that keeps cross-cultural workers humble and dependent on Him. In every aspect of training, God's grace is at work.

10. *How can an understanding of grace help tentmakers be more effective in ministry?*

_____

_____

_____

Contribution to the church

The role of tentmakers is to contribute to the body of Christ, the church. In some countries, churches are already established. However, there is still a lot to be done in reaching out to the lost. Sometimes tentmakers can reach out to peoples that the national churches find difficult to reach. Tentmakers can also strengthen the work of national churches by bringing fresh motivation and encouragement.

> **In countries where there is an established church, tentmakers need to serve more as facilitators and encouragers rather than trying to be leaders.**

In countries where there is an established church, tentmakers need to serve more as facilitators and encouragers rather than trying to be leaders. They need to remember that the church will continue its strategic outreach long after they have left the country.

In areas where there is no established church, tentmakers can lay the foundations for new churches to be planted. Here, tentmakers often work together as a team. Team members have varying gifts and strengths. It would be good if at least one member is a good pioneer and is also a good personal evangelist.

A case in point is a team of tentmakers who are working among a difficult people group. Difficult, so they thought. One of the team members, Jon, said that at first the people appeared to him like a ship made of impenetrable steel—impossible to pierce. Then he decided to "enter the ship" to find out what the people were really like on the inside. He found them to be like wax—soft, friendly, and reachable. More than 20 people have since trusted Christ. Jon, a gifted pioneer, and his team are discipling this group. A church has been planted.

Summary

There are many elements which contribute to tentmakers' success. Among these are a multifaceted nurturing environment and a tenacious hold on one's calling. Once tentmakers are on the field, skills in personal evangelism and discipling are essential to ministry effectiveness. It is important that these skills be developed in one's own culture before attempting to exercise them in another.

Even those who are skilled evangelists in their own culture must recognize specific principles and concepts necessary to successful cross-cultural witness. The message must be contextualized through tentmakers' lifestyles, words, and actions. Evangelism should also be viewed as both sowing and reaping. Winning one person can have a multiplying effect. Evangelism should be learned through active practice. These activities include developing friendships, giving a testimony, leading an investigative Bible study, presenting the gospel, and answering questions.

Discipling new believers follows evangelism. The goal is to see new Christians grow and mature in their own cultures and be effective witnesses among their own families and communities. The discipling process contributes to the planting of new fellowships and churches or to the growth of existing churches. Areas to cover as part of discipleship include the Lordship of Christ, the intake of the Scriptures, prayer and devotion to God, fellowship and the church, Christian character, relationships, and witnessing. Ultimately, the role of tentmakers is to contribute to the development of the body of Christ, the church, in the target area.

Action Plan Assignment

1. *How well have you been discipled? Think about the people, programs, and circumstances that have most helped you to become a disciple of Christ. List the most important elements for helping a new Christian grow in Christ. Determine to begin discipling at least one person.*

2. *Is there a program in your church which trains people in how to share their faith? What process should be used to best learn these elements of evangelism?*

3. *The modeling aspect of discipling cannot be overemphasized. Rate yourself on how well you model the items listed in the rating scale below (for an explanation of each item, refer to pages 8-9 and 8-10). Then determine how you will improve in the areas in which you are weakest.*

Discipleship Modeling Rating Scale

How well do you model each of the following?   **Poor   Excellent**

	Poor → Excellent
1. The Lordship of Christ	1 2 3 4 5 6 7 8 9 10
2. The intake of the Scriptures	1 2 3 4 5 6 7 8 9 10
3. Prayer and devotion to God	1 2 3 4 5 6 7 8 9 10
4. Fellowship and the church	1 2 3 4 5 6 7 8 9 10
5. Christian character	1 2 3 4 5 6 7 8 9 10
6. Relationships	1 2 3 4 5 6 7 8 9 10
7. Witnessing	1 2 3 4 5 6 7 8 9 10

Figure 8-1

CHAPTER 9

Team Dynamics and Spiritual Warfare

Bible knowledge, discipling, and evangelism skills are indispensable for personal ministry effectiveness. Nevertheless, it is only as workers band together in ministry teams that an ongoing and lasting contribution to the work of God can be accomplished in most creative access countries. In order to produce long-term results, tentmakers need to see themselves as part of the "big picture." This can be accomplished through working with others who have similar goals.

Teaming with others, however, is a two-edged sword. Sometimes, we can't succeed without it, but we can't succeed with it either! In some cases, relationships have been the primary factor for missionary discouragement and drop-out. Additional stress from cross-cultural adaptation, lack of appreciation for gifting and calling, absence of agreed-upon procedures for resolving conflicts, poor communication, and Satan's astute way of using these situations for his own purposes have caused the demise of many, many missionary teams. In the following article, James Tebbe explores the vital issues of teamwork and spiritual warfare.

❏ *Teaming Up for Victory*

James Tebbe *

"I don't know what we're doing here," Duane remarked bitterly to his wife, Diana. "I had more of a ministry with Arabs when I was back home—at least I could lead Bible studies and invite my friends to church. Here, none of that is happening!"

---

* James Tebbe was born and raised in Pakistan, where his parents were missionaries. Since 1977 he has worked with InterServe, a tentmaker mission. He is presently the International Director of the mission and is based in Cyprus.

Duane was an economics professor at a large Middle East university. He had done his Ph.D. on a subject related to the country where he served. Both he and his wife had a strong sense of calling to tentmaking. Duane had even given up the opportunity for professional advancement in his home country to take up this ministry. He was extremely frustrated over his failure to accomplish what he had intended.

In another large Middle East university, Joseph taught computer mathematics. He and his wife, Nancy, were older and had come to this job a few years before retirement. Joseph was the only Christian professor (that he was aware of) at his university. Life was hard. Course preparation was hard. There was little or no fellowship, and there were few opportunities for relaxation.

Joseph, however, shared a dream with other Christians who wanted to see an international church established and recognized by the government in that large city, where no other churches had been allowed. "I don't mind being thrown out of the country," Joseph confessed, "but I want it to be for a good reason." Joseph

> *The church was not his doing, but he was a part of it. It had become his vision as he served as part of a larger team.*

was willing to sign his name to a petition requesting permission for the international church to be set up. He stayed in the country long enough to see the church very successfully established. Even some local believers attended. The church was not *his* doing, but he was a part of it. It had become his vision as he served as part of a larger team.

1. What made the difference in these two scenarios as to the sense of satisfaction the tentmakers received from their service?

_____

_____

_____

A Cause Bigger Than Oneself

Joseph and Nancy were part of a mission that worked with tentmakers. Duane and Diana had considered joining a similar mission, but they had found the mission's policies were not suited to them, so they went to the field independently. Both couples faced similar difficulties in their work and similar restrictions in terms of ministry. Joseph and Nancy felt at peace and were effective despite the difficulties, while Duane and Diana had a sense of hopelessness about what they were doing—even though they may have been more effective than they realized.

The difference was not in experience, spiritual maturity, or commitment. The contrast was that Joseph and Nancy were conscious of belonging to something greater than themselves—a team that was doing the work of God in that land. In this case, the team was a mission geared for tentmakers. Joseph and Nancy didn't need the mission to help them financially, but they felt they needed such a relationship spiritually. Therefore, they joined the mission—in spite of its seeming restrictiveness and limitations.

Duane and Diana, although equally committed, were on their own. Local fellowship was available, but commitment and mutual responsibility were lacking. After the first year, Duane and Diana realized this lack, and they worked at becoming part of a team.

2. What are the primary reasons a tentmaker might consider joining a mission which works with tentmakers before going overseas?

_____

_____

_____

The Elijah syndrome

It is so very easy to fall into what some have called "the Elijah syndrome," in which Christians feel that they are the only ones who have obeyed God—yet what they have done seems to have made no difference. In 1 Kings 19:10-18, God pointed out to Elijah that there were still 7,000 people in Israel who had remained faithful to Him, the true God, and who had not bowed down to Baal.

> **The biggest reason tentmakers leave the ministry to which they have felt called is that what they are doing seems to accomplish nothing.**

God spoke directly to Elijah to encourage him. Today, God generally uses other Christians to encourage believers and show them the reality of what He is doing. For tentmakers, encouragement begins with their relationship with their home church. Do other church members share the vision that tentmakers have, and do they pray regularly for those involved? It is vital for tentmakers to establish this link before going to the field.

Once tentmakers are on the field, the biggest reason they leave the ministry to which they have felt called is that what they are doing seems to accomplish nothing. Encouragement from others is vital to keep workers going.

In the past 150 years, many institutions, such as schools, colleges, and hospitals, have been established through mission efforts. These institutions have borne a corporate witness. The total Christian witness that has gone forth is much greater than the sum of the parts. Individuals who have worked in such institutions have been able to take satisfaction in being part of an overall witness that has been seen by the whole community. Contrast this situation to the one facing a Christian individual working in a government university in a country where open witness is not allowed. A sense of futility is common in such an environment.

3. How is the Elijah syndrome best overcome?

_____

_____

_____

Several years ago a woman was working for the Bible Society under the auspices of an international church, which was serving many different language groups in a creative access country. In that country, there were both tentmakers and a few full-time Christian workers,

> **Tentmakers must be motivated to learn how they are a part of God's agenda for the country where they serve; otherwise, purposelessness can overwhelm them.**

who were able to get their visas through the international church. This woman provided Bibles and Christian materials for distribution. She commented that a person working openly with the church distributed, on an average, four times as much literature as a person who was a tentmaker. Of course, quantity is not always quality, but it is this sense of restriction to ministry which can be so discouraging to tentmakers.

Tentmakers must be motivated to learn how they are a part of God's agenda for the country where they serve; otherwise, purposelessness can overwhelm them. The Lord's answer to the prophet Habbakuk's complaint against Him for failing to act is most appropriate for today's tentmakers: "'Look at the nations and watch—and be utterly amazed. For I am going to do something in your days that you would not believe even if you were told'" (Hab. 1:5). God's agenda is much greater than that of most Christians. Tentmakers are called to see things from God's perspective. Joining with God's people is one way tentmakers can enlarge their vision.

4. What pitfalls exist in pursuing one's own objectives, without trying to discern God's bigger picture?

_____

_____

_____

Becoming Part of a Team

Regular mission agencies usually place missionaries on a team and into a church situation that gives a broader picture than individual ministry. For tentmakers, such placements do not happen automatically. In fact, they will not happen at all unless tentmakers choose strongly and clearly to make them happen.

The restrictions of working with other believers and submitting to them as the body of Christ can require a lot more effort for tentmakers than simply getting a job and performing it on their own. The body of Christ, however, is something Christians simply cannot do without. No believer can live without support and pastoral care. In their home countries, tentmakers may not be consciously aware of this need. Many Christians may not even have identified a particular person or group that nurtures them, because this sustenance can be obtained in many different ways. The need is not always easy to see—but when it is missing, the problems are obvious.

How do tentmakers go about becoming part of a team? The first and most obvious way is to go out with a mission or group they respect. There are many different organizations involved in tentmaking. It should not be hard to obtain a list of agencies that offer possibilities

for teamwork centered around a particular calling. This is the preferred method of forging a team, since tentmakers cannot always be sure they will find the "material" for a team after they arrive on the field.

> **From the very first day on the field, tentmakers should seek out fellowship and look for a group with whom they can relate and be accountable.**

The second way for tentmakers to become part of a team is to join a team once they are on location. Tentmakers should not postpone this step until they arrive on the field. Instead, they should write to agencies and people they know who might have Christian contacts in the place where they are going. From the very first day on the field, tentmakers should seek out fellowship and look for a group with whom they can relate and be accountable. Work patterns and habits can quickly be established in a new location that can lead tentmakers away from fellowship and accountability relationships; therefore, a search needs to be handled with conscious effort.

In either case, it is important for tentmakers to research what Christian work is going on in their target country. Knowledge of such work gives encouragement, provides a sense of perspective, and helps tentmakers channel their energies in a way that complements other work in the country.

5. *Why is it important for tentmakers to find out as much as possible about Christian work in their target country and to become part of a team as soon as possible?*

_____

_____

_____

In the section above, the author has brought up the idea of mission teams. This concept has its basis in several biblical examples. Jesus sent out His disciples two by two, modeling the principle of teamwork for gospel workers. Strength, protection, and accountability are provided through healthy relationships in the work. The church in Antioch also modeled this teamwork principle by sending Barnabas, Paul, and John Mark as their first missionary team. They later sent Paul and Silas, and Barnabas and John Mark as separate pairs. Paul demonstrated the broader concept of teamwork as he incorporated many other believers from the cities and lands where he worked as a missionary. The team was never static. It was always changing, with people coming into it and being sent out from it.

Too often, modern missions make the "us/them" distinction when thinking of teams. The expatriate task force maintains its own distinctiveness and agenda, and it expects the national Christians to do the same. Breaking out of this mold, tentmakers may find their team among the nationals where they are serving, or the team may support the work of a largely expatriate task force. In either case, tentmakers should cultivate the broader concept of a team, as God calls out individuals from different nations and adds them to the body of Christ.

For Christian workers, teamwork and interpersonal relationships are closely linked to spiritual warfare. Mission work is primarily a spiritual struggle. Missionaries are warriors who advance into enemy-held territory. Satan is the enemy, who has enslaved millions through vain philosophies and religions. Missionaries are primary agents in carrying out Christ's purpose to destroy the work of Satan (1 John 3:8). Their main task is to turn men and women from darkness to light and from the power of Satan to God (Acts 26:18).

Satan resists God's warriors and attacks them at their most vulnerable point. He seeks to discredit them through fleshly desires and immoral behavior. When that tactic fails (as it most often does with mature Christians), Satan attempts to minimize the powerful witness of Christian love. Since love for other believers is the primary proof before the world of Christian discipleship (John 13:34-35), Satan most often aims his counter-attacks at interpersonal relationships. If he can damage these, he can greatly reduce the effectiveness of the mission effort. In the following sections, Mr. Tebbe comments on this sobering reality.

Spiritual Warfare

Spiritual warfare is a reality in mission work, just as it is a reality in the Christian life. Satan is real and his attacks are real, but the manifestation of his work can be quite different from culture to culture. Understanding the reality of spiritual warfare goes a long way in helping Christians prepare for Satan's attacks. Some cultures clearly demonstrate the overt power of Satan through their belief systems, as in the case of Tibetan Buddhism. In other cultures, Satan exerts his power through disbelief, e.g., communism. In still other places, one can see the influence of Satan in the violence of ethnic and political disputes. In all cases, one can safely say that the less the influence of the gospel, the stronger the enemy's hold.

Christians are called to pray and work against the power of Satan. Attention needs to be given to the hold Satan has on a country or culture. In non-Christian cultures, the enemy is clearly

> **The less the influence of the gospel, the stronger the enemy's hold.**

identifiable—tentmakers can see him, hear him, and point him out. There are also other, less obvious ways that Satan works. In general, it is these subtle attacks that tentmakers are most likely to experience.

6. What are some of the most obvious ways Satan manifests his control over cultures and peoples?

_____

_____

_____

Satan's disabling tactics

The biggest problem for Christian workers abroad is their relationship with each other. Mutually understood social norms are often not relevant in the new culture. The possibilities for misunderstandings and broken relationships are enormous!

God has given a mandate to the world to judge the reality of the gospel by how Christians relate to one another. John 13:34-35 says, "'A new command I give you: Love one another. As I have loved you, so you must love one another. By this all men will know that you are My disciples, if you love one another.'" Jesus was confident that Christians' love for one another would show the world the truth, because such love does not happen naturally in a fallen world where Satan reigns supreme.

Satan does not limit his work to other religions. He is working just as hard against the Christian church and within teams of tentmakers. Ephesians 6:12 reminds us, "For our struggle is not against flesh and blood, but against rulers, against the authorities, against the powers of this dark world, and against the spiritual forces of evil in the heavenly realms." This spiritual battle is easy to understand when tentmakers are praying against Islam or Tibetan Buddhism, but what about when they have fights with those closest to them? The battle is not against other people—especially

other believers—but against Satan. The implication of this fact is that when there are difficulties between believers, tentmakers must remember that the battle is against Satan and not against one another. Together, believers can fight the potential destructiveness that comes through broken relationships.

7. How can tentmakers be on guard against Satan's attempts to bring conflict into the team dynamic and destroy relationships?

_____

_____

_____

Attacks on tentmaker teams

Two couples were part of a team of tentmakers. Both were older, mature couples with effective ministries and years of experience working in difficult places. One couple were very professionally oriented, and their ministry and lives revolved around the husband's more-than-full-time job. The other couple were the team leaders. They felt strongly that tentmakers should work as little as possible in order to be free for ministry. Weekly team meetings in the evenings typically began an hour late and went two hours overtime, making it difficult for the professionally oriented couple to attend. The interpersonal difficulties arising out of this tension dominated these couples' thoughts and energies and led to difficulties within the rest of the team. The situation threatened the well-being and effectiveness of the whole group. Fortunately, these couples had the maturity to work through their problems. Their relationship to each other took constant hard work, but it improved greatly over time.

For Christians engaged in cross-cultural ministry, the sphere which is most vulnerable to Satan's attacks is that of interpersonal relationships. Potential target areas for attack are a couple's marriage, the team, the mission, and the church. No one is exempt from attack. Disagreements and conflicts are unavoidable. The issue is not how to escape attack, but how

> **Disagreements and conflicts are unavoidable. The issue is not how to escape attack, but how to deal with conflict and what to do to conserve and restore relationships.**

to deal with conflict and what to do to conserve and restore relationships. This is an area of training which is often neglected, to tentmakers' great detriment. Because the world is supposed to see that Christians are Jesus' disciples by the way they love each other, the area of relationships is often the primary and most ongoing target of spiritual attack. Victory does not come just once—it must be achieved again and again. Repeated victory is possible only by God's grace.

8. *What kinds of prefield training would be most helpful to prepare tentmakers to defend themselves successfully against Satan's attacks?*

_____

_____

_____

Developing sensitivity to spiritual warfare

Beyond simply defending themselves against Satan's blows, tentmakers are often called to take the offensive in events that are happening outside their personal lives. The reality of spiritual warfare, however, can often be missed if those on the team have not developed a sensitivity in this area.

An uneducated Nepali believer once shared her testimony. She told how she had been ostracized from her family and village for her faith. Finally, through Christian contacts, she came to the capital city of Kathmandu, where a missionary woman took her in and gave her a place to stay. At this point in the testimony, the Nepali woman's face broke into a toothless grin, and with a cackle she said (totally without malice), "Do you know what that woman of God did? That first night she put me in a place that was possessed by demons. I fought with them all night." She then went on to describe the battle and how God gave her victory through Jesus—something that could not have been possible before she became a Christian. It was inconceivable to this Nepali sister that someone as godly and educated as this Western missionary should not have been able to tell in an instant that there were demons in that house. She thought she had been put there intentionally as a test to her new faith.

> *It was inconceivable to this Nepali sister that someone as godly and educated as this Western missionary should not have been able to tell in an instant that there were demons in that house.*

Houses and people possessed by demons were fully a part of the experience of the Nepali woman, but they were alien to the Western missionary. As a result, there was an entire area of ministry to which the missionary was insensitive. Knowing the reality of the spirit world and applying the power of God to it were vital to successful ministry, yet ignorance through lack of experience hampered the missionary's ability to deal with the situation.

9. *In what ways can tentmakers who do not have experience with demonic manifestations develop sensitivity in this area?*

_____

_____

_____

Because tentmakers may be called to engage in spiritual warfare in situations outside their experience, it is vital that they prepare properly. Talking with people who have worked in the country is a good way to gain an understanding of the spiritual realities. Reading about the experiences of others in ministry (starting with Christ and the apostles) is also helpful. In addition, contact with cultures that are very different from tentmakers' own may reveal opportunities for ministry not previously imagined.

A Western tentmaker was working with a group of college students. Most were from non-Christian backgrounds, and several had recently come to believe. In the dormitory where several of the students lived, two boys were engaged in witchcraft. They knew the Christians and said they would cast spells on them to make trouble. One of the Christian boys, in particular, was affected. He had terrible dreams at night of wind in the room, curtains blowing, the floor creaking, etc. This boy related his experiences to the Bible study group, and several others told similar stories. Two boys from Hungary, who came from a communist background, were utterly amazed and unbelieving. A Nigerian student listened to the stories and only nodded. Finally he spoke. "Yes, these things happened all the time in Nigeria. Spiritual warfare is fierce there." He had several things to say about how to fight, emphasizing again and again the fact that "you must always speak the name of Jesus."

The Nigerian brother had come to the group to learn, but his culture had given him experience that spoke to this situation. The group learned together how to deal with this spiritual attack. Tentmakers must be humble and willing to learn from others in cultures where Christians have to deal with overt spiritual warfare that is beyond tentmakers' experience.

10. What are the weapons of spiritual warfare, and how are they used?

_____

_____

_____

Putting on the full armor of God

In Ephesians 6:10-18, Paul encourages Christians to "put on the full armor of God." He goes on to describe the different pieces of armor that need to be included, so that Christians may be fully equipped to engage in spiritual warfare—just as Roman soldiers were completely protected by their armor and prepared to fight.

There are three important points to note here. First, the armor of God does not just fall onto individuals when they become Christians. Rather, the armor of God is something that is "put on" through the disciplines of the Christian life. "Work at it," Paul is saying. "It won't just happen to you."

The second point is that whether we like it or not, as Christians we are active participants in the battle. The choice isn't whether or not we

> **The choice isn't whether or not we fight, but whether or not we put on the armor of God.**

fight, but whether or not we put on the armor of God. The battle will take place even if we are not prepared. Paul enjoins us not to sit, but to put on God's armor and stand, stand, stand! If we don't do these things, we will be wounded, because the fiery darts of the devil are aimed at us!

Finally, prayer is the most strategic of spiritual weapons. In Ephesians 6:18, Paul ends the section on spiritual warfare by encouraging the recipients of his letter, "Pray in the Spirit on all occasions with all kinds of prayers and requests. With this in mind, be alert and always keep on praying for all the saints."

11. In what ways can prayer be used as a strategic weapon in spiritual warfare?

_____

_____

_____

It is easy for tentmakers to fall into the trap of thinking, "What am I doing here? Surely, given different circumstances, I could be *doing* more." In fact, most of the time it is not the physical activities that tentmakers perform which count in the spiritual battle. Tentmakers' most effective work is to put on the armor of God and use prayer as their primary weapon. God has chosen to work in this world through the prayers of the saints. All Christians are called to be involved in praying. Beyond praying themselves, tentmakers also have opportunities to share prayer requests with other believers and thus encourage others to engage in this vitally strategic enterprise with them.

Summary

Tentmakers can be overwhelmed by a sense of futility in what they are doing. This can be particularly true of individuals who are not members of a team that shares a larger vision for what God is doing in the country. Belonging to a team is an important way to gain a sense of belonging to something much bigger than oneself. Team members can encourage each other and provide an accountability structure on the field.

Tentmakers are counted among the ranks of Christ's warriors on the front lines of spiritual warfare. Because the demonstration of love to other believers is so vital to effective Christian witness, Satan tries to disrupt these relationships and diminish the effectiveness of mission teams. This vulnerable area is often neglected during tentmaker preparation. Tentmakers need to be equipped to thwart Satan's tactics.

Beyond defending themselves against the attacks of the enemy, tentmakers are called on to take the offensive. This may take them outside the realm of their own experience. The manifestations of Satan and his demons are varied throughout the world, and satanic activity is more evident in some places than in others. Tentmakers must be willing to learn about spiritual warfare from others who have more experience. They must be prepared in their own minds and hearts. They must put on the full armor of God. They must also utilize the most strategic of mission weapons—prayer.

Action Plan Assignment

1. *What options are available to you as a tentmaker in teaming up with others before going to the field? Explore the possibilities of working with mission agencies or with those already serving in your target area. Pray and work towards establishing some kind of relationship with these people. Initiate communication with them as soon as possible.*

2. *How do you handle conflict? Do you identify it and deal with it quickly? Do you prefer to avoid it? Do you hide your disagreements in public, but carry resentment with you and poison others with your feelings in private? Handling conflict is not entirely a matter of personality. Skills and attitudes are involved which are only developed through God's grace and through conscientious practice. The Bible sets forth some guidelines for confronting our brothers and sisters. We are to approach them in love and are to be ready to pardon, because love covers a multitude of offenses (1 Pet. 4:8). Matthew 5:21-24 and 18:15-17 set forth the procedures for resolving conflicts. Meditate on these passages and write out a covenant of relationship which you will attempt to keep. If you are part of a team, discuss this issue and draw up a covenant with other team members. Then begin practicing what you have set forth.*

3. *Ephesians 6 contains the familiar passage regarding "the armor of God," which we are to put on in order to stand firm. The Christian's weapons, however, are not strictly defensive. Paul states with confidence, "The weapons we fight with are not the weapons of the world. On the contrary, they have divine power to demolish strongholds" (2 Cor. 10:4). These strongholds are the systems of spiritual bondage which enslave major portions of mankind. Through prayer, fasting, the use of the powerful name of Jesus, and precise wielding of the Sword of the Spirit, Christians are called to the offensive. The battle demands skills which must be developed and cultivated. If you are not adept in this area, study the examples of Christ and the apostles as they dealt with overt manifestations of demonic power. By means of conversations, literature, or seminars, tap those who have experience in spiritual warfare. Plan to develop sensitivity and ability in this area.*

CHAPTER 10

Understanding
the Host Culture

The story is told of a young American evangelist who visited Japan. A series of meetings was set up for him, and through an interpreter, he preached his first sermon with great excitement and anticipation. When he asked those who wanted to accept Jesus to raise their hands, he was amazed when nearly every hand in the room went up! In city after city, the evangelist got the same response. Based on his tremendous success, he determined to move to Japan to continue this great harvest. It was only after he had gone to great trouble and expense to relocate that he learned that his Japanese audiences were responding in politeness to his invitations, not in repentance and faith.

Understanding the host culture is critical to successful ministry. It is also the key to successful adaptation in a foreign setting. Learning about a culture can begin long before one arrives on location. Cultural anthropology is the study of cultures and is dedicated to analyzing the components of specific cultures, utilizing what are known as *ethnographic* tools. From these studies, a general understanding of how cultures function has been derived. In the following article, Elizabeth Goldsmith outlines the meaning of culture and indicates some sources of information we can seek in order to become more knowledgeable about our target people.

❑ *Understanding Culture*

Elizabeth Goldsmith *

"How did you get on this morning with your Bible class?" my husband asked one of our newly arrived workers. He and Bernard were chatting together over lunch, while the whirl-

---

* Elizabeth Goldsmith is an instructor at All Nations Christian College on the outskirts of London.

ing ceiling fan did its best to dispel the oppressive tropical heat of Singapore.

"Oh, they were a nice bunch," Bernard replied, "all keen Christians and fluent in English, which is marvelous!" Then he frowned slightly. "But I couldn't get them to tell me what they wanted to study. I started by asking them to choose what we'd look at.... I didn't know what they'd done already. But no one would say. I tried several times. To encourage them, I told them I had some suggestions written down, but I really wanted them to say first."

> **If we really want to communicate the message of Jesus Christ effectively in the country in which we hope to work, we need to take the time and trouble to learn about the new culture.**

"So you couldn't wrangle anything out of them!" Martin said smiling. "Shall I tell you what was going on? They see you as their teacher, so they're much too polite to speak up straight away. In Asia, you have to ask several times and really show you mean it before someone will respond. When you said you actually had a list already, that clinched it! They saw you as just being polite, but you'd obviously made up your mind already what you wanted to do."

How we sympathized with Bernard! My husband and I had often made similar mistakes during our early years in Asia. It's so easy to imagine that other people react and think and decide just in the same way as *we've* always done. It's only when we actually live in another culture and relate to the people there that we begin to realize how things can appear so different from another viewpoint.

Some years ago, someone new to Singapore was handing out tracts in a Malay market.

With only a couple of months of language study, he still couldn't say much. But he longed to be of use. Then he happened to read in a book on Malay culture that he should only use his right hand. The left was for toilet purposes only. Not thinking much about the advice, the next week he switched from using his left hand, as he was accustomed, to handing out tracts with his right hand. A dignified Malay man approached him, stiffened, and said haughtily in perfect English, "I'm glad to see you have learned some manners!" and stalked off. Horrified, the Christian realized that the use of his left hand had been tantamount to saying, "These tracts are vile and dirty!" ... and yet his motives had been so good!

If we really want to communicate the message of Jesus Christ effectively in the country in which we hope to work, we need to take the time and trouble to learn about the new culture. The people won't automatically understand even our best intentions. We need to get right into their shoes and see things from their perspective.

1. Why would Bernard have been more effective if he had known the culture?

_____

_____

_____

Biblical models

Have you ever thought that Jesus integrated Himself into the culture when He came to tell us about the good news of the kingdom? As the eternal Son of God, His viewpoint and way of doing things were very different from ours. He

> **Jesus knew that the only way to make His message clearly understood and relevant was to take on all the various aspects of the culture of the people to whom He was sent.**

didn't arrive dressed in a heavenly spacesuit, with an oxygen mask linking Him to the pure air of the supernatural. Nor did he have headphones wired to receive direct messages from God, which he could then pass on untainted by this world's influences. In order to relate effectively, Jesus not only became a human being, but He totally fitted into the first century Jewish culture of His day. In His dress, appear-

ance, and behavior, He fully identified with the local people. His teaching style was that of a contemporary rabbi, with its use of story-telling *haggadic* forms, together with the more concrete and legal *halacha*. Jesus was relevant to the Jewish debates, such as, "Does God work on the Sabbath? If He stopped, wouldn't the whole universe collapse?" He knew that the only way to make His message clearly understood and relevant was to take on all the various aspects of the culture of the people to whom He was sent.

Interestingly, in the account of the apostles' missionary travels in Acts, the two places where Paul was completely misunderstood were where he was attempting to cross cultural barriers. In Lystra, he and Barnabas were mistaken for gods (Acts 14:8-13). In Athens, the Greeks thought Paul was talking about two new gods—Jesus and the resurrection (Acts 17:18). Paul thought he was speaking clearly, but his audience heard something quite different.

2. In what ways did Christ model identification with His host culture?

_____

_____

_____

The Meaning of Culture

So what exactly is *culture*, and how do we begin to understand it? Any society's culture is that people's whole way of life—their way of looking at things, the customs they follow, and the values and ideas which lie behind their actions. The Lausanne Working Group gave a useful definition which might help us to understand culture more clearly:

Culture is an integrated system of:

- beliefs (about God, reality, etc.)

- customs (how to behave, relate to others, talk, pray, dress, etc.)

- values (what is true, good, etc.)

- institutions which express these beliefs, values, and customs

which binds a society together and gives it a sense of identity, dignity, security, and continuity.

It may be helpful to look at each of these aspects in turn.

Beliefs

The underlying beliefs of a people influence their goals in life. For instance, for centuries Western culture has never considered the possibility that the world is anything but tangible and real. Traditional Hindu philosophy, on the other hand, holds that there is only one supreme reality called *Brahma*. Everything else is illusion, called *maya*. Therefore, deeply religious Indians will spend long hours in meditation. Activist Westerners want to explore and experiment, and they focus on technology and other inventions which increase their capacity to control the material world.

Similarly, a Hindu who takes for granted the idea of reincarnation will have a different understanding from a Westerner of the question, "Have you been born again?" "Everyone has been reborn—hundreds of times!" would be the Hindu's reaction. "What I want is to escape from the cycle of birth and rebirth! Can't you offer me something new?"

A large Christian conference of leaders from all over the world was held in Thailand a few years ago. One of the delegates felt burdened at his first sight of Buddhist monks with their shaven heads and saffron robes. Passing an ornate temple, he suddenly stopped and shouted, "Jesus is Lord!" This is a sentiment we would all echo. Indeed, it is the heart of our faith, and in early centuries the cry was used as a touchstone to prove genuine commitment to Christ. But what did the man's actions say to the Buddhist monks going into the temple?

> *"Have you been born again?"*
> *"Everyone has been reborn—hundreds of times!" would be the Hindu's reaction.*

First of all, the Thai speak in low voices, and to shout is considered extremely rude. The Buddhist monks must have wondered why this foreigner was behaving so impolitely. Fortunately, not many of them understood English, so little notice was taken of the man. If the people had understood, the message would have been offensive. "Lord" is the title Buddhists give to the Buddha: was the foreigner actually putting Jesus on a par with the Buddha? Who is this Jesus anyway? They did not know. He could not be equal to the Buddha, since the Buddha had realized that all existence is illusion. The Buddha knew that what appeared to exist did not really exist. Jesus could not have been enlightened like the Buddha, because the foreigner claimed that "Jesus is...."

We see that a lack of knowledge of Thai religious beliefs led to a complete miscommunication in this cross-cultural situation.

3. *Why is the statement "Jesus is Lord" a seeming contradiction to a Buddhist monk? From the information given, how might the Lordship of Christ be expressed to a Buddhist?*

_____

_____

_____

Values

The more we begin to understand people from another background, the more we will see that their underlying values may be quite different from our own. The difference may show itself in small ways, such as in what is considered beautiful. Many African men prefer to marry a robust girl—a fuller body is considered beautiful, and the girl will probably be able to work hard in the fields and bear her husband many children. In contrast, in the West a slim figure is often admired.

I was amused in northern Sumatra, when I asked a dynamic church elder what attracted him to Christianity. "My best friend was very fat," he replied, "and I wanted to be fat and contented like him. He was a Christian, so I became one too!"

As another example of values, the ethnic group among whom we worked had a completely different idea from ours of what were "major" sins and what were "minor" sins. My background had stressed that violence and physical assault are out of the question for a Christian, even if one is feeling angry. To pass on a bit of gossip, on the other hand, especially if prefaced with, "We really ought to pray for so-and-so,"

might be quite normal. However, the Bataks despised anything underhanded or deceitful or done behind another's back, and yet to punch someone in the nose was no big deal.

> **The more we begin to understand people from another background, the more we will see that their underlying values may be quite different from our own.**

The first weekend my husband spent in Sumatra, fighting broke out during a large church service, with two different ministers each trying to gain control of the pulpit! The violence spread to many in the congregation, so that the police had to be called. After one minister was forcefully installed and the other was thrown out, what amazed us was that several people were converted through the ensuing sermon! Were our ideas of "big" sins and "little" sins perhaps wrong, and does the Holy Spirit sometimes use people in spite of all their weaknesses?

4. *Why can tentmakers' own values interfere with communicating scriptural truth?*

_____

_____

_____

Customs

Any reasonably alert person arriving in a new country will immediately see that many local customs are different from those at home. For instance, how do you greet people? Do you bow? If so, how low should you bow? Does the bow differ according to your relationship with the other person? Or do you shake hands? Are you free to do this with both men and women? How do you shake hands? Is it with a firm grip or a light touch? What do you do with the other hand? Or is it the custom to embrace warmly or even kiss on the lips, as is done between men in Russia? The permutations are endless, and not to behave appropriately shows you are uncouth.

To fit in with the ways of the local people can actually commend the gospel. A Chinese farmer once told my father that he had first been drawn to Christ because when he went as a patient to the mission hospital, my father (the doctor in charge) had stood up and had very courteously bowed in greeting.

Most cultures have conventions about dress, as to what is decent. Some ethnic groups are offended by miniskirts, and for a woman to show more than her ankle is sexually provoca-tive. I remember as a child in Hong Kong noticing the women's stiff, high collars and being told it was indecent for a Chinese woman to show her collarbone. At the same time, I was baffled by the almost thigh-length slits to their skirts. Apparently their idea of propriety was different from the way I had been brought up.

> **To fit in with the ways of the local people can actually commend the gospel.**

Fifteen years later, when I went to live in northern Sumatra, I had to grow my hair. For a woman, short hair was considered quite out of place. The girls wear their hair long and flowing, often hanging below the waist. However, a married woman must put her hair up and not have any ends showing. Fortunately, my short hair grew quite quickly, so I was just able to pin the ends under when I arrived. A new German lady, arriving with her husband some time after us, refused to grow her hair. In Germany at that time, long hair was a sign of being very pious and old-fashioned.

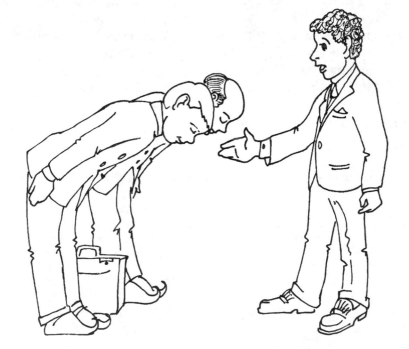

I remember a very embarrassing lunch to which the head of the church invited us four missionaries and several church leaders. Our host solemnly told us all how shocking it had been in the old days: a missionary wife had actually kept her hair cut short! Unfortunately, the German lady never took the hint. Apparently she could only see the issues involved from her own point of view. Her attitude led to very difficult relationships.

5. Why can disregard for customs hinder tentmakers' witness?

_____

_____

_____

Sometimes we are tempted to feel that local conventions are too restrictive. Surely the people understand that we are foreigners and that we follow different customs! We might even feel that if we change we're being dishonest, not true to ourselves: "They ought to accept us as we come, warts and all!" But isn't this actually implying that our own culture is superior and should be clung to at all costs? Looked at honestly, this attitude really springs from a sense of pride. Fundamentally, we are saying, "My way of doing things is best. I don't care how you see things."

No one culture has the monopoly on how things should be done. Each has its strengths and its weaknesses. Each looks at situations from its own viewpoint. I was chatting with a friend who had worked for a Japanese firm in the U.K. for some years. He had found his work very difficult, until he got used to the Japanese way of doing things. In their overall planning, the Japanese seemed to work from the details of each person's task, and so built up the whole picture. My friend had been used to planning long-term goals and basic strategy and then working down to the details. He told me he was

> **No one culture has the monopoly on how things should be done. Each has its strengths and its weaknesses. Each looks at situations from its own viewpoint.**

nearly sacked for getting two figures interchanged in a lengthy statement of accounts. He didn't usually slip up over such things, but he still felt they were mere details. However, his Japanese boss was of the opinion, "If you can't get the details right, how can you be trusted with the whole?" The incident involved two completely different ways of looking at an issue, but neither was "right" or "wrong."

6. Are cultural perspectives ever "wrong"? By what standard should we judge questionable cultural practices?

_____

_____

_____

Institutions

Because of the underlying cultural differences, we find that institutions and their way of working vary from country to country. To be able to work smoothly and effectively in your new host country, you will need to understand the lines of communication, whom you need to consult when things go wrong, and who has authority to act in any situation.

> **To be able to work smoothly and effectively in your new host country, you will need to understand the lines of communication.**

Decision-making procedures may be very different from what you are used to. They may need to be preceded by long and courteous inquiries into family members' health before the "business" can begin. Some societies make decisions by consensus, after long and detailed discussions during which everyone has the right to express an opinion. (As a Westerner, I had to force myself to sit patiently through hours of what I felt to be tedious debate in northern Sumatra.) Other societies work on a hierarchy of authority. Only the person at the top can say what must happen. This hierarchy will often be linked with seniority, so that a younger person must always defer. Last summer in an Asian country we happened to mention that we were older than the principal of the college we work with, All Nations Christian College in Herts, U.K. Our friend looked shocked. "What's the matter?" we asked. "Couldn't that happen in your country?" "Oh, no!" came the reply. "You couldn't appoint a younger person as principal... and if it were to happen, you would be forced to resign!"

It is also very important to understand family and kinship ties in your host country. These may be very complex, as extended family relationships are often preserved, involving many obligations and duties. The whole family may have joined together to pay for the brightest child to become a doctor or a lawyer. This is a form of investment, because once such children have graduated, their salary will not be entirely their own. It must be used for the good of all.

We were often intrigued riding on a bus in the Karo-Batak region, listening to the conversation between two strangers. They would exchange where they came from and the names of relatives, tracing the genealogy further and further back, until finally they discovered what kinship ties lay between them. One would then be established as *kalimbubu* (the senior relation) and the other as *anak beru* (the junior relation). A *kalimbubu* had rights over the *anak beru*. He could borrow the junior relative's things and make use of the person's home. Our Christian friends would often do this when wanting to start up evangelism in a new village: they would find some *anak beru* there, who would quite willingly open up his home for meetings.

7. Why is it important for tentmakers to understand the host culture's institutions and way of doing things?

_____

_____

_____

Looking back over the above brief description of cultures and how they affect every side of the life of any society, we can see why the Lausanne Working Group report ends with the statement, "Culture... binds a society together and gives it a sense of identity, dignity, security, and continuity." Knowing a society's culture helps the newcomer feel at home,

> **Culture binds a society together and gives it a sense of identity, dignity, security, and continuity.**

understand what is going on, and, to some extent, predict the outcome of events. Failure to take the time and care to learn the culture may result in disastrous mistakes, not only proving to be embarrassing, but also bringing the name of Christ into disrepute.

A Christian Peace Corps worker we knew in Malaysia was baffled why he was never asked to speak at any meeting in the local church. He attended it regularly, gave generously, and participated in the prayer meetings. My husband knew these leaders well, and one day he was able to inquire tactfully about the situation.

"We never ask non-Christians to speak!" they expostulated.

"He isn't a non-Christian! He really loves the Lord!" my husband urged.

"How can he be a Christian if he never mentions God in his lessons? He teaches science, doesn't he? And all science comes from God! Why does he never say so?"

That Peace Corps worker was carrying his Western worldview with him into the classroom and so separating life into "religious" and "secular." However, the Malaysians did not see it like that. I would suggest, neither does the Bible!

8. How can understanding the host culture's worldview help tentmakers gain a more accurate biblical perspective?

_____

_____

_____

_____

Finding Out About Other Cultures

So how can we find out about other cultures? Where can we look for advice and insight, before setting out for our new country?

Missionary societies

Most countries in the world have had missionaries working in them, and many missionary societies will have taken great care to research the local situation. Many of their findings have been set down in readable, short pamphlets, as well as in more detailed books and journals. Find out which missionary societies have worked in your new area and write to them for advice. In the U.K., a list of missionary societies can be found in the *U.K. Christian Handbook* or can be obtained from:

> Evangelical Missionary Alliance
> 186 Kennington Park Road
> London SE11 4BT
> ENGLAND

In the United States, a list can be obtained from:

> Evangelical Fellowship
> of Mission Agencies
> 1023 15th Street, N.W.
> Washington, DC 20005

Many other nations have their own associations of missionary societies as well.

Subscribing to a missionary magazine will give you a fund of information on the people, their customs and history, and very importantly, their religious beliefs. Writing to a missionary already working in that country can be a great help too, and the missionary might be able to answer many of your questions.

Before you go, it is vital to find out about the national church, so that you can cooperate with what the national Christians are doing.

> **Before you go, it is vital to find out about the national church, so that you can cooperate with what the national Christians are doing.**

As a guest in their country, you should not try to impose on them your own ideas, areas of theological debate, or methods of working.

---

9. *From a tentmaker's perspective, why can mission agencies be one of the best sources of information about a region, country, or people?*

Embassies

Embassies are often keen to inform other nations of their own cultural heritage. A visit to an embassy or a letter will often yield much useful information. Since brochures and other printed information will be written by nationals, these items will also give a feel of how the people see themselves.

Public libraries

Public libraries are worth consulting about your host country. The librarian will be able to furnish you with a list of titles, and you can browse through these and see which are worth taking home. Don't overlook valuable periodicals such as *National Geographic*. The sort of information books might provide would be the geography, history, and economics of the host country; its ethnic make-up; and the various religions adhered to. Books will also describe the political structures and cultural features such as festivals, marriage customs, etc. It can often be fascinating to read novels written by local authors, so as to see life through their eyes.

Nationals in your own country

Have you begun to make contact with nationals living in or visiting your own country? There may well be students from your target country studying at a nearby college or language school. Look for ethnic neighborhoods where you might be able to visit and get acquainted with the people. Nationals are often very pleased when someone takes an interest in them. You might be able to help with any problems they are facing in your country, as well as learning from them. If you live in a large city, there might be a church from your target country. Even if you do not speak their language yet, you would often be welcome to attend. Cross-cultural friendships could be formed. But remember, those settling into *your* country will already have begun adapting to *your* culture. It will not be the same as relating to them in their home territory.

Mass media

Keep your eyes open for articles about your target country in newspapers and magazines. You could cut these out and build up a file to refer to later. Radio programs can often be a mine of information, and a television documentary will provide many insights as to what life in the country is like.

10. In your particular circumstances, what are the best sources of information about different peoples and the regions in which they live? How can you access these resources?

_____

_____

_____

_____

To summarize, it is essential that we go to the mission field with an attitude of humility and a willingness to learn. There will be much that is unexpected and different and also much that will be fascinating and exciting. If you want to communicate the message of Jesus Christ effectively, you will need to do what Jesus did: get right alongside people in your new country, learn to sit where they sit, and see things from their point of view.

Summary

Effectiveness in ministry depends on a clear understanding of the host culture. Without such knowledge, tentmakers stand to accomplish less than they hope for. Misunderstandings are bound to occur. If tentmakers really want to communicate the message of Jesus Christ effectively, they must take the time to learn the new culture. They must understand and identify thoroughly with the people. Jesus Christ is the perfect example in this endeavor.

Culture is composed of a number of different elements. *Beliefs* determine how people view reality. *Values* influence every aspect of life, especially how events and relationships are perceived. *Customs* are the external conventions of a culture which provide a pattern for social and daily interaction, including greetings, foods, and dress. *Institutions* determine how the people organize themselves and carry on functional activities, such as religion, government, business, kinship, and other relationships. These elements bind the people of a specific culture together, giving them a sense of identity, dignity, security, and continuity.

Finding out about other cultures involves accessing the resources that are available. *Mission societies* may be a good source of information about a particular group, and they usually have the added advantage of a genuine interest in seeing that group reached. *Embassies* are often eager to inform others about their people and culture. *Public libraries* are worth consulting, and depending on the size and scope of their collection, they may be able to provide titles from books, periodicals, and other media. *Nationals* in one's own country are often a good source of information. They also provide opportunities to develop cross-cultural friendships. *Mass media* such as newspapers, magazines, radio, and television also offer a good source of current news about the target country. If all these sources are used, a reasonable understanding of the host culture will be achieved.

Action Plan Assignment

1. *The best way to become a student of culture is to begin understanding your own! While it may be outside your ability to produce a complete ethnographic report of your own culture, write a one- or two-page description using the following topical outline and the suggested questions:*

   - *Customs. What are the norms in your culture for greeting others? What is the dress code for different activities? When and how often do people generally eat?*

   - *Values. What values does your culture give to kinship relationships, efficiency, cleanliness, mobility, education, and other aspects of everyday life?*

   - *Beliefs. How does your culture think about reality, eternity, and God?*

   - *Institutions. How do institutions (religious, governmental, educational, and social) affect the way you are, the way you think, and the way you behave?*

2. *Have you identified a part of the world where you want to serve as a tentmaker? Using a people group from this region or one you select arbitrarily, describe their culture in the same way you have described your own. Then contrast and compare each general area of culture with your own. Share your work with someone who has cross-cultural experience.*

CHAPTER 11

Dealing With Stress

Juggling the dynamics of work, cross-cultural adaptation, ministry, team relationships, and spiritual warfare can produce a tremendous amount of stress in the lives of tentmakers. The intensity of this stress is conveyed to us in the following true account of a tentmaker couple. Some might think this material is too strong. It is an attempt to face with honesty the real issues tentmakers are forced to deal with in their cross-cultural service. This chapter also gives a *feel* for the capacity of a cross-cultural situation to overwhelm those who are not prepared to deal with the inevitable stress. In the following article, Carlos Calderon shares from his intimate knowledge of this true case study.

❏ *Cross-Cultural Coping*

*Carlos Calderon ***

With three degrees in engineering, a firm sense of calling to the Muslims, solid prayer support, and stable and adequate financial backing, Jose Rubio (a Latin American tentmaker) and his wife were jointly commissioned by their two local churches (one in Latin America and the other in the United States) to lead a team of four young adults with the same calling. Married for four years and experienced in church planting, Jose felt confident that he was prepared to function as a tentmaker and team leader. He was anxious to plant a church in a Muslim context.

Jose did well in school. Coming from a poor family, he was used to having to work hard to make his own way in life. Difficulties or limitations were not equated with a lack of God's blessing or with an indication that one was being punished. "Jose has lots of common sense," commented one of his professors. "Endurance is his main characteristic," was the

---

* Carlos Calderon is the Middle East representative for Partners International. He has been active in mobilizing Latins for missions and has lived and worked in the Middle East as a tentmaker.

final comment in the psychological test Jose took just before departing for the mission field.

Jose's wife, Maria, was in many ways her husband's mirror image. She had four university-level degrees and was accustomed to functioning as a fellow worker in the ministry.

> *A sense of spiritual oppression was a daily reality, and the lack of fellowship with other believers added to a sense of displacement.*

Finally the day of departure arrived. Flight delays made Jose and Maria miss their contact person in the Middle East airport when they arrived, but this inconvenience did not cause them much anxiety. They just stayed in a hotel for a few days. Real stress began to build some six weeks later, when the excitement of the new language, new friends, new sights, new flavors, and new smells gave way to everyday existence. Life was not easy in this new land and city that was to become the Rubios' home. A sense of spiritual oppression was a daily reality, and the lack of fellowship with other believers added to a sense of displacement. The couple began to compensate by deepening their personal relationship with the Lord.

Meanwhile, Jose was facing the realities of his occupational task. His tentmaking work required him to establish a branch office for his home company that would open a new market for the firm's products. Jose soon discovered that he was not the only qualified person in the city in this field. Even worse, big multinational companies were also breaking into the same market. The ideal job that was to generate Jose's income, provide him with "contacts,"

and let him share the gospel had to be carried out in an environment of stiff, professional, and well-funded competition.

Beyond his secular job, Jose was expected to learn the language so he could communicate the gospel more effectively to Muslims and nurture new disciples. He was also expected to provide leadership to his "church planting team," a group of university-educated, professional Christians who were full of zeal. He would keep the churches back home properly informed about the progress of the ministry. He would measure up to his family responsibilities and would engage in all the time-consuming visits with friendly neighbors (the couple's real target audience). On top of these responsibilities, he would cheerfully provide tours for visiting church members from his home congregation.

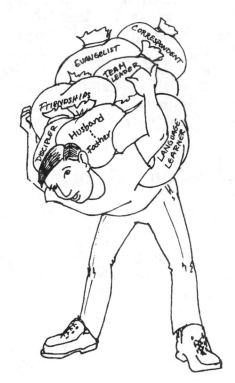

1. Evaluate the expectations set on the Rubios. What were they? Who set them? Were they realistic?

_____

_____

_____

_____

Cross-Cultural Stress

Tentmaking missionaries are not the only ones who take cross-cultural assignments. Graduates from every world class university are well-prepared to work in foreign countries. With commitment and effective training, these individuals are capable of functioning as professionals in new cultural environments. These positions do not necessarily demand deep personal relationships. They are more oriented to the accomplishment of a primary task, the performance of a job, or the completion of a project. The positions are usually well-compensated, with a good salary, medical insurance, yearly paid home leave, a generous housing allowance, and other benefits.

Multinational corporations attempt to alleviate the levels of stress by housing their short-term visiting workers in luxurious hotels or by offering long-term workers the opportunity to live in compounds—places that simulate the workers' original home environment, architecture, eating habits, and dress code. Professional performance is usually geared to the accomplishment of a task.

Christian tentmakers, in contrast, aim at sharing the gospel, which is a scent of death to those who do not believe and the fragrance of

> *Sharing the gospel necessitates sharing life—spending time with unbelievers and opening one's home to outsiders.*

life to those who believe (2 Cor. 2:14-16). Sharing the gospel necessitates sharing life—spending time with unbelievers and opening one's home to outsiders. These relationships, even in one's own culture, can produce a high degree of stress... a short word for *distress!*

2. What important distinction exists between a non-ministry-minded professional who is employed to work overseas and a tentmaker?

_____

_____

_____

Multiplying stress

On a relational level, tentmakers operate under a multiplying stress factor. Initially, one might be led to believe that stress develops out of language limitations. At a deeper level, stress comes from the inability to communicate with others because of their different ways of looking at life, doing things, solving problems, writing letters, and conveying ideas. In short, stress is produced by the inability to relate in a healthy way to the new environment.

Stress is compounded when friends and family back home do not seem to understand tentmakers... and tentmakers do not understand

their friends either! Stress hits at the very core when natural gender differences, intensified by new cultural realities, cause a husband and

> **Stress is produced by the inability to relate in a healthy way to the new environment.**

wife to speak seemingly different languages. Concerns about the children's present safety and uncertain future are also added to the equation.

3. Why does the author claim that tentmakers operate under a "multiplying" stress factor with regard to relationships?

_____

_____

_____

Job-related stress

Over the course of several months, Jose worked hard at establishing his business. However, the multinational corporations from the Pacific Rim were deliberately killing the competition in "Jose's" market. There was no doubt that Jose was losing money. His home company did not understand such international business practices. The company was not willing to put up with these problems, coupled with the ongoing financial losses. All the time and energy that Jose had put into the effort were lost. It seemed a bad investment all around.

There was one piece of good news, however. Since the company had finally been established legally, at least Jose's and Maria's residence permits were secure for the next year.

The police had not come to visit the couple, and they had not asked Jose and Maria to visit them either. But now that Jose was basically out of business, what would happen to him and his family? How could they stay in the country? What about their passion and vision for reaching Muslims in that land?

Since the job was less and less demanding, most of Jose's time was now free to do ministry—but now this tentmaking family began to experience an identity crisis. Nationals asked, "Why are you home so much of the time now?" "I work out of the house," Jose replied. In his heart, he began to wonder if he hadn't settled for being a missionary with a "cover" instead of a tentmaker with a job.

4. *What kind of stress was Jose experiencing with the loss of viability as a businessman?*

_____

_____

Family stress

At this point, the whole family was experiencing stress. More "free" time meant more "ministry" activities, which involved more money. For all practical purposes, Jose's official job had dried up. Simple questions such as, "Where do you get your money?" became difficult to answer. It was impossible and dangerous to explain fully. Every visit to the police to renew their residence permits was a nerve-wracking experience.

The family was making other adjustments. Constantly entertaining people from the host culture in their home brought ongoing friction, particularly when their visitors' social hours differed from their own.

One evening, the telephone rang at 8:30 p.m., just about the time Maria was trying to put their child to bed. "Can I come and visit you?" the voice asked. "Well, I'm putting my baby to bed," Jose replied. "Fine, my mother is also coming, and I have my father's car. We'll be there in 30 minutes." Maria tried to make their daughter go to sleep, and Jose began brewing the tea and checking their cookie supply. (Local culture dictated that tea and cookies always be served to visitors.) Two hours later, the visitors arrived. It was 10:30 p.m. The cookies were served, and the tea was poured. By 2:00 a.m., Jose could hardly stay awake, and Maria was tired of the smell of tea.

The couple's budget was exhausted after the rounds of ever-present visitors who always expected something to eat. That was the culture, however, and the Rubios were making progress with their contacts. Jose and Maria adapted to the local dishes of food, but that "different" social schedule was another issue!

> **The couple's budget was exhausted after the rounds of ever-present visitors who always expected something to eat.**

The Rubios were also a center of attention. Two of their neighbors met in their home and began a friendship. Jose and Maria wondered how it was that two such friendly people had not met before, especially since they lived in the same building. One day things changed. One of the women did not greet her new "friend" and gave her a mean look, which ended their relationship. They began to fight for Maria's attention by giving her gifts and vying for her time. Needless to say, this situation put Maria in a very awkward position.

5. *What implications does a commitment to fostering redemptive relationships have for personal lifestyle preferences?*

_____

_____

_____

The months passed by. Rampant inflation was eating away at the Rubios' budget. Their contacts were making only marginal progress. By this time, it was obvious that if they were to obtain any ministry results, it was going to take many years and a serious language-learning program.

Maria was expecting another baby. With some reservations, the Rubios decided to return to the doctor they had seen during her first pregnancy. As Maria's pregnancy progressed, a washer and dryer were becoming pressing needs. The couple settled for a used "semi-automatic" washer, but they could not afford a dryer. At least this was not a hot summer

> *It was obvious that if they were to obtain any ministry results, it was going to take many years and a serious language-learning program.*

pregnancy. Jose and Maria were thankful there was some heat during the cold winter nights. Even the smell of the coal-based heating system was no problem, considering the freezing alternative.

Budget limitations, constant visitors to entertain, market competition, an identity crisis, the birth of children, changes imposed by seasonal variations, air pollution, slow progress with their contacts, the need to write ever-positive reports back to the home churches and supporters, and language difficulties produced

their cumulative effect. For Jose, hanging around the house doing nothing became a refuge. Jose would enjoy these precious moments until he was interrupted, perhaps by one of his team members who would come to ventilate personal frustration. The situation usually called for prayer and Scripture, followed by more prayer. It was difficult for Jose to counsel others when his own situation was in such flux and turmoil.

The question weighed heavily on Jose and Maria as to the impact of raising their children in this country. They wondered what effect the cross-cultural environment would have on their children and how it would shape their children's futures. There seemed to be arguments pro and con. The children would study in this new culture; they would be bilingual, with options to learn yet other languages; they would see the world through the eyes of the poor; they would understand cultural realities and might develop bonds with other cultures; and they would grow up in the context of spiritual ministry and spiritual warfare which, Jose and Maria hoped, would make them strong believers. If the children married and stayed in the country, they would have to be sensitive to their own children as they grew up, helping them to develop a secure personal, family, and cultural identity in this complex world of cross-cultural life. Ultimately, it seemed that the advantages of raising a multicultural family outweighed the monocultural alternative. The children would not be disadvantaged, but making this choice for them was difficult.

6. *What are your impressions regarding tentmakers' raising children in another culture? What are the major issues that produce stress?*

_____

_____

_____

_____

Dealing With Stress

The complexity of stress factors in a tentmaking ministry can reduce the experience to emotional "survival." High personal, family, and vocational stress can seriously impact tentmakers' sense of calling, purpose, and accomplishment. Are there ways for tentmakers to deal with these concerns before the stresses overcome them? Yes, but the solution is not an easy one. Thank God that others have gone before in these cross-cultural assignments. Tentmakers can learn from these forerunners, as well as from those who have studied these issues deeply.

The first major principle in dealing with stress is to face reality with honesty, humility, and transparency. Stress is a part of life, but cross-cultural servants face a particularly heavy dose of the condition. If tentmakers understand beforehand the stress milieu they are likely to face, they will be better able to recognize stress for what it is and limit its effects. Paul Hiebert's description of the three stages of cross-cultural adaptation (summarized below) is a good point of reference to keep in mind.*

As Hiebert notes, almost all tentmakers go to their assignment with a high sense of calling and peaked enthusiasm. There is a sense of, "Finally! I'm here where I have wanted to be for so long! Thank God! Wow! Look at all this marvelous diversity of sights, sounds, tastes, peoples, customs, and culture! We want to stay here all our lives!" This is the *tourist* or *honeymoon* stage. It can last quite some time, depending on the person. But the day will come when the excitement wears off. For some people, the culture crashes in on them suddenly; for others, there is a more gradual awareness of problems.

The second stage then sets in with *culture shock*. Hiebert defines culture shock as "...the sense of confusion and disorientation we face when we move into another culture.... It is the fact that all the cultural patterns we have learned are now meaningless. We know less about living here than even the children, and we must begin again to learn the elementary things of life—how to speak, to greet one another, to eat, to market, to travel, and a thousand other things." **

> **If tentmakers understand beforehand the stress milieu they are likely to face, they will be better able to recognize stress for what it is and limit its effects.**

If tentmakers realize that culture shock is normal to all cross-cultural workers, and it is not evidence of spiritual problems, then they can relax and face it realistically. Here we see the importance of tentmaker teams, where honest sharing allows all to open up and work through the stress of culture shock. Many times an experienced missionary in the same area can be of tremendous encouragement to younger tentmakers. Relieving stress will come as tentmakers relax the expectations which they, their families, the company, the home church, and others have imposed on them.

---

* Hiebert, P. G. (1992). Culture and cross-cultural differences. In R. D. Winter & S. C. Hawthorne (Eds.), *Perspectives on the world Christian movement: A reader* (rev. ed.) (pp. C9-C23). Pasadena, CA: William Carey Library.

** Hiebert, p. C13.

Hiebert emphasizes that the third stage of cultural adaptation, that of the *adjusted bicultural person*, takes time. Tentmakers should not assume that this adjustment can be made quickly! Too many tentmakers stay for such short periods that they never move into this stage of trust, knowledge, and language freedom—all of which lead to significant identification and bonding with the host culture and people.

7. If adaptation is an expected outcome, why is it unwise for tentmakers to take a relatively short assignment?

_____

_____

_____

Adaptation becomes the key issue in handling stress. Adaptation comes as tentmakers understand that most cultural variants are neither right nor wrong, neither angelic nor demonic. They simply identify deep-seated historic differences between the peoples of the world. *Different* is not bad or wrong! Adaptation comes with *communication*, and if tentmakers are not committed for a long-term ministry,

> **Adaptation comes as tentmakers understand that most cultural variants are neither right nor wrong, neither angelic nor demonic.**

there will be a tendency to avoid the hard task of learning the local or national language. Language is the window into the heart of a people, but such a window opens gradually. Adaptation comes with time; it requires long-term investments with a culture, with the people, with families, and with individuals.

Facing the realities honestly

Missionary work in a Muslim context is not easy. Holding a secular job in the host country where Jose and Maria went to work was an experience in exploitation. Combining both ministry and job activities in a healthy balance was harder than Jose had ever read about. The task seemed overwhelming.

A turning point came when the Rubios finally realized that their host culture was not merely a variation of their own, but was indeed a radically different culture in its own right. It was not merely that local people acted or thought differently, but they had a pattern of conduct, a different rhythm, a song with its own singular beauty.

To solve a problem, one must realize that the problem exists. The same is true with culture. Once tentmakers recognize, accept, and embrace the reality that different cultures do exist, they are on their way to beginning to feel at home in the new country. An interesting aside to this personal discovery is that as tentmakers embrace another culture, their own culture comes under closer scrutiny.

The touristic fascination with the new country soon fades away, transformed into rejection, with outbursts of heavy criticism. There are two possible outcomes of this criticism. One is a growth period, during which tentmakers discover the essence of the local culture and come to a deeper awareness of their own culture. The other possible outcome is total rejection of the new culture, which often ends in tentmakers' making an abrupt return to their home country—at a heavy emotional, spiritual, and even physical cost.

The Rubios entered the growth phase. They continued to learn the culture, adapting and incorporating its features into their way of life, trying to make it as much their own as possible. The smells, the cold, the lack of running water, stiff professional competition, slowly progressing contacts, limited fellowship with believers, a shrinking budget, the crowded streets, and packed public transportation made up real life. It was *their* life... and it was slowly becoming more enjoyable!

Not all tentmakers make this cultural transition.

8. Why is it that as tentmakers adapt to the new culture, stress is reduced?

_____

_____

_____

The Role of the Home Church

During the Rubios' term on the field, letters, visitors, phone calls, and faxes arrived regularly. Money, or the lack of it, was not as important as the emotional and spiritual support Jose and Maria felt from their home churches. An added blessing was the fact that these churches also were faithful in sending the promised finances.

The Rubios had been raised in a conservative Latin American evangelical church, where spiritual warfare was not emphasized. In their new home, they realized that they were fighting a war of attrition, in which they were constantly under attack from the forces of darkness. They felt like Joshua fighting in the valley, totally dependent on Moses' keeping his arms up to heaven on their behalf (Ex. 17:8-13). The home churches, the Rubios' "Moses," were still holding their arms up. Jose and Maria were most grateful for this ongoing support.

The Rubios' American pastor and some elders came to visit the team—always at the right time and at great financial sacrifice on the part of the church. These visits were like a cold, thirst-quenching drink in the middle of a hot afternoon. Jose's pastor had been a businessman himself. The church provided not only finances, prayer support, and pastoral visits, but also business counsel from the pastor and other professionals in the congregation.

It was these counselors who first told Jose that he had to change course if he wanted to remain in business. It was his pastor who was around for that intensive counseling session when Jose most needed it. When an emergency demanded that the Rubios make an immediate trip out of the country, the church had the flexibility not only to pray, but also to underwrite the required action financially.

9. In what ways was the Rubios' church involved in helping the Rubios cope with stress?

_____

_____

_____

_____

The best pastoral care from the home church comes under the following conditions:

1. The church has sent out tentmakers as its own missionaries.

2. The church identifies with tentmakers through serious and informed prayer.

3. The church invests financially (where this is needed) for the tentmaking family to do an effective work.

4. The church ensures that *on-site* strategizing, shepherding, and supervising are provided for the family. (Few churches can do these things themselves, so it becomes critical that other arrangements be made. Anything short of this is a travesty.)

5. The church provides for periodic renewal and refreshment for the family, making available all that is necessary for these needs to be met.

Reentry

Several years older, Jose and Maria with their expanded family return "home" to beautiful memories. Some faithful friends come to welcome them at the airport. One thoughtful person blesses them with a gift representing a modest monthly amount put aside in a separate account for the family's "personal reentry expenses." Jose and Maria have almost lost that magic aura that new missionaries have, but they are welcomed back.

They are not the same, however. Life is different here. Their "home" city has grown, with new streets, new houses, new shops and fads, and almost a different church (people move about so much!).

The Rubios find that their stomachs reject the food that used to be their own ("too many chemicals," they say). They have running water, a really automatic washer and dryer, doctors they feel good about, and basically the same job. They miss their friends, however, in their Middle East "home."

Folks assume that Jose and Maria are still the self-confident professionals they always were. As time passes, Jose gradually realizes that the Lord and the devil are somehow becoming more distant. He has fought in a spiritual war in a remote land. The smell of the battle begins to give way to more mundane discussions of church strategy. His debriefing session with the pastor is excellent and personally reaffirming. Jose takes back his old responsibilities at the church. Life is to continue as before.

Jose and Maria find that they have to work through reverse culture shock. They try to overcome their criticism and unexpected rejection of this "home world." It is not easy to embrace the home culture again. The large church worship meeting is a joy—how unusual to be with so many Christians in one place!—but the seeming shallowness of brothers' and sisters' commitment is baffling. Deep spiritual life seems rare, but full schedules and busyness are common. The ministry pace is more relaxed and more inward-focused than Jose is used to... Jose's spiritual battles are being replaced by intellectual battles. The congregation is experiencing growth and leadership difficulties requiring major change. Jose won-

> *The large church worship meeting is a joy, but the seeming shallowness of brothers' and sisters' commitment is baffling.*

ders whether he will be expected to carry this burden while holding down his other staff position. He faces an uphill battle in his new ministry, under the heavy weight of his missionary medals and radical image.

10. Why were the Rubios feeling a sense of alienation in their readjustment to life in their home church and culture?

_____

_____

_____

_____

The church did a good job of debriefing the Rubios. Jose was given ministry opportunities. The Rubios were fortunate that their church was walking with them through the reentry stage with patience, support, personal concern, and an ongoing commitment to help the family make the proper decisions for the future. Should they return to the overseas assignment? Jose's original company had folded, but the Rubios' passion remained. What were they to do now? Care and concern by the church were going a long way to help the Rubios work through these difficult questions and readapt to their home culture.

Summary

The stress level for tentmakers begins to build, once the initial honeymoon phase of adaptation has been completed and everyday routines begin to take hold. Disorientation sets in as tentmakers lose touch with their own cultural norms. On the surface, a lack of ability in the language of the host culture seems to be the main difficulty. A deeper incongruity with the new environment exists, though, which compounds the stress.

Tentmakers differ from other professionals working overseas in that, beyond their jobs, they focus on the development of redemptive relationships. This focus requires tentmakers to open their homes and lives to the people. The impact of the new culture affects all these relationships—including those within the family. Adapting to the business or professional environment is another area of stress, as tentmakers attempt to cope with different culturally determined practices. A combination of all these stresses can ultimately overwhelm tentmakers and their families.

Adapting to the culture becomes the key to reducing the overall stress. This process begins with an understanding of the complexity of the situation into which tentmakers are stepping. It is important that the home church be aware of the potential for stress and that the members support tentmakers by whatever means possible. The home church also has a tremendously important role to play when tentmakers return home. Members should be available to support tentmakers through the sometimes difficult time of readjustment to the home culture.

Action Plan Assignment

1. *The initial expectations set on the Rubios were daunting. What expectations do you have of yourself as a tentmaker? What expectations do others have? Identify these. Think through your capability of handling each of these sets of expectations. Discuss these with a mentor or someone in missions leadership. Plan in such a way that you will not be dealing with more than you can handle.*

2. *Every individual has ways of relieving stress. Some people exercise. Others relax by reading a book or watching television. Other people develop hobbies. Still others engage in destructive practices, such as drinking or overeating. Identify how you relieve stress constructively. If you are not strong in this area, develop ways of relaxing. These activities should be ones that you can incorporate into your lifestyle once on the field.*

3. *Many churches which do a very conscientious job of sending missionaries fail miserably when their missionaries return from the field. The assumption is that the missionaries will be glad to be back and will fit into the current way of life. Often, this reentry period can be very disorienting and discouraging to families who have returned from what to them has been a transforming experience. Church leadership needs to give adequate time to hearing what the tentmaker family has been through and helping them readjust. This process, often called debriefing, is essential to missionaries' health and well-being. List what you think would be important to you as a tentmaker upon returning to your home town and church after a three-year overseas assignment.*

CHAPTER 12

Becoming a Belonger

Learning all about another culture while in one's own country is similar to learning all about swimming without ever entering the water. We can study the composition of water, the different types of places where people swim, and the motion of swim strokes. We can even anticipate what swimming will be like, but real knowledge comes only through actual experience.

Previous chapters have emphasized the importance of knowing the host culture. We have even suggested how one can learn about the host culture while still at home. In this chapter, we make the transition to the field. When workers arrive, with whom will they identify? How much effort will they make to adapt to the culture? How vulnerable will they become in trying to communicate? As we shall see, these questions will be answered largely in the initial approach used by tentmakers upon arrival on the field.

The long-term effectiveness of cross-cultural ministers depends to a large extent on how they approach the difficult and challenging task of becoming part of the new culture. To continue with our swimming analogy, many new missionaries try to shelter themselves from the struggle and shock of a new culture by wading near the shore. Others, with a clearer understanding of the importance of *swimming*, are willing to plunge into the deep end. In the following article, Marcelo Acosta highlights principles of cultural integration from his own experience.

❏ *Experiencing Cultural Integration*

Marcelo Acosta *

Petrovsky was a Russian tentmaker sent by his local church to work among unreached peoples in Africa. When he arrived at the airport in the city of Uga-Bunga, his Russian compatriots, long-term workers in Africa, greeted him enthusiastically. Immediately they took him to one of the workers' houses and, wanting him to feel right at home, did all they could to make him comfortable—just as if he were back in Russia. In the weeks that followed, they gave him the best of Russian food, spoke Russian, and showed him around in a Lada (a Russian car). He even met some Africans who spoke Russian fluently, and to his surprise, he was able to establish a good relationship with them quickly.

Petrovsky was impressed. He did not understand why so many people had told him during his years of theological and missiological preparation that he would have difficulties in adapting to African culture. It was just the opposite! He was feeling as if he were back in Russia, with no sign of culture shock at all.

Of course, Petrovsky had not yet tried eating the "horrible" typical African foods, nor the "detestable" drinks made of local fruits. "But," thought he, "little by little I will become a part of this culture with its strange habits. For now, I will listen to my missionary friends' advice to get a good house, a car, and learn the language,

---

* Marcelo Acosta and his wife are Latin Americans who have pioneered as tentmakers in a creative access, Muslim context. In addition to their own personal ministry, they conduct annual training and orientation programs for new workers entering their area of the world. They serve with a Latin American mission agency to Muslim peoples.

and then I will be ready to confront these people." *

The above story is not true. It well illustrates, however, a pattern for many cross-cultural missionaries and tentmakers. When workers do not involve themselves with the culture from the first day, and when they are protected by their missionary colleagues, they often fail to learn to speak the language fluently—even after years in the country. They also tend to avoid contact with nationals, and they are generally limited socially to foreign friends who happen to reside nearby.

1. *Although the Russian tentmaker's behavior may seem a bit extreme, it is typical of the approach and attitudes of many to a new culture. Why might the approach the Russian used seem "normal" to many who go overseas?*

_____

_____

_____

Entry Strategy

Identifying with the host culture: The initial bonding experience

Knowing the dangers of non-identification, my wife and I sought ways to minimize cultural differences by undertaking a structured process of adaptation** in Madon,*** an Arabian country in North Africa, where propagation of the gospel is forbidden.

As soon as we arrived, we felt the impact of cultural diversity. Even though the people of Madon were physically similar to Latin Americans, they spoke a different language, dressed differently, and even looked at us in a different manner.

Poverty was evident everywhere. The streets were narrow and dusty, lined with small shops. Hundreds of people, mainly men and boys, walked around as if they had no destiny and were looking for a reason for life. Children asked for money, and dozens of tourist guides tried to show us the city. The places where we ate were small, offering juices and food that we had never seen before. All these things made a deep negative impression, even though we were trying to fit in as well as possible. Our natural reaction was to distance ourselves from the people, trying to protect ourselves in order to avoid feeling the pain of adaptation.

In spite of the pain that started that first week and went on for about five months, we virtually immersed ourselves in the culture. We knew that not doing this from the beginning would

* The problem of cultural adaptation is well treated by Thomas and Elizabeth Brewster. This illustration is inspired by the Brewsters' article. See Brewster, E. T., & Brewster, E. S. (1982). *Bonding and the missionary task: Establishing a sense of belonging.* Pasadena, CA: Lingua House.

** This process of cultural adaptation was guided by Richard and Connie Smith of Wycliffe Bible Translators.

*** For security reasons, this name is fictitious.

weaken our adaptation process. According to specialists, those first weeks are crucial—when the missionary has the ideal physical and emotional stamina to adjust to a new situation. We did not have our own house, but lived very simply with a Muslim family, eating, sleeping, and learning with the people to whom God had sent us.

When we arrived in Madon, it was very rainy and cold. We got up early each morning to travel with our infant son in an overloaded bus to Arabic classes. Everything was new; we felt very insecure.

> **Those first weeks are crucial—when the missionary has the ideal physical and emotional stamina to adjust to a new situation.**

In spite of these difficulties, we began to experience the first good results. Little by little, we began to break the barriers and cultural differences that existed between us and the local people. Slowly the people started to appreciate our efforts to live and talk with them, and after a short time of intense language and cultural studies, we began to feel more comfortable.

Since we knew that in this society the men were very religious, I told the family where we lived that I was not a Muslim, but a Christian. Because I was a Christian, I would read the Bible, fast, give handouts to the poor, and refrain from smoking or using alcoholic beverages. My statement was a surprise to the people, since the image they had of a Christian or anyone from the West (to them, both are the same) is of a person with no moral principles.

I considered the fact that if I prayed differently from the local people, I could cause them to think I had no respect for God. Not seeing anything in the Bible that would prevent me, every day I washed as they did and followed their lead by praying prostrate on a piece of clean cloth, with my head bowed to the ground.

When *Ramadan*, the Muslim month of fasting, came around, my wife and I fasted with the people, making sure they understood that our motives for doing so were different from theirs.

With all these activities, we were gaining the respect of our host family. In a few days the whole neighborhood knew that staying in that family's house was a non-Muslim man who was, even so, correct. When we conversed about religion, the people were much more willing to listen to us; they had seen something different in our lives. They did not look at us as just some more strangers, but as people who tried to do everything possible to become integrated with their way of life, accepting them as they were.

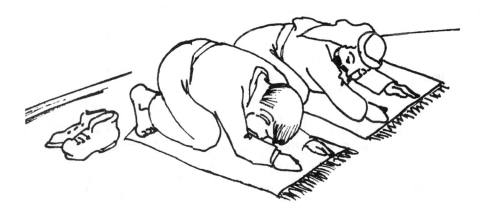

2. *How did the author's entry into the culture differ from the Russian's?*

_____

_____

_____

3. *Which approach, the Russian's or the author's, is likely to be more effective for tentmakers in the long run? Why?*

_____

_____

_____

Lifestyle decisions which affect identification

Because preaching the gospel is prohibited in Madon, our official reason for being in the country was rug exportation to Europe. Madon is a society of attributed status, meaning that the people expected all residents to conduct themselves, dress, and relate to others according to their status or position in life. Because of this value system, the families with whom we lived expected from us a lifestyle commensurate with my position as a businessman—something difficult to achieve since we lived with poor families and used public transportation. This discrepancy without a doubt limited our ministry.

It is very important for all Christian workers in creative access countries to understand that the type of work they do will probably determine the group of people with whom they will be able to work. If missionary tentmakers want to work with needy communities, they will have to arrange some kind of secular employment that will put them in contact with members of these communities.

A good example of this principle is a worker in our mission who is now engaged in a project to take drinkable water to needy communities.

This project puts the missionary in contact with persons of various social levels—principally the most needy—and gives him a chance to share the Word with them.

In contrast, a tentmaker whose job involves selling computers will have trouble ministering to less privileged social classes, because there isn't a market for his product among the poor.

> *If missionary tentmakers want to work with needy communities, they will have to arrange some kind of secular employment that will put them in contact with members of these communities.*

Such a worker should try to live in a middle class neighborhood, dress as a middle class person, and minister to middle class people. If he insists on selling computers and ministering to the poor, he will be extremely frustrated, and his chances of leaving the field within a short time are great.

4. Why did the discrepancy which existed between the author's occupation and his lifestyle affect his ministry?

_____

_____

_____

Communicating

The importance of learning the language

One of the greatest tasks that cross-cultural workers face is learning the language well. In our process of adaptation, it was very important for us to remember that communication should start from the first day in the new country. In our case, we were immediately forced to communicate the few words we knew, because we lived with a family who spoke only Arabic. This forced communication was very important to our acquiring fluency in the new language.

Of course, the process was not easy. We were afraid we would speak wrong words or communicate something we did not mean. Every day we studied for four hours in a local school. One day I wrote the following in my diary:

> This last week was really difficult. On Monday I did well in my Arabic classes, on Tuesday I did okay, but on Wednesday I couldn't get anything right and I became completely confused. Also, I can hardly stand what goes on with the family where we live. Almost every day our host invites two or three friends to come and talk with me, and as the culture demands that men and women don't mix, my wife and I almost never have

time to talk. We have to find new ways to have privacy.

In addition to going to language school, we found someone who would help us three or four times a week as we wrote down and also recorded phrases and sentences.* Then we would listen over and over to what we had recorded, trying to assimilate the new words and sentence construction. When we felt secure with the material, we would go out into the streets and talk with different people (clerks, street sellers, store owners, etc.), constantly practicing what we had learned.

In spite of the difficulties we faced, little by little we gained the confidence of the people and fluency in the language. People's reactions to us were varied. Some began to laugh at us and others avoided us, but many were intrigued and ready to help. One day when my wife was in the *medina* (the old part of the city) talking with a group of women, one of them invited us to her home. It was a house with only one room, where the entire family of six lived. In a short time, we had developed a good friendship with this family, eating with them and even sleeping in their house. Our friendship was a direct result of our trying to communicate, in spite of knowing very little.

5. *Most people try to "study" a language before attempting to converse in it. What advantages and disadvantages does the author's approach (mixing language school with a practical approach and the LAMP method) offer over just formal study?*

_____

_____

_____

_____

Communicating across cultures

When we think of communication, we have to be aware that communication is not accomplished only through words, but also through attitudes, behavior, gestures, body movements, and facial expressions (smiles, eyebrow movements, the way we look at others). When cross-cultural workers neglect these nonverbal aspects of communication, they will without a doubt create misunderstandings, making communication all the more difficult. To overcome this problem, we need to look at the world from the perspective of the nationals, trying to understand their worldview and customs.

One time I invited my friend Mohammed to go on a business trip with me. We were going to buy rugs. When we arrived at the city, he

> **When cross-cultural workers neglect nonverbal aspects of communication, they will without a doubt create misunderstandings.**

helped me for two days in buying good rugs at the best prices. I thanked him very much, but

---

* This method is known as the "LAMP Method," developed by Thomas and Elizabeth Brewster. See Brewster, E. T., & Brewster, E. S. (1976). *Language acquisition made practical: Field methods for language learners.* Colorado Springs, CO: Lingua House.

on the way home I felt a tension between us. I asked him what was wrong, but he did not respond. After much insistence, Mohammed said, "It's true that I am your friend, but I left my work and stayed two days with you so you could get the best prices. You will make a lot of money from these rugs. And what will I get?"

> **Because we think that our way of life is superior and more desirable, we begin to look down on others, even losing respect for our national friends.**

At first, Mohammed's response shocked me. I said to myself, "Wow, I thought Mohammed was really my friend, and now he's trying to take advantage of me!"

After thinking over the situation, however, I came to the conclusion that I was the one who was wrong. I was assuming that the rights and obligations of a friend in Madon were the same as in my own country, where a true friend would never expect payment for his efforts. In Madon, even though Mohammed was my friend, I should have given him some type of financial compensation for his help. Because of my lack of knowledge of the culture, I communicated something that I did not want to and almost lost my best national friend.

Another difficulty for me was the type of physical contact common between men. When a friend would come and give me three kisses on the cheek, as is the custom between men in Madon, I wanted to lean back away from him, obviously communicating rejection. At other times, when walking with male friends, I would put my hands in my pockets, fearing that one of the men would try to hold hands with me as we walked along. To the men in Madon, holding hands was a perfectly natural expression of friendship; to me as a Latin, it signified something very different. Again, without speaking a word, I was communicating things that would make sharing the gospel more difficult.

Many times our ethnocentrism* creates barriers to cross-cultural communication. Because we think that our way of life is superior and more desirable, we begin to look down on others, even losing respect for our national friends. We think that the way they do things is wrong, that their moral values are lower, etc. With this viewpoint, even though we may try to communicate acceptance through words and gestures, our attitudes will show just the opposite and will hinder our attempts at communication.

6. *Why does good communication encompass more than a command of the language?*

_____

_____

_____

_____

---

* Ethnocentrism is the innate belief in the superiority of one's own culture.

Continuing Adaptation to the Cultural Context

Culture shock

According to some specialists, culture shock can be divided into four stages (see Figure 12-1). The first is the *honeymoon* stage, during which everything is beautiful and wonderful. The second is the *critical* stage, when we think everything is wrong. The food is bad, the people are dishonest, and nothing works right. We are tempted to go home. The third phase is the initial *recuperation* stage, which starts when we begin to speak and understand the language. We begin to accept what we initially considered to be strange customs. Our sense of humor starts to return, and slowly we learn to laugh at our own errors. The fourth stage is the full *adaptation* stage, when we feel at home in the new culture and our ministry begins to show fruit.

Paul Hiebert explains culture shock.* He says that when we receive our acceptance notice from the mission agency to which we've ap-plied, our level of personal satisfaction is high; our dreams have come true. The farewell at our church brings us even more satisfaction. Now we are the center of attention, even more than the pastor. At the airport, emotions continue. We feel a mixture of sadness at departing and the excitement of a new adventure. Arriving overseas, we at first continue to feel excited. Soon, however, we discover that we cannot communicate very well, we can't get around the city, we have a hard time liking the food, we get sick easily, we are afraid to go to a local doctor, and in a very short time we want to sign in at the closest five-star hotel where we can escape these "strange nationals with their strange customs." When we arrive at this point, we surely are beginning to experience *culture shock*, a disorientation that comes when all our cultural maps and the guidelines we learned as children no longer function.

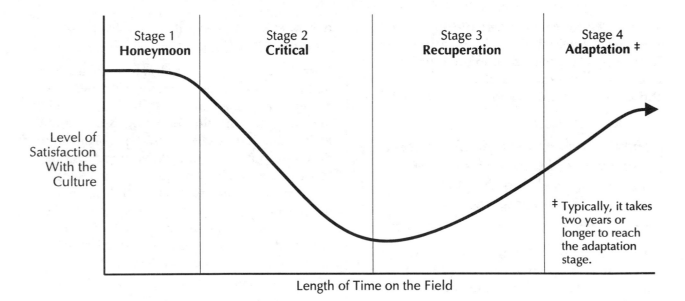

Figure 12-1. Stages of Culture Shock

---

* Hiebert, P. (1985). *Anthropological insights for missionaries.* Grand Rapids, MI: Baker Book House.

In Madon, we felt culture shock strongly. In the beginning, we did not know how to get a bus or a taxi, we did not know how to eat, people did not understand us, and we felt ridiculous dressing in the kind of clothes the local people wore. Before long, our world began to crumble. In the eyes of the nationals, we acted like children who knew very little.

One day I wrote in my diary:

> Today is our son's birthday. Even so, it was not a good day for me. Arabic classes were a problem, but that wasn't all. I would love to be in a place where I didn't have to talk to anyone and I could just do what I wanted. Now I understand what everyone told us about culture shock. It is painful to break our habits, learn a new language, and at the same time relate to people who are so different from us. That's why I have the impression that if we don't do this from the beginning, it will be more difficult later on. Also, as a family we are having to adjust, complicating our own relationships with each other. Even so, I believe that this is a unique experience in our lives and we are doing the correct thing in getting to know the culture where the Lord has sent us.

7. *What is culture shock, and at what stage of adaptation is it most likely to occur?*

_____

_____

_____

_____

In confronting so many new things at once, new missionaries find that their attitudes start to change. They become impatient and critical and more vulnerable to sickness. In spite of these difficulties, it is very important not to give

> **The first step in the right direction is to recognize that culture shock exists, that it is natural, and that it is not a sign of lack of spirituality.**

up at this stage. The first step in the right direction is to recognize that culture shock exists, that it is natural, and that it is not a sign of lack of spirituality. With perseverance, new missionaries will find that the shock will eventually pass!

Correct attitudes and a willingness to resist the temptation to escape situations that create fear or embarrassment are important. We need to face threatening situations head-on. In the most difficult times, we should be able to count on the support of more experienced workers. However, we should never use such relationships as a means of escape, hiding in each other's homes and avoiding contact with the nationals and their culture. Such retreat will never get us beyond the critical stage of culture shock and will make an effective ministry almost impossible.

8. *What made it possible for the author to continue working through the pain and discomfort of cultural adaptation?*

_____

_____

If, on the other hand, we are careful to maintain contact with the nationals, participate in their parties, and learn their language, little by little we will begin to feel comfortable in the new culture and will be able to function effectively and without anxiety. Not only will we accept the local food and customs, but we will grow to like them. Our need for friendship and companionship will begin to find fulfillment in nationals and not just in our compatriot friends. We will continue loving our own country, but we will grow to love our new country and our new friends to the point that we will miss them when we return home. In other words, we will become bicultural—*belongers* in two cultures.

9. *What dangers exist for tentmakers in looking for friendships and relational fulfillment primarily from other foreigners?*

_____

_____

_____

Summary

The approach tentmakers use in adapting to a foreign situation has a great effect on the success of their integration into that culture. While it is easy for new workers to insulate themselves from the new culture, it is only as identification with the new culture is attempted that bonding can occur. Total immersion in the new culture is a difficult and often insecure approach to adaptation. Nevertheless, those who endure this acculturation process gain the respect of their hosts and, in the long run, pave the way for effective ministry in the culture. An important part of identifying with the new culture is for tentmakers to create a fit between their social position and the social position of those with whom they are identifying.

One of the greatest challenges to effectiveness is learning the target language well. Besides attending language school, those who employ an immersion approach to acculturation will continually practice what they learn. This method will result in acceptance by the people, and relationships will be built. Communication, however, is not just words. Gestures, body language, and cultural expectations are all important factors. One of the biggest barriers to true communication is ethnocentrism, the feeling that one's own ways are superior to those of the host culture.

Cultural adaptation encompasses several stages. Tentmakers may pass through an initial *honeymoon* stage. Next, a feeling of disorientation sets in during the *critical* stage. From this low point, workers begin to enter the *recuperation* stage. Finally, they reach the *adaptation* stage. Most long-term workers pass through culture shock. Identifying with the nationals and bonding with them effectively will go a long way to minimize the effects of this difficult transition. Once the transition has been made, tentmakers will have successfully passed through cultural adaptation, becoming truly bicultural people.

Action Plan Assignment

1. *From what you have read, describe what you feel is the best entry situation into a new culture for yourself (and, if applicable, for your spouse and family). Think through the implications of your choices. This description can become a specific item for prayer as you plan to head overseas.*

2. *For effective communication in another culture, there is nothing more important than learning the language. Not only does facility with the language give you a way to converse, but it also demonstrates to your hosts that you have a real interest in them, and it opens the door to relationships. Language study can be undertaken formally or informally. In many countries around the world, knowledge of more than one language is useful. For example, in North Africa, French is still widely used in legal and governmental matters, but colloquial Arabic is most useful for getting around the commercial sector. Classical Arabic is used for reading and writing. The nomadic population, however, prefer to use their own language with each other.*

   Identify the trade or official language of the area you have targeted. Think through what you need to do to become competent in this language. If possible, begin to study the language.

3. *Most people experience a slight degree of culture shock even when they move from one place to another in their own country! The loss of friends and a sense of disorientation can produce depression, irritability, and other symptoms of culture shock. Reexamine the four stages of culture shock described on page 12-9. For each stage, pick one or more verses or passages from Scripture which can help you gain the right perspective when passing through this difficult transition. Memorize these verses.*

Conclusion

I have a sense of where your pilgrimage through this course has brought you.... I also have a sense of where it will continue to take you. As I gaze up at the world map on the wall of my office, I see the outline of 195 political nations of our world. Behind that image are five and one-half billion people.

As a missions leader, I can't help but translate those numbers into hundreds of millions of men, women, and children in 6,000 currently identified unreached people groups. More than 4,500 of these groups have no Scripture in their language. Many are in countries which do not permit access to career missionaries. The picture would be bleak if it were not for you, because you hold the keys to reaching these multitudes.

You are called tentmakers. You are called by the sovereign missionary God into this life, because you have a holy concept of vocation. You are committed to living in the marketplaces of our creative access countries, excelling in your work. You are Christ's ambassadors to the lost.

You are not alone. You are a Filipino contract worker in the sensitive Arabian Peninsula; a Korean medical technician serving on contract in China; a Guatemalan engineer digging wells in North Africa; a business woman in Central Asia; a European sanitary engineer in the Middle East; a Nigerian petroleum consultant in North Africa. You are many faces—red, yellow, black, brown, and white—Christ's servants to every continent from every continent.

You have studied the material in this manual and have come to understand what it takes to be a successful tentmaker. The Personal Action Plan you've developed gives you an adequate idea of what it will take to arrive at your destination. Follow that map. God has given it to you to lead you to the place to which He is calling you.

Be encouraged! There are thousands of believers who share your passion, and thousands of others who are actively serving as God's gracious, skilled, and discipling tentmakers.

Be serious! This is not a game. You have a long road to follow as you develop and reach your goals. Be an avid reader and self-motivated student. Gather other resources and grow in all areas of your life.

Be accountable! Cultivate a relationship with a mentor to whom you can be responsible and who can guide you in your current development plan. Become part of a small group of men and women with the same dream—even if you have to help start the group. Meet regularly with your mentor and support group for prayer, evaluation, mutual encouragement, and equipping.

Do it! Implement your Personal Action Plan as you've outlined it. Trust God to confirm your plans and direct your steps.

As I look at the map on my wall, I see you with the eyes of faith, and I rejoice in what God has done and what He will do. We shall meet at the great celebration around the throne, and together we will worship the Lamb. We will be there because we know Christ, and others will also praise our God because, through you, they came to a redeeming knowledge of the only Savior, Jesus Christ our Lord.

William D. Taylor
Executive Director
WEF, Missions Commission

Personal Action Plan

The items in the chart on the following pages are keyed to the Action Plan Assignments (APA). While the assignments are intended to be completed while you are studying this manual, some of the goals you set may take years to achieve. It is important to project these goals in order to create a general timeline for reaching your destination. The timeline will help you keep things in perspective and order your way to the nations as a well-equipped tentmaker.

The APA NUMBER is listed in the first column of the chart. Next is the ACTION REQUIRED of you. The GOAL STATEMENT expresses how you will complete the action. (A complete discussion of goal setting is found in chapter 1 of this manual.) The next two columns are for the TARGET DATES for beginning and finishing the goal. The last column is to indicate the PERSON to whom you will be accountable in completing the goal. Two sample chart blocks are given below.

APA NUMBER	ACTION REQUIRED	GOAL STATEMENT	TARGET START DATE	TARGET FINISH DATE	PERSON TO RESPOND TO WHEN DONE
2-1	Memorize the Great Commission (Matt. 28:18-20).	*Write verses on card. Memorize 5 minutes each morning.*	1/12	1/17	*Paul Smith*
5-3	Outline goal-oriented steps to define your own vocational tentmaking path.	*Talk with voc. counselor. Write for information on job opportunities in Saudi Arabia. Call tech schools for catalogs.*	2/13 3/4 3/4	3/3 3/4 3/4	*Laura Johnson* " "

Figure A-1

Chapter 1: Planning for Success					
APA NUMBER	**ACTION REQUIRED**	**GOAL STATEMENT**	**TARGET START DATE**	**TARGET FINISH DATE**	**PERSON TO RESPOND TO WHEN DONE**
1-1	Talk to one or more of the persons responsible for missions leadership in your church about your commitment to accountability.				
1-2	Memorize the components of SAMM and use them in writing goal statements for your Personal Action Plan.				
1-3	With the help of your church's missions leader-ship, identify a person who is willing and able to mentor you.				

		Chapter 2: Getting Perspective			
APA NUMBER	**ACTION REQUIRED**	**GOAL STATEMENT**	**TARGET START DATE**	**TARGET FINISH DATE**	**PERSON TO RESPOND TO WHEN DONE**
2-1	Memorize the Great Commission (Matt. 28:18-20).				
2-2	Share a sound rationale for becoming a tentmaker with at least three persons in your church.				
2-3	Find out about your church's tentmaker policy. Examine a copy of your church missions policy or talk to someone in leadership.				

		Chapter 3: Cross-Cultural Servants			
APA NUMBER	**ACTION REQUIRED**	**GOAL STATEMENT**	**TARGET START DATE**	**TARGET FINISH DATE**	**PERSON TO RESPOND TO WHEN DONE**
3-1	Share your calling with a person in missions leadership in your church.				
3-2	List concrete steps you can take to test your calling and bring it into balance.				
3-3	Make plans with concrete goals for improving your rating on the Spiritual Life Rating Scale.				

\multicolumn{6}{c}{**Chapter 4: The Crucial Role of the Local Church**}					
APA NUMBER	**ACTION REQUIRED**	**GOAL STATEMENT**	**TARGET START DATE**	**TARGET FINISH DATE**	**PERSON TO RESPOND TO WHEN DONE**
4-1	List concrete, goal-oriented actions which will help your church improve its missions role.				
4-2	Write out a site agreement proposal with someone in missions leadership from your church.				
4-3	List the steps (goals) which will improve the communications process between your church and its tentmakers.				

Chapter 5: Critical Considerations of Deployment					
APA NUMBER	**ACTION REQUIRED**	**GOAL STATEMENT**	**TARGET START DATE**	**TARGET FINISH DATE**	**PERSON TO RESPOND TO WHEN DONE**
5-1	Share your "ethics of tentmaking" statement with at least three other Christians.				
5-2	Discuss the evaluations of Rating Scales 5-2, 5-3, and 5-4 with someone who can counsel you and keep you accountable in improving in these areas.				
5-3	Outline goal-oriented steps to define your own vocational tentmaking path.				

Chapter 6: Biblical and Doctrinal Foundations					
APA NUMBER	ACTION REQUIRED	GOAL STATEMENT	TARGET START DATE	TARGET FINISH DATE	PERSON TO RESPOND TO WHEN DONE
6-1	Outline a goal-oriented plan which demonstrates an increased commitment to read the Word of God.				
6-2	Define how, when, and where you are going to study areas of biblical and theological knowledge in which you are weak.				

		Chapter 7: Personal Readiness				
APA NUMBER	**ACTION REQUIRED**	**GOAL STATEMENT**	**TARGET START DATE**	**TARGET FINISH DATE**	**PERSON TO RESPOND TO WHEN DONE**
7-1	Make goal-oriented plans to meet new non-Christians and look for opportunities to meet their needs.				
7-2	Share your thoughts about your identity in Christ with three other people.				
7-3	Write to two or three mission agencies.				

Chapter 8: Two Essential Skills					
APA NUMBER	**ACTION REQUIRED**	**GOAL STATEMENT**	**TARGET START DATE**	**TARGET FINISH DATE**	**PERSON TO RESPOND TO WHEN DONE**
8-1	Outline goal-oriented steps to become a discipler.				
8-2	Outline goal-oriented steps to become proficient in personal evangelism.				
8-3	Outline goal-oriented steps to improve modeling aspects of discipling.				

| \multicolumn{6}{c}{**Chapter 9: Team Dynamics and Spiritual Warfare**} |
APA NUMBER	ACTION REQUIRED	GOAL STATEMENT	TARGET START DATE	TARGET FINISH DATE	PERSON TO RESPOND TO WHEN DONE
9-1	Outline a goal-oriented plan for establishing communication with potential team members.				
9-2	Draw up a "relationship covenant" and discuss it with potential team-mates, a mentor, or someone in church leadership.				
9-3	Outline goal-oriented plans to understand the dynamics of spiritual warfare and gain increased competence in this area.				

APA NUMBER	ACTION REQUIRED	GOAL STATEMENT	TARGET START DATE	TARGET FINISH DATE	PERSON TO RESPOND TO WHEN DONE
		Chapter 10: Understanding the Host Culture			
10-1	Outline elements of your own culture.				
10-2	Outline steps for researching elements of your target culture and comparing them to your own culture. Share this work with your mentor and/or someone who has cross-cultural experience.				

Chapter 11: Dealing With Stress					
APA NUMBER	**ACTION REQUIRED**	**GOAL STATEMENT**	**TARGET START DATE**	**TARGET FINISH DATE**	**PERSON TO RESPOND TO WHEN DONE**
11-1	Discuss field expectations with your mentor and outline a plan which will not overwhelm you.				
11-2	Outline goal-oriented measures to help you relax and relieve stress in constructive ways.				
11-3	Outline reentry steps with church missions leadership.				

\begin{tabular}{c} APA \\ NUMBER \end{tabular}	ACTION REQUIRED	GOAL STATEMENT	TARGET START DATE	TARGET FINISH DATE	PERSON TO RESPOND TO WHEN DONE
Chapter 12: Becoming a Belonger					
12-1	Outline your "entry" plan into your target culture.				
12-2	Outline steps for learning the trade language or official language of the area in which you plan to serve.				
12-3	Memorize verses which will sustain you when passing through culture shock.				

Resources

The resources listed in this appendix are arranged topically as follows*:

- General tentmaking
- Mission awareness
- Integration of faith and work
- Apologetics and world religions
- Ministry principles
- Cross-cultural sensitivity
- Language learning
- Placement/referral agencies

General Tentmaking

‡ Aldrich, J. C. (1983). *Lifestyle evangelism: Crossing traditional boundaries to reach the unbelieving world.* Portland, OR: Multnomah Press.

Anthony, R., & Roe, G. (1984). *Educator's passport to international jobs.* Princeton, NJ: Peterson's Guides.

Beckman, D. M., et al. (Eds.). (1985). *The overseas list: Opportunities for living and working in developing countries.* Minneapolis, MN: Augsburg Press.

Bramlett, J. (Ed.). (1986). *Finding work: A handbook.* Grand Rapids, MI: Zondervan.

---

* We gratefully acknowledge P. Marman of the Discipleship Training Centre in Singapore and Don Hamilton of TMQ Research in California for their bibliographic contributions.

‡ Recommended by one or more of the authors of this course.

Casewit, C. W. (1984). *Foreign jobs: The most popular countries*. Washington, DC: Seitar International Publication.

Copeland, L., & Griggs, L. (1985). *Going international: How to make friends and deal effectively in the global marketplace*. New York, NY: Random House.

‡ Hamilton, D. (1987). *Tentmakers speak*. Ventura, CA: Regal Press.

Hesselgrave, D. J. (1984). *Communicating the gospel cross-culturally*. Grand Rapids, MI: Zondervan.

Hybel, B. (1986). *Christians in the marketplace*. Wheaton, IL: Victor Books.

InterCristo. *Career kit*. (Available from: InterCristo, P.O. Box 33487, Seattle, WA 98133).

International Employment Gazette. (Available from: 1525 Wade Hampton Blvd., Greenville, SC 29609).

‡ Martin, D. *Tentmakers in mission: Put your vocation to work*. Kent, WA: Mission to Unreached Peoples.

‡ Parshall, P. (1989). *Tentmaking: Crucial issues for today*. Columbia, SC: Columbia Bible College.

‡ Peabody, L. (1974). *Secular work is full-time service*. Fort Washington, PA: Christian Literature Crusade.

‡ Price, D. J. (1991). *Twentieth century tentmakers: Mission, mandate, motivation*. Lilydale, Victoria, Australia: Commodore Press Pty. Ltd.

Shelly, J. A. (1985). *Not just a job*. Downers Grove, IL: InterVarsity Press.

‡ Siemens, R. *Global Opportunities compendium*. Pasadena, CA: Global Opportunities.

‡ Taylor, G. (1992). *Trailside companion: A guide for creative access missionaries*. Woodland Park, CO: Strategic Ventures.

‡ Tentmakers International. (1992). *The tentmaker's resource guide: A compendium of information*. Seattle, WA: Issachar.

Turner-Gottschang, K. (1987). *China bound*. Washington, DC: National Academy Press.

Wharton, J. (1986). *Jobs in Japan*. Denver, CO: Global Press.

‡ Wilson, J. C., Jr. (1979). *Today's tentmakers: An alternative model for world evangelization*. Wheaton, IL: Tyndale.

Win, D. (1986). *International careers*. Charlotte, VT: Williamson Publishing.

Mission Awareness

Adeney, M. (1984). *God's foreign policy*. Grand Rapids, MI: Eerdmans.

Bryant, D. (1984). *In the gap: What it means to be a world Christian*. Ventura, CA: Regal Books.

Costas, O. E. (1974). *The church and its mission: A shattering critique from the Third World*. Wheaton, IL: Tyndale.

Culver, R. D. (1984). *A greater commission: A theology for world missions*. Chicago, IL: Moody Press.

Dayton, E. R. (Ed.). (1976). *Missions handbook: North American Protestant ministries overseas*. Monrovia, CA: MARC.

Dyrness, W. O. (1983). *Let the earth rejoice!* Westchester, IL: Good News.

Evangelical Missions Quarterly. (Available from: EMIS, P.O. Box 794, Wheaton, IL 60189).

Griffiths, M. C. *What on earth are you doing?* Grand Rapids, MI: Baker Book House.

International Bulletin of Missionary Research. (Available from: 6315 Ocean Ave., Ventnor, NJ 08406).

‡ Johnstone, P. (1993). *Operation world.* Waynesboro, GA: Send the Light Publishers.

Kane, J. H. (1976). *Christian missions in biblical perspective.* Grand Rapids, MI: Baker Book House.

Kane, J. H. (1978). *A concise history of world missions.* Grand Rapids, MI: Baker Book House.

Kane, J. H. (1981). *The Christian world mission: Today and tomorrow.* Grand Rapids, MI: Baker Book House.

Kane, J. H. (1981). *Life and work on the mission field.* Grand Rapids, MI: Baker Book House.

Latourette, K. S. (1975). *History of the expansion of Christianity.* New York, NY: Harper & Row.

McQuilkin, J. R. (1984). *The great omission.* Grand Rapids, MI: Baker Book House.

Murray, A., & Choy, L. (1980). *The key to the missionary problem.* Fort Washington, PA: Christian Literature Crusade.

Neill, S. (1964). *History of Christian missions.* Middlesex, England: Penguin Books.

Nicholls, B., & Kantzer, K. (1986). *In word and deed: Evangelism and social responsibility.* Grand Rapids, MI: Eerdmans.

‡ O'Donnell, K. (1992). *Missionary care: Counting the cost for world evangelism.* Pasadena, CA: William Carey Library.

Pentecost, E. C. (1982). *Issues in missiology.* Grand Rapids, MI: Baker Book House.

Pulse. (Available from: EMIS, P.O. Box 794, Wheaton, IL 60189).

Sine, T. (1981). *The mustard seed conspiracy.* Waco, TX: Word.

Taylor, J. H. (1982). *Hudson Taylor's spiritual secret.* Chicago, IL: Moody Press.

Troutman, C. (1976). *Everything you want to know about the mission field but are afraid you won't learn until you get there.* Downers Grove, IL: InterVarsity Press.

‡ Wagner, C. P. (1983). *On the crest of the wave: Becoming a world Christian.* Ventura, CA: Regal Books.

Westing, H. J. (Ed.). (1977). *I'd love to tell the world: The challenge of missions.* Denver, CO: Accent Books.

Wilson, S., & Aeschliman, G. (1982). *The hidden half: Discovering the world of unreached peoples.* Monrovia, CA: MARC.

A winning combination: ABC/DBC—Cultural tensions in the Chinese church. Chinese Christian Mission.

‡ Winter, R. D., & Hawthorne, S. C. (Eds.). (1992). *Perspectives on the world Christian movement: A reader* (rev. ed.). Pasadena, CA: William Carey Library.

‡ Yamamori, T. (1987). *God's new envoys: A bold strategy for penetrating "closed countries."* Portland, OR: Multnomah Press.

Yamamori, T. (1993). *Penetrating missions' final frontier: A new strategy for unreached peoples.* Downers Grove, IL: InterVarsity Press.

Integration of Faith and Work

Bolles, R. N. (1981). *The three boxes of life: And how to get out of them.* Berkeley, CA: Ten Speed Press.

Bramlett, J. (Ed.). (1986). *Finding work: A handbook.* Grand Rapids, MI: Zondervan.

Business Life Digest. (Available from: Christian Business Life, Inc., 8100 Penn Ave. S., Minneapolis, MN 55431).

Campolo, T. (1983). *It's Friday but Sunday's coming.* Waco, TX: Word.

Campolo, T. (1984). *You can make a difference.* Waco, TX: Word.

Christianity at Work. (Available from: Career Impact Ministries, 711 Stadium Dr. E., #200, Arlington, TX 76011).

‡ Danker, W. J. (1971). *Profit for the Lord.* Grand Rapids, MI: Eerdmans.

Diehl, W. E. (1982). *Thank God it's Monday!* Philadelphia, PA: Fortress Press.

Estes, S., & Estes, V. (1986). *Called to die: The story of American linguist Chet Bitterman slain by terrorists.* Grand Rapids, MI: Zondervan.

Foster, R. J. (1981). *Freedom of simplicity.* New York, NY: Harper & Row.

Hefley, J., & Hefley, M. (1976). *The church that takes on trouble.* Elgin, IL: David C. Cook.

Holmes, A. E. (1985). *Contours of a Christian world view.* Grand Rapids, MI: Eerdmans.

Holmes, A. E., et al. (1984). *The making of a Christian mind.* Downers Grove, IL: InterVarsity Press.

InterCristo. *Career kit.* (Available from: InterCristo, P.O. Box 33487, Seattle, WA 98133).

Kane, J. H. (1975). *The making of a missionary.* Grand Rapids, MI: Baker Book House.

Kane, J. H. (1981). *Life and work on the mission field.* Grand Rapids, MI: Baker Book House.

Kane, J. H. (1986). *Wanted: World Christians.* Grand Rapids, MI: Baker Book House.

Lutzer, E. (1977). *Failure: The backdoor to success.* Chicago, IL: Moody Press.

‡ Lykins, J. (1991). *Values in the market place: A biblical alternative of doing business.* Fullerton, CA: R. C. Law & Co.

‡ Munger, R. B. (1954). *My heart Christ's home.* Downers Grove, IL: InterVarsity Press.

‡ Paul, J. (1990). *Ethical issues for individual professionals: Corporations committed to the Great Commission.* Oak Park, IL: Midwest Center for World Mission.

‡ Peabody, L. (1974). *Secular work is full-time service.* Fort Washington, PA: Christian Literature Crusade.

Perkins, J. M. (1976). *Let justice roll down: Perkins tells his own story.* Ventura, CA: Regal Books.

Perkins, J. M. (1976). *A quiet revolution.* Waco, TX: Word.

Scott, W. (1980). *Bring forth justice.* Grand Rapids, MI: Eerdmans.

Sine, T. (1981). *The mustard seed conspiracy.* Waco, TX: Word.

Sine, T. (Ed.). (1983). *The church in response to human need.* Monrovia, CA: MARC.

Sproul, R. C. (1983). *Stronger than steel: The Wayne Alderson story.* New York, NY: Harper & Row.

Stott, J. R. (1976). *Christian mission in the modern world.* Downers Grove, IL: InterVarsity Press.

Stott, J. R. (1985). *Involvement: Vol. 1. Being a responsible Christian in a non-Christian society.* Old Tappan, NJ: Fleming H. Revell.

‡ White, J. E., & White, M. E. (1976). *Your job: Survival or satisfaction?* Grand Rapids, MI: Zondervan.

‡ Wilson, J. C., Jr. (1979). *Today's tentmakers: An alternative model for world evangelization.* Wheaton, IL: Tyndale.

Yoder, R. A. (1983). *Seeking first the kingdom.* Scottdale, PA: Herald Press.

Apologetics and World Religions

Anderson, E. (1981). *History and beliefs of Mormonism.* Grand Rapids, MI: Kregel.

Anderson, J. N. (1976). *The world religions.* Grand Rapids, MI: Eerdmans.

Anderson, J. N. (1984). *Christianity and world religions.* Downers Grove, IL: InterVarsity Press.

Budd, J. *Studies on Islam.* (Available from: Red Sea Team, 33/35 The Grove, Finchley, London, England).

Chapman, C. (1984). *The case for Christianity.* Grand Rapids, MI: Eerdmans.

Christian witness among Muslims. (Available from: Africa Christian Press, 16 Morwell St., London WC1B 3AP, England).

Conn, H. (1984). *Eternal Word and changing worlds: Theology, anthropology and mission in trialogue.* Grand Rapids, MI: Zondervan.

Cooper, H. (1985). *Reaching the unreached.* Phillipsburg, NJ: Presbyterian and Reformed Press.

Hanna, M. (1975). *The true path: Seven Muslims make their greatest discovery.* Colorado Springs, CO: International Doorways.

Hanna, M. (1981). *Crucial questions in apologetics.* Grand Rapids, MI: Baker Book House.

Hopfe, L. M. (1983). *Religions of the world.* New York, NY: Macmillan.

Martin, W. (1985). *The kingdom of the cults.* Minneapolis, MN: Bethany House.

Matheny, T. (1981). *Reaching the Arabs: A felt need approach.* Pasadena, CA: William Carey Library.

McCurrey, D. M. (1979). *The gospel and Islam: A compendium.* Monrovia, CA: MARC.

McDowell, J. (1979). *Evidence that demands a verdict.* San Bernardino, CA: Campus Crusade for Christ.

McDowell, J. (1981). *More evidence that demands a verdict.* San Bernardino, CA: Campus Crusade for Christ.

McDowell, J. (1983). *Handbook on today's religions.* San Bernardino, CA: Campus Crusade for Christ.

McDowell, J., & Gilchrist, J. (1982). *The Islam debate.* San Bernardino, CA: Campus Crusade for Christ.

McDowell, J., & Stewart, D. (1982). *Understanding non-Christian religions.* San Bernardino, CA: Here's Life Publishers.

Montgomery, J. W. (1986). *History and Christianity.* Minneapolis, MN: Bethany House.

Neill, S. (1984). *Christian faith and other faiths.* Downers Grove, IL: InterVarsity Press.

Newbigen, L. (1986). *Foolishness to the Greeks.* Grand Rapids, MI: Eerdmans.

Parshall, P. (1980). *New paths in Muslim evangelism: Evangelical approaches to contextualization.* Grand Rapids, MI: Baker Book House.

Parshall, P. (1985). *Beyond the mosque.* Grand Rapids, MI: Baker Book House.

Pinnock, C. (1980). *Reason enough: A case for the Christian faith.* Downers Grove, IL: InterVarsity Press.

Rahman, F. (1979). *Islam.* Chicago, IL: University of Chicago Press.

Ramm, B. (1965). *Varieties of Christian apologetics.* Grand Rapids, MI: Baker Book House.

Ramm, B. (1989). *Protestant biblical interpretation.* Grand Rapids, MI: Baker Book House.

Reaching Muslims today. North Africa Mission.

Rosen, M. (1976). *Share the new life with a Jew.* Chicago, IL: Moody Press.

A shorter encyclopedia of Islam. (1974). Ithaca, NY: Cornell University Press.

Sire, J. (1976). *The universe next door: A basic worldview catalog.* Downers Grove, IL: InterVarsity Press.

Tanner, J. (1981). *The changing world of Mormonism.* Chicago, IL: Moody Press.

Yamamoto, J. I. (1982). *Beyond Buddhism.* Downers Grove, IL: InterVarsity Press.

Zwemer, S. *The Muslim Christ.* (Available from: Frontiers, 325 N. Stapley Dr., Mesa, AZ 85203).

Ministry Principles

‡ Aldrich, J. C. (1983). *Lifestyle evangelism: Crossing traditional boundaries to reach the unbelieving world.* Portland, OR: Multnomah Press.

Allen, R. (1962). *Missionary methods: St. Paul's or ours?* Grand Rapids, MI: Eerdmans.

‡ Coleman, R. (1978). *The master plan of evangelism.* Old Tappan, NJ: Fleming H. Revell.

Conn, H. (1982). *Evangelism: Doing justice and preaching grace.* Grand Rapids, MI: Zondervan.

‡ Crabb, L. (1988). *Inside out.* Colorado Springs, CO: NavPress.

Dayton, E. R. (Ed.). (1979). *That everyone may hear.* Monrovia, CA: MARC.

Dayton, E. R., & Fraser, D. (1980). *Planning strategies for world evangelization.* Grand Rapids, MI: Eerdmans.

‡ Eims, L. (1978). *The lost art of disciple making.* Grand Rapids, MI: Zondervan.

Engel, J. F., & Nurlen, W. H. (1975). *What's gone wrong with the harvest?* Grand Rapids, MI: Zondervan.

Getz, G. A. (1984). *Sharpening the focus of the church.* Wheaton, IL: Victor Books.

Glasser, A. (1976). *Crucial dimensions in world evangelization.* Pasadena, CA: William Carey Library.

Green, M. (1970). *Evangelism in the early church.* Grand Rapids, MI: Eerdmans.

Henrichs, W. A. (1974). *Disciples are made, not born.* Wheaton, IL: Victor Books.

Hesselgrave, D. J. (1980). *Planting churches cross-culturally.* Grand Rapids, MI: Baker Book House.

Howard, D. M. (Ed.). (1974). *Jesus Christ: Lord of the universe, hope of the world.* Downers Grove, IL: InterVarsity Press.

Innes, R. (1985). *I hate witnessing.* Ventura, CA: Regal Books.

Law, L. (1984). *The world at your doorstep.* Downers Grove, IL: InterVarsity Press.

Little, P. (1979). *How to give away your faith.* Oxnard, CA: Vision House.

‡ Lum, A. (1971). *How to begin an evangelistic Bible study.* Downers Grove, IL: InterVarsity Press.

Lum, A. (1978). *Jesus the life changer.* Downers Grove, IL: InterVarsity Press.

Lum, A. (1984). *A hitchhiker's guide to missions.* Downers Grove, IL: InterVarsity Press.

Lutz, L. (1986). *Destined for royalty: A Brahmin priest's search for truth.* Pasadena, CA: William Carey Library.

McGavran, D. A. (1980). *Understanding church growth*. Grand Rapids, MI: Eerdmans.

‡ The Navigators. (1973). *Leader's guide for evangelistic Bible studies: Using the Gospel of John*. Colorado Springs, CO: Navigators.

The Navigators. (1978). *Growing strong in God's family*. Colorado Springs, CO: NavPress.

The Navigators. (1978). *The 2:7 series*. Colorado Springs, CO: NavPress.

Packer, J. I. (1961). *Evangelism and the sovereignty of God*. Downers Grove, IL: InterVarsity Press.

Patterson, G. (1981). *Church planting through obedience oriented teaching*. Pasadena, CA: William Carey Library.

‡ Petersen, J. (1980). *Evangelism as a lifestyle*. Colorado Springs, CO: NavPress.

‡ Pippert, R. M. (1980). *Out of the saltshaker and into the world*. Downers Grove, IL: InterVarsity Press.

Sine, T. (1985). *Taking discipleship seriously*. Valley Forge, PA: Judson.

‡ Stafford, T. (1984). *The friendship gap: Reaching out across cultures*. Downers Grove, IL: InterVarsity Press.

Trotman, D. E. (1981). *Born to reproduce*. Colorado Springs, CO: NavPress.

Verwer, G. (1983). *No turning back*. Wheaton, IL: Tyndale.

Wagner, C. P. (1979). *Your spiritual gifts can help your church grow*. Ventura, CA: Regal Books.

Wagner, C. P. (1981). *Church growth and the whole gospel: A biblical mandate*. New York, NY: Harper & Row.

Winter, R. D. (1978). *Penetrating the last frontiers*. Pasadena, CA: William Carey Library.

‡ Winter, R. D., & Hawthorne, S. C. (Eds.). (1992). *Perspectives on the world Christian movement: A reader* (rev. ed.). Pasadena, CA: William Carey Library.

Yohn, R. (1982). *First hand joy*. Colorado Springs, CO: NavPress.

Cross-Cultural Sensitivity

Austin, C. N. (1986). *Cross-cultural reentry: A book of readings*. Abilene, TX: Abilene Christian University Press.

Beckmann, D. M., et al. (Eds.). (1985). *The overseas list: Opportunities for living and working in developing countries*. Minneapolis, MN: Augsburg Press.

‡ Brewster, E. T., & Brewster, E. S. (1982). *Bonding and the missionary task: Establishing a sense of belonging*. Pasadena, CA: Lingua House. (Available from: SIL Dallas Center Bookstore, 7500 W. Camp Wisdom Road, Dallas, TX 75236).

Condon, J. C., & Yousef, F. S. (1975). *An introduction to intercultural communication*. New York, NY: Macmillan.

Copeland, L., & Griggs, L. (1985). *Going international: How to make friends and deal effectively in the global marketplace*. New York, NY: Random House.

Goldstein, S. M., & Sears, K. (1984). *The People's Republic of China: A basic handbook*. New York, NY: LRIS.

Greeley, A. M. (1980). *Why can't they be like us? Facts and fallacies about ethnic differences and group conflicts in America*. New York, NY: American Jewish Committee.

Hall, E. T. (1973). *The silent language*. New York, NY: Doubleday.

Hall, E. T. (1977). *Beyond culture*. New York, NY: Doubleday.

Hess, J. D. (1980). *From the other's point of view.* Scottdale, PA: Herald Press.

Hesselgrave, D. J. (1984). *Communicating Christ cross-culturally.* Grand Rapids, MI: Zondervan.

Hesselgrave, D. J. (1984). *Counseling cross-culturally.* Grand Rapids, MI: Baker Book House.

Hiebert, P. G. (1983). *Cultural anthropology.* Grand Rapids, MI: Baker Book House.

Hiebert, P. G. (1986). *Anthropological insights for missionaries.* Grand Rapids, MI: Baker Book House.

Hopler, T. (1981). *A world of difference: Following Christ beyond your cultural walls.* Downers Grove, IL: InterVarsity Press.

International business travel and relocation directory. (1986). Detroit, MI: Gale Research.

Kohls, L. R. (1984). *Survival kit for overseas living.* Yarmouth, ME: Intercultural Press.

Kraft, C. H. (1979). *Christianity in culture.* Los Angeles, CA: Orbis Books.

Kraft, C. H. (1983). *Communication theory for Christian witness.* Knoxville, TN: Abingdon Press.

Ligenfelter, S. G., & Mayers, M. K. (1986). *Ministering cross-culturally.* Grand Rapids, MI: Baker Book House.

Luzbetak, L. J. (1970). *The church and cultures: An applied anthropology for the religious worker.* Techny, IL: Divine Word Publications.

Nida, E. (1975). *Customs and cultures: Anthropology for Christian missions.* Pasadena, CA: William Carey Library.

Nida, E. (1979). *Religion across cultures.* Pasadena, CA: William Carey Library.

Nida, E., & Reyburn, W. D. (1981). *Meaning across cultures: A study on Bible translating.* Los Angeles, CA: Orbis Books.

Preheim, M. K. (1969). *Overseas service manual.* Scottdale, PA: Herald Press. (Available from: Institute of Mennonite Studies, 3003 Benham Ave., Elkhart, IN 46514).

Prior, I. (Ed.). (1980). *The Christian at work overseas.* Teddington, Middlesex, England: Tear Fund.

‡ Richardson, D. (1974). *Peace child.* Ventura, CA: Regal Books.

Richardson, D. (1984). *Eternity in their hearts.* Ventura, CA: Regal Books.

Seamands, J. T. (1981). *Tell it well: Communicating the gospel across cultures.* Kansas City, KS: Beacon Hill Press.

Smalley, W. A. (Ed.). (1978). *Readings in missionary anthropology II.* Pasadena, CA: William Carey Library.

Stewart, E. C. (1972). *American cultural patterns: A cross-cultural perspective.* Chicago, IL: Intercultural Press.

Stott, J. R., & Coote, R. T. (1980). *Down to earth: Studies in Christianity and culture.* Grand Rapids, MI: Eerdmans.

Sugden, H. F. (1980). *Sharing Jesus in the Two Thirds World.* Grand Rapids, MI: Eerdmans.

Ward, E. W. (1984). *Living overseas: A book of preparations.* New York, NY: Macmillan.

Language Learning

Blatchford, C. (1982). *Directory of teacher preparation programs in TESOL and bilingual education.* Washington, DC: TESOL.

Brewster, E. T., & Brewster, E. S. (1982). *Bonding and the missionary task: Establishing a sense of belonging.* Pasadena, CA: Lingua House. (Available from: SIL Dallas Center Bookstore, 7500 W. Camp Wisdom Road, Dallas, TX 75236).

Brewster, E. T., & Brewster, E. S. (Eds.). *Community is my language classroom!* (Available from: Lingua House, 135 N. Oakland, #91, Pasadena, CA 91182).

Brewster, E. T., & Brewster, E. S. (1976). *Language acquisition made practical: Field methods for language learners.* Colorado Springs, CO: Lingua House. (Available from: SIL Dallas Center Bookstore, 7500 W. Camp Wisdom Road, Dallas, TX 75236).

Burling, R. (1984). *Learning a field language.* Ann Arbor, MI: University of Michigan Press.

Larson, D. N. (1984). *Guidelines for barefoot language learning.* St. Paul, MN: CMS Publishing.

Larson, D. N., & Smalley, W. A. (1984). *Becoming bilingual: A guide to language learning.* Lanham, MD: University Press of America.

Rubin, J., & Thompson, I. (1982). *How to be a more successful language learner.* Boston, MA: Heinle & Heinle.

Stevick, E. W. (1988). *Teaching and learning languages.* Cambridge, England: Cambridge University Press.

Placement/Referral Agencies*

AIMS
P.O. Box 64534
Virginia Beach, VA 23464
(804) 523-7979

Excalibur Intl. Employment Agency
P.O. Box 114
La Marque, TX 77568
(409) 935-4214

Global Opportunities
1600 Elizabeth Street
Pasadena, CA 91104
(818) 398-2393

InterCristo
P.O. Box 33487
Seattle, WA 98133
(800) 251-7740 and (800) 426-1343

International Employment Gazette
1525 Wade Hampton Blvd.
Greenville, SC 29609
(800) 882-9188

Marketplacers International
P.O. Box 51538
Pakuranga, Auckland
NEW ZEALAND
(64) (9) 576-8403

Strategic Ventures Network
P.O. Box 220
Woodland Park, CO 80866
(719) 687-6818

Tentmakers International Exchange
P.O. Box 48665
Seattle, WA 98108
(206) 524-4600

U.S. Association of Tentmakers
743 Gold Hill Plaza, Suite 190
Woodland Park, CO 80866
(719) 687-6818

* These agencies vary widely in their scope. Their services may or may not be compatible with the individual employment concerns of prospective tentmakers.